Perspectives in American History

No. 45
THE PROTESTANT CLERGY AND PUBLIC ISSUES
1812-1848

THE PROTESTANT CLERGY

AND PUBLIC ISSUES 1812-1848

BY *JOHN R. BODO*

PORCUPINE PRESS
Philadelphia

First edition 1954
(Princeton: Princeton University Press, 1954)

Reprinted 1980 by
PORCUPINE PRESS INC.
Philadephia, PA 19107
By arrangement with Princeton University Press

©copyright 1954 by Princeton University Press.
All rights reserved.

Library of Congress Cataloging in Publication Data

Bodo, John R.
The Protestant clergy and public issues, 1812-1848.

(Perspectives in American history ; no. 45)
Reprint of the 1954 ed. published by Princeton University Press, Princeton, N.J.
Bibliography: p.
Includes index.
1. United States—Church history. 2. Church and state in the United States—History. 3. Protestant churches—United States—Clergy. I. Title.
II. Series: Perspectives in American history (Philadelphia) ; no. 45.
[BR525.B63   1979]   261   79-12849
ISBN 0-87991-854-3

Manufactured in the United States of America

TO JEANNE

PREFACE

THIS study is concerned with the patriotism of the American Protestant clergy during one of the formative periods of the nation's history. It is an attempt to trace the efforts of the clergy to make the United States into a "city which hath foundations, whose builder and maker is God." It is the story of a dream—the dream of an American theocracy.

The subject requires certain definitions. Such key words as "theocrat," "patriotism," "clergy," must be defined, if the treatment is to be safeguarded from misconstruction. A simple statement of these definitions will make their necessity apparent.

We shall be dealing with the *patriotism* of a specific social group. We have defined patriotism as love of country in the most inclusive sense, as the desire for one's country to conform to an ideal, as the holy zeal to make one's country what it ought to be. The use of the word "nationalism" would be anachronistic and would not do justice to all these implications.

The group under consideration are the American *Protestant* clergy. Applying the term Protestant to the body of Christians holding, with some variations, the doctrinal heritage of the Reformation, we eliminated, on the one hand, the Quakers, Unitarians, and Universalists, and on the other hand, the "high church" Episcopalians. Since the Lutherans were not yet in the mainstream of American life during our period, we might say that our use of "Protestant" is identical with *Calvinistic*. An exception was made for the Methodists, whose doctrinal divergence on the matter of Arminianism did not seem materially to affect our investigation.

A further significant limitation was necessary with regard to the word *clergy*. In a country where freedom of religion and freedom of speech were well-nigh complete, it would have been ill-advised and impossible to include all who took it upon themselves to preach. We chose to restrict our inquiry to the Protestant clergy as a self-conscious social group, that is, to ministers and Christian leaders with a college and seminary education or its equivalent. In this way we excluded thousands of uneducated frontier preachers and revivalists, mostly Methodists, Baptists, and Presbyterian schismatics, whose views, if at all accessible in print, would be "frontier" views rather than "clerical" views in the more professional sense of the term. On the other hand, we did consider the educated elements in the Baptist and Methodist denominations, whose opinions we found to be in substantial agreement with those of their Congregational, Presbyterian, and "low church" Episcopalian colleagues.

A geographical restriction also appeared inevitable. Clergymen, according to our definition, were found predominantly in the northern and middle states, or tended to represent the point of view of this area. They were graduates of colleges like Yale, Brown, Bowdoin, Williams, and Amherst in New England; Princeton, Union, Hamilton, Rutgers, and the University of Pennsylvania in the middle states; or, if they were Southerners, most of them would still come to Andover or Princeton Seminary for their formal theological training. As for the West, the founding of the first western colleges and seminaries which occurred during our period was the work of graduates of these eastern institutions of learning.

In short, the *American Protestant clergy* comprises, with some exceptions, the educated ministry of New England and the middle states, whose theology was largely Calvinistic, and whose patriotism, while rooted in their sectional background, embraced the whole nation as a *nation*. This is our basic contention: that the American Protestant clergy thus defined had a definite pattern for America to which they wanted the nation to conform. We shall refer to it as the *theocratic pattern*, because the allusion to a theocracy, with its Calvinistic

PREFACE

background, seems best to describe what they had in mind. Anchored firmly in their belief in the universal sovereignty of God and in his particular concern for the United States, they sought to bring the young nation under his rule and into conformity with his will. By contrast, those Christian groups which criticized or opposed the *theocrats*, widely divergent though they were among themselves, shared a certain basic individualism, which led them to reject any thought of a pattern for the national life.

We believe that if the Protestant clergy's pattern for an American theocracy had remained merely an opinion, expressed in writings and public utterances, it would still be worth investigating, because it would reveal how the clergy reacted to the loss of their status as a privileged class, which occurred when the Federal Constitution forbade religious establishment. But the theocratic pattern was more than a distinctive body of thought: it was a pattern for action. The theocrats not only cherished an ideal of what America should be like, but also evolved a strategy to make that ideal come true, to establish God's rule over the United States. By the nature of their calling, they were anxious to make individuals Christian. Their patriotism impelled them to look beyond the individual at the country as a whole, and to work for its Christianization in accordance with a coherent pattern. The choice of a strategy, however, did not stem directly either from their evangelistic fervor or their patriotic concern, but was a result of their practical wisdom, which early led them to see the power of *associations* for the attainment of their goal. These associations were moral and religious voluntary societies, most of them interdenominational, or rather, undenominational in character. Nothing was more characteristic of the theocrats than such banding together in national societies in order to transform the United States into the theocracy which they envisaged.

It will be the object of this work to analyze the ideological

PREFACE

foundations of the theocratic pattern, to describe the pattern in relation to some of the major public issues which confronted the American nation during this period, and, finally, to attempt a fair critique of the pattern, of its success or failure, and of its relevance to our own mid-twentieth century predicament.

It must be admitted that most of the problems facing the young nation were not unique and that most of the solutions proposed by the theocrats were conservative rather than radical and had been tested, or were then being tested, in continental Europe and particularly in England. However, from our point of view a study of the period seemed justified because the problems were arising within a new nation, at once the offshoot and the compound of many European nations, and because the impact of organized Protestantism on the nation's "growing pains" during this period has never been fully investigated.

One more word may be in order concerning the choice of the dates 1812 and 1848. There are three main reasons for selecting 1812 as our starting-point: the absence of real national feeling in the United States prior to that date; the inability of the clergy before that date to realize the full significance of the separation of church and state; and the emergence of American nationalism during the War of 1812. The closing date 1848 was suggested by the following factors: it marked the end of the Mexican War and the rise of the United States to the rank of a true continental empire; it witnessed a series of revolutions in Europe which had important repercussions in America; and, above all, it opened that short and turbulent span of years, in which, though there was still nominally one United States, there were in spirit "two nations under one flag."

My deepest thanks are due to President John Alexander Mackay and Dean Edward Howell Roberts, who made it possible for me to do postgraduate work at Princeton Theological

PREFACE

Seminary; to Dr. Frederick William Loetscher and Dr. Norman Victor Hope, under whose guidance my interest in church history was deepened and my horizon enlarged; and to Dr. Lefferts Augustine Loetscher, whose genius for making the past come alive and disclose its meaning is matched only by the generosity of his person.

JOHN R. BODO

Princeton, New Jersey
March, 1952

CONTENTS

CHAPTER I. THE THEOCRATIC PATTERN IN THE MAKING   3

CHAPTER II. THE THEOCRATS AND THE STATE   31
Disestablishment. The National Government. National Holidays. Sabbath Controversy. The Clergy in Politics. The Real Roots of the Pattern. The Real Causes of Opposition. Summary

CHAPTER III. THE THEOCRATS AND THE CATHOLIC PROBLEM   61
Anti-Catholicism in America. The Colonial Background. The Peaceful Twenties. The "Foreign Conspiracy" and Nativism. Summary

CHAPTER IV. THE THEOCRATS AND THE INDIAN PROBLEM   85
The Missionary Impulse. Jedidiah Morse's Master Plan. The Story of Elias Boudinot, Cherokee. Isaac McCoy, Realist. Jeremiah Evarts, Idealist. Expulsion and A New Beginning. Summary

CHAPTER V. THE THEOCRATS AND THE NEGRO PROBLEM   112
Early Voices. Ideological Background. *1812-1831*: Founders of the American Colonization Society. Official Response of the Major Denominations. The Fourth of July Collection. Clerical Leadership in the Auxiliary Societies. The Missionary Motive. The Philanthropic Motive. National Security. National Unity. Ultimate Abolition. Summary. *1831-1848*: The Slaveholder's View. The Abolitionist's View. Theocrats versus Abolitionists. The

CONTENTS

Southern Clergy after 1831. The Education of the Slaves. Continued Southern Support of Colonization. Summary

CHAPTER VI. THEOCRATIC SOLUTIONS TO OTHER SOCIAL PROBLEMS   152

Ideological Background. Evangelizing the West. Educating the West. The Public School Issue. The Challenge of the City. Theocratic Paternalism. The Temperance Crusade. Summary

CHAPTER VII. THE THEOCRATIC PATTERN FOR TERRITORIAL EXPANSION   191

Expansion before 1812. The Causes of the War of 1812. Anti-War Arguments of the Theocrats. Clerical Support of the War of 1812. The Theocrats and the Peace of Ghent. American Expansion, 1815-1844. American Expansion, 1844-1850. The Mexican War. California and Beyond. The Theocrats and War. Summary

CHAPTER VIII. THE THEOCRATIC PATTERN FOR AMERICA'S WORLD ROLE   233

America and Europe. World Mission by Example. The Missionary Outreach. The Millennial Perspective

CHAPTER IX. THE THEOCRATIC PATTERN IN THE RETROSPECT   253

BIBLIOGRAPHY   261

INDEX   285

CHAPTER I

THE THEOCRATIC PATTERN IN THE MAKING

IN 1812, on the eve of war, there appeared in Boston the sixth edition of one of the best scientific books of the age, *The American Universal Geography* by the Rev. Jedidiah Morse, pastor of the First Congregational Church of Charlestown and one of the leading theocrats. Into its two massive volumes, first published in 1789, Morse had crammed a wealth of information about America and the rest of the universe. Every page breathes the spirit of a rising national self-consciousness, with heavy emphasis on the New England past. But even more significant is the order of topics: the section on religion precedes the section on government, even the text of the Constitution of the United States![1]

The patriotism of the theocrats was not of the "my country right or wrong" variety. It was a patriotism conditioned upon the nation's obedience to God's will, and it rested on the basic conviction that God's will for the nation was clearly revealed in the Bible. The absolute sovereignty of God and his revelation in the Bible, particularly in the Old Testament, of his specific demands on all matters of national as well as individual concern, was the cornerstone of the theocratic pattern. Deeply aware of the utter corruption of human nature, the theocrats affirmed that man could not be governed by the law of nature without the aid of the law revealed in Scripture. Preaching on the Nineteenth Psalm, Lyman Beecher flatly rejected the "disclosures of heaven" as being insufficient to "restrain the depravity of man," and went on to extol the "law of the Lord." "Adapted to the exigencies of a lost world, it speaks on all those subjects, on which no speech is heard from the heavens, and is attended with glorious efficacy."[2]

[1] I, 188-192.
[2] Lyman Beecher, *The Bible a Code of Laws* (1817). In *Works* (3 vols., Boston, 1853), II, 154.

3

PATTERN IN THE MAKING

This Biblical legalism made correct belief essential to national security and national welfare, since God would prosper the nation only if his commandments were carried out. Every professor at Andover Theological Seminary—founded in 1808 as a reaction to the defection of Harvard to Unitarianism and destined to remain the stronghold of the theocrats throughout our era—had to sign the "Associate Creed," consisting of thirty-six points of doctrine, the thirty-third of which reads: "I will maintain and inculcate the Christian faith, as expressed in the Creed, by me now repeated . . . and in opposition, not only to Atheists and Infidels, but to Jews, Papists, Mahometans, Arians, Pelagians, Antinomians, Arminians, Socinians, Sabellians, Unitarians, and Universalists, and to all heresies and errors, ancient or modern. . . ."[3]

Echoing Beecher's phrase, Heman Humphrey, President of Amherst College, made the connection between the Bible and the nation explicit by reminding his hearers "that the Bible contains the only code of laws, or rather the elements of the only code, which can sustain our free government, or any other like it. It is only by teaching the rising generation to 'fear God and keep His commandments,' that we can induce them to 'obey magistrates,' to 'lead quiet and peaceable lives in all godliness and honesty,' and thus to maintain the great pillars of the state."[4]

This belief in God's direct rule of nations was characteristic of the theocrats. It was built on Calvin's theology which in this respect draws almost exclusively on the Old Testament. Statements of this belief were numerous and articulate. "There is a personality in nations as in men, and as every individual has peculiar responsibilities, arising out of his peculiar circumstances and character, so have nations. . . ."[5] "There are duties and sins which are strictly national, and which are cognizable

[3] As cited in Edwards A. Park, *The Associate Creed of Andover Theological Seminary* (Boston, 1883), p. 23.
[4] Heman Humphrey, *The Way to Bless and Save Our Country* (New York, 1830), p. 24.
[5] Charles Hodge, "Anniversary Address," *The Home Missionary*, II (July, 1829), 17.

PATTERN IN THE MAKING

by those laws which regulate the relation we sustain to God."[6] "God exercises a righteous retribution over nations in the present life...."[7] "They are punished here for national sins, because they will have no individual existence in the next. There we shall be tried as individuals."[8]

Having thus established the principle of God's direct rule of nations by means of a "code of laws" contained in the Bible, the theocrats went on to claim that the United States had a special destiny to fulfil as heir of ancient Israel, God's Chosen People.

The application of the concept of the Chosen People to the American nation had been bequeathed to them by the founders of New England. How God had separated unto himself a saving remnant for the creation of a people to whom he would devote peculiar attention, was the theme of William Bradford's *History of Plymouth Plantation*,[9] Edward Johnson's *Wonder-Working Providence of Sions Saviour*,[10] and Cotton Mather's monumental *Magnalia Christi Americana; or, the Ecclesiastical History of New England*[11] as well as of countless sermons and political orations.

"I write the *Wonders* of the CHRISTIAN RELIGION, flying from the *Depravations* of *Europe*, to the *American Strand*: And, assisted by the Holy Author of that *Religion*, I do ... Report the *Wonderful Displays* of His Infinite Power, Wisdom, Good-

[6] Samuel G. Winchester, *The Religion of the Bible, the Only Preservative of our Civil Institutions* (Natchez, Miss., 1838), p. 8.
[7] Samuel S. Schmucker, *The Christian Pulpit, the Rightful Guardian of Morals, in Political no less than in Private Life* (Gettysburg, Pa., 1846), p. 23. Schmucker was the outstanding theocrat of his denomination. He differed radically from the majority of the Lutheran clergy in his wholly American viewpoint and in his cooperative spirit toward other denominations. It is probable that his Princeton Seminary training did much to influence him along these lines.
[8] Asa Cummings, *A Discourse Delivered at Brunswick, Maine, ... on the Day of the Annual Fast* ... (Brunswick, 1820), p. 24.
[9] Written between 1630 and 1650. Text in part in Perry Miller and Thomas H. Johnson, *The Puritans* (New York, 1938), pp. 91-116.
[10] First published anonymously in London, 1654. Text in part in Miller and Johnson, *op.cit.*, pp. 143-161.
[11] Published in London, 1702. Text in part in Miller and Johnson, *op.cit.*, pp. 163-179.

5

ness, and Faithfulness, wherewith His Divine Providence hath *Irradiated* an Indian Wilderness."[12] In these opening words of Mather's *Magnalia* we detect the three related strands of Puritan belief concerning America, which were to form the basis of the theocratic pattern of the nineteenth century: God had rescued his people from the "Depravations of Europe," just as he had delivered Israel out of Egypt; he meant to use them as an instrument of salvation for this "Indian Wilderness" and ultimately for the world; and for this purpose he had guided them and continued to guide them by means of "Wonderful Displays" of his providence.

The belief in the divine selection of America for a special destiny among the nations was prominent among the early Puritans, but never had much influence in the middle and southern Colonies, until it was powerfully revived on a national scale after the triumph of the American Revolution.

If it is true that America became a political reality before the concept had an opportunity to take firm root in the minds of most Americans, the Protestant clergy at once set about fostering its growth along theocratic lines. The closing of the revolutionary century and the opening of the new gave rise to a flood of sermons and discourses intended "not to raise our national vanity, as if we had an indefeasible title to peculiar divine favour; but rather to excite our pious caution, that we may not forfeit it. . . ."[13]

The note of surprise at the sudden achievement of nationhood was present for a long time. A New Hampshire theocrat wrote: "When the collected wisdom of our country had formed a national constitution, so various was the public opinion, does it not seem a matter of astonishment, that it was not finally rejected, and our country ruined by civil commotions?"[14]

[12] *ibid.*, p. 163.
[13] Abiel Abbott, *Traits of Resemblance in the People of the United States of America to Ancient Israel* (Haverhill, Mass., 1799), p. 6.
[14] Timothy Alden, *The Glory of America* (Portsmouth, N.H., 1801), p. 23.

PATTERN IN THE MAKING

Most theocrats, however, did not take time to reflect on the element of wonder, but did their utmost to publicize the doctrine of the "American Israel," of the providential election and destiny of the United States. "In the discovery and settlement of this country God had some great end in view," wrote a Congregational clergyman. "As the eastern continent was honoured with the birth of a Saviour . . . so this land may be favoured with the dawn of the millennial sun, which may return to the east, shining with growing brightness unto the perfect day."[15]

That such was God's design could be amply illustrated by referring to his "special providences." The heirs of Cotton Mather continued to interpret natural events as media of divine guidance and instruction. "History, when rightly written, is but a record of providence; and he who would read history rightly, must read it with his eye constantly fixed on the hand of God."[16]

Timothy Dwight's *Travels in New England and New York*[17] reveal the same point of view as Cotton Mather's *Magnalia*. "What hath God wrought! Every detail of the creation is full of manifest providences. The rich vegetable mould on the surface of new lands, for example, which yields an abundant crop to the pioneer almost without effort on his part, has been placed there for that very purpose, to support him during the first years of his settlement. . . . Then, when the beneficent mould has disappeared, the poor soil has its providential purpose, too, for by now the settler has time to cultivate it, indeed must cultivate it if he is to live; so that he has a motive for industry and the other virtues which make him respectable. Thus both the presence and the absence of vegetable mould are effects of the final causes which make the world for men."[18]

[15] Stephen Chapin, *The Duty of Living for the Good of Posterity* (Portland, Me., 1821), p. 40.
[16] Hollis Read, *The Hand of God in American History* (Hartford, Conn., 1848-1850), p. iv.
[17] New Haven, 1821-1822. Four volumes.
[18] As cited in article on Timothy Dwight in *The Cambridge History*

In the same vein another outstanding cleric interpreted a cholera epidemic as a divine warning to the United States. "It has been believed by wise and good men of this land and other lands, that God designs to accomplish great events in the earth . . . through the instrumentality of the American people. If so, he will make us virtuous. And if he forms us a people to his praise, he will probably yet do great things and terrible before our eyes."[19]

Thus the theocrats were certain that God who had led their forefathers across the ocean and who had a special destiny in store for them, was manifesting the same care for the nation which their descendants had formed, and that he desired this nation to be consecrated to him by a constant, public acknowledgement of his sovereignty and by the practice of all the Puritan virtues. For this reason it seemed imperative to them that the nation should be thoroughly Christianized, not only as an aggregate of unconverted individuals in need of conversion, but specifically *as a nation*. Nathanael Emmons expressed this point of view succinctly: "It is our imperious duty to diffuse the knowledge and spirit of the gospel as far as possible through the United States, in order to secure our highest temporal as well as spiritual interests. These are interests which God undoubtedly intended to promote by giving us a national existence; and by the great and peculiar privileges and blessings which he has already conferred upon us. What he has done for us is a presage of what he still intends to do for us."[20]

Another theocrat fixed this obligation on the level of the individual citizen by stating: "He who cultivates personal re-

---

of American Literature (ed. W. P. Trent *et al.*, 3 vols., New York, 1917-1921), II, 204.

[19] Gardiner Spring, *A sermon . . . on account of the malignant cholera* (New York, 1832), pp. 29-30. For other sermons interpreting natural events in this vein, see Archibald Alexander, *A Discourse Occasioned by the Burning of the Theatre in the City of Richmond, Virginia* (Philadelphia, 1812), and William Alger, *Inference from the Pestilence and the Fast* (Boston, 1849).

[20] Nathanael Emmons, *New England's Second Century* (1820). In *Works* (6 vols., Boston, 1840), II, 336.

8

PATTERN IN THE MAKING

ligion and obeys the gospel, is the best friend to his country. Christian piety is practical patriotism."[21]

This, then, was the underlying structure of the theocratic pattern: Biblical legalism, drawn largely from the Old Testament, whence it derived the assurance of God's concern with nations as nations; the belief in the election of the United States as God's new Israel; and the resulting sense of duty to make the United States conform to God's law and to her own God-given destiny. It followed as a matter of course that the clergy considered themselves divinely commissioned to cast the United States in the theocratic mould and that, in the tradition of the Hebrew prophets, they sought to regulate the morality of the nation. The greatest difficulty in attempting to impose this pattern arose from the clergy's loss of prestige during the first two decades of our national existence.

The clergy, with the exception of the Tory Anglicans, had staunchly supported the cause of independence. The Congregationalists and the Presbyterians were in the forefront of the Revolutionary struggle.[22] But the defection of the Anglican clergy of the South, the infiltration of radical thought from France, the beginning of the movement across the Alleghenies, away from the organized community life of the East, in short, the growing secularization of American society greatly curtailed the clergy's influence and prestige. Just at the time when they felt that the nation needed them most, the theocrats had to admit that their ascendancy was largely a thing of the past. Two important additional reasons for their plight were their lack of sufficient numbers and their lack of a spiritual dynamic.

In the eighteenth century there had not been any widespread upsurge of religious interest since the time of White-

[21] John Chester, *A sermon in commemoration of the landing of the New England pilgrims* . . . (Albany, 1820), p. 22.
[22] Cf. Alice M. Baldwin, *The New England Clergy and the American Revolution* (Durham, N.C., 1928). John Witherspoon, President of the College of New Jersey, was the only minister to sign the Constitution, but his influence upon its formation was extensive.

9

field, but a great deal of theological bickering among the conservative Calvinists, the "Edwardians," the "Hopkinsians," and the liberal element who were going to develop into the Unitarian denomination. To recover their position of leadership and to regain ideological control over the nation whose destiny, they believed, depended on their ability to make it Christian, the theocrats needed not only a more dynamic theology but also more dynamic methods.

Calvinism had acted upon the early Puritans as a "powerful incentive to faith and activity." But this initial impact could not last, because "it so conceived the sovereignty of God and so obscured human freedom that it exercised, when operating in any locality for a long period, a paralyzing effect upon human initiative. . . . Theology was gradually strangling life."[23] The theology of Jonathan Edwards was the first great protest against this influence. Superficially his system might be viewed as a step in the direction of Arminianism. One might assume that the natural thing for the theocrats of the early nineteenth century would have been to adopt the Wesleyan doctrine of free will in order to spark their efforts to bring the nation under God's rule. Some of them did incline in this direction, but the majority used as the theological vehicle of their pattern for an American theocracy the so-called "consistent" Calvinism of Samuel Hopkins, whose thought marked a decided return to Calvin and even exceeded Calvin's rigor in claiming that "one must be willing, nay even anxious, to spend his eternity in hell, if it should chance to please God to send him there."[24] This ascetic theology instilled a new vigor into the endeavors of the theocrats. It inspired Samuel J. Mills and most of the other pioneers to launch the American missionary enterprise. Another theological alternative considered by the theocrats, though adopted only by a few, was the deliberate avoidance of doctrinal controversy for the sake of

[23] Frank Hugh Foster, *A Genetic History of the New England Theology* (Chicago, 1907), pp. 543-544.
[24] Hopkins, as cited in Oliver W. Elsbree, *The Rise of the Missionary Spirit in America, 1790-1815* (Williamsport, Pa., 1928), pp. 147-148.

the nation's needs. Lyman Beecher epitomized this alternative. In his sermon on *The Faith Once Delivered to the Saints*,[25] he drew up an undogmatic, conciliatory statement of belief, through which he hoped to enlist all the orthodox clergy in a comprehensive effort to bring about an American theocracy.

One more factor, the effect of the so-called "Second Awakening," has to be taken into consideration. Known largely as a frontier revival and notorious for its eccentricities, it provided a great stimulus to church life in New England and the middle states as well. Its theological contribution was insignificant, apart from the rise of some schismatic groups like the "Cumberland Presbyterians," but its spirit was contagious. Some of the older theocrats were flexible enough to embrace it and to make use of its methods for starting new life in their own churches. Bennet Tyler, Ebenezer Porter, Edward Dorr Griffin, and the pioneer colonizationist Robert Finlay, showed its fruits in their respective parishes. At the same time, and in an exactly parallel way, the clerical members of the faculties of most New England colleges followed the example of Timothy Dwight of Yale in an effort to stamp out "infidelity" and to revive interest in orthodox Christianity on their campuses. It was through these evangelistic endeavors that the theocrats gained some of their outstanding younger men, such as Samuel J. Mills, Justin Edwards, James Richards, Jeremiah Evarts, and Elias Cornelius. The influence of the revivals carried on through the first half of the nineteenth century, and was attested by a surprising increase in church membership which was double that of the population's rate of growth and exceeded in its proportions any such growth in ancient or modern times.

This, then, was the theological orientation adopted by the theocrats: a restatement of Calvinism in terms of Hopkins' thought, stressing the heroic virtues of the system in the doctrine of "disinterested benevolence"; but, above all, a practical,

[25] Preached in 1823. Text in *Works* (3 vols., New York, 1852), II, 243-300.

Biblical approach to theology, replacing the sterile, unnerving tendency of Calvinistic dogmatism, and a corresponding dynamic evidenced in their approval of, and participation in, the Second Awakening.

But if the parish revival became a characteristic method of the theocrats, it was by no means their most characteristic method. As a matter of fact, they soon retreated from their earlier revivalistic position on account of their rejection of the "New Measures." These innovations were initiated largely by Charles G. Finney. A disciple of Nathaniel W. Taylor, founder of the "New Haven Theology," Finney preached a modified Calvinism, epitomized in his sermon, "Sinners Bound to Change their Own Hearts."[26] His theological views might have been acceptable, but his aggressive evangelistic devices, such as the use of the "anxious bench," the "inquiry room," and the "protracted meeting" estranged most of the theocrats from him. The saintly Richard Channing Moore, Bishop of Virginia, who was strongly evangelical in spirit and unusually broad-minded in his denominational sympathies, remarked with distaste: "If Christianity is a system founded on truth, the work of grace must be God's work; and I cannot believe that the Almighty stands in need of the cunning craftiness of men to promote His designs."[27]

Far more denunciatory, however, was a list of letters appended to William B. Sprague's *Lectures on Revivals,* in which some twenty theocrats representing five leading denominations agreed in drawing a sharp line between "true" and "false" revivals without once mentioning Finney's name.[28]

[26] In *Sermons on Various Subjects* (New York, 1836), pp. 1-58.
[27] "Letter to William Meade" (1832). Text in J. P. K. Henshaw, *Memoir of . . . Richard Channing Moore . . .* (Philadelphia, 1843), p. 97.
[28] Published at Glasgow in 1832. Writers of these letters include Archibald Alexander, Samuel Miller, Henry Davis, Ashbel Green, Edward Dorr Griffin of the Presbyterian Church; Congregationalists Joel Hawes, Edward Payson, Nathan Lord, Heman Humphrey, Jeremiah Day; and Francis Wayland, Philip Milledoler, and Charles P. McIlvaine representing respectively the Baptist, Reformed Dutch, and Protestant Episcopal communions. It is difficult to imagine a more representative roster of theocrats.

PATTERN IN THE MAKING

Because of his rejection by the theocrats, Finney's interest for our investigation is peripheral, but he remains significant as added evidence of the resurgence of orthodox aggressiveness. As for the theocrats, they had inaugurated their own distinctive method—the use of voluntary societies—during the quarter century before Finney's appearance, but had been prevented from making any spectacular advances for lack of manpower.

The opening of the nineteenth century found the ranks of the Protestant clergy dangerously depleted. At the same time, the population was growing and spreading across the mountains from the New England and seaboard states of the South into the new West. The Episcopal Church in the South was so short of ministers, that in 1813 the Rev. William Meade, later Bishop of Virginia, "returned from a diocesan convention, which he thought might be the last, with the words of the page in the *Lay of the Last Minstrel*, 'Lost, lost, lost' running through his ears."[29] The Congregationalists were still largely localized in New England. "The Methodist Church was in its feeble infancy. . . . The Baptist churches, although they had gained heavily in both New England and the South . . . had achieved their growth mainly among the poor and uneducated classes; and had accepted the ideal of a 'lowly ministry' of uneducated men."[30] Of the five major denominations only the Presbyterians had a truly national constituency in addition to that major theocratic prerequisite: an educated clergy. But even their numbers were far from adequate to their opportunities. Statistics are more impressive than general statements. The group of theocrats who first realized the tremendous need for more educated ministers were aware of this fact when they appointed the Rev. Eliphalet Pearson to estimate the number of clergymen in relation to the population of the country. Assuming the necessity of having "one minister

---

[29] W. W. Manross, *The Episcopal Church in the United States, 1800-1840* (New York, 1938), p. 39.

[30] Robert E. Thompson, *A History of the Presbyterian Churches in the United States* (American Church History Series, New York, 1895), vi, 68.

13

to a thousand souls," Dr. Pearson's search revealed that Louisiana, Kentucky, Tennessee, Ohio, Mississippi, Indiana, Missouri, Illinois, and Michigan had only 116 ministers for a population of 1,078,815; Georgia, the Carolinas, and Virginia only 126 for 2,197,670 people; that even the New England States, with their population of 1,471,927, had only 803 "liberally educated ministers"; and that the states of New York, New Jersey, Pennsylvania, Delaware, Maryland, and the District of Columbia, had only 955 "clergymen of liberal education" for their population of 2,495,955. Dr. Pearson concluded: "In round numbers: present population, eight and a half million; ministers 2,000; destitute, six and a half million."[31] He went on to show that if the trend continued, there would be in 65 years a population of 65 million with 60 million of them destitute of the services of an educated clergy.

The American Education Society was both the sponsor and the outcome of this investigation. It became the coordinating agency of the theocrats, supplying information about the clergy and the work of the churches. In harmony with the theocratic ideal, it kept itself relatively free from sectarian bias, though primarily Congregational and Presbyterian in leadership.[32] Above all, it secured scholarships for young men who felt called to enter the ministry, but did not have the means for a college and seminary education, and it gave a vigorous impulse to the expansion of existing facilities for theological training and to the building of new Christian colleges and seminaries. The value of this last service to the realization of the theocratic pattern cannot be overestimated. In the twenties alone, the Presbyterians founded Lafayette College by themselves and Western Reserve University in cooperation with the Congregationalists; the Baptists organized Colby College in Maine, George Washington University in Washing-

[31] Eliphalet Pearson, *Address of the American Society for Educating Pious Youth for the Gospel Ministry* (Andover, 1815), pp. 10-11.

[32] The Congregational and Presbyterian Churches had been cooperating in the so-called Plan of Union since 1801.

ton, D.C., and Georgetown College in Kentucky; the Episcopalians moved to the frontier with the founding of Hobart and Kenyon Colleges in New York and Ohio respectively; and the Congregationalists launched Amherst in Massachusetts which became the largest "feeder" for Andover and other seminaries.[33]

Amherst College, founded in 1821, kept its supremacy during the first thirty years of its existence with a ratio of one minister to every 1.96 students, representing seventeen and a half ministers per year. The Christian emphasis of the college was highlighted by the number of campus revivals. Under the presidency of Heman Humphrey (1823-1845) there were no less than seven full-fledged revivals, all yielding impressive numbers of decisions for the ministry.[34]

Second to Amherst in its importance for the theocratic pattern was the College of New Jersey at Princeton. While its ratio of preministerial students was considerably lower, it had a much wider geographical representation among its students. It was favored by Southern students and contributed disproportionately to Southern leadership, and to the Southern clergy in particular.[35]

The other colleges most extensively attended by ministerial candidates were Yale, Dartmouth, Harvard (Unitarian), Brown (Baptist), and the University of Vermont; though Hampden-Sidney in Virginia, Dickinson in Pennsylvania, and Centre in Kentucky also trained a respectable number. The Methodists were the slowest to develop denominational colleges. Wesleyan University in Connecticut was not founded

[33] *American Quarterly Register* (Boston, 1828), I, 75, 103. This was the official organ of the American Education Society, edited first by Elias Cornelius, then by Bela Bates Edwards, both of whom were prominent theocrats.

[34] Edward Hitchcock, *Reminiscences of Amherst College* (Northampton, Mass., 1863), pp. 160-162, 191. Hitchcock, the successor of Humphrey, was president of Amherst from 1845 to 1855.

[35] Charles F. Thwing, *A History of Higher Education in America* (New York, 1906), pp. 254-255. Statistics compiled by this author reveal that between 1820 and 1860 one-third to one-half of the students at Princeton came from the Southern States.

until 1831. Most of the other Methodist colleges organized before 1848 were in the South and West. Thus the effects of a formal education on the Methodist ministry (and, to a lesser extent, on the Baptist ministry) did not, for the most part, become manifest until after our period.[36]

The college movement, initiated by the theocrats through the American Education Society, led to the founding of theological seminaries. Up to the turn of the nineteenth century, theological education was rather haphazard, consisting largely of a period of apprenticeship served under a parish minister, though the curriculum of the eighteenth-century college was heavily flavored with theology, and the outstanding ones had special chairs of divinity. The filling of this chair at Harvard in 1803 by an advocate of Unitarian views forced a showdown between the orthodox and the liberal parties of the New England clergy, and resulted in the founding of Andover Seminary in 1808. Uniting the two leading factions of the orthodox—the "Hopkinsians" and the "Old Calvinists"—Andover became the headquarters of the theocrats as well as the nation's first fullfledged seminary. Founded by men of the caliber of Eliphalet Pearson, Jedidiah Morse, Timothy Dwight, Samuel Spring, and Samuel Abbot, Andover left an indelible stamp on American Protestantism during the first half of the nineteenth century. Averaging sixty-two entering students annually during the first thirty years of its existence, it cast hundreds of influential clergymen in the theocratic mould. Its professors—Leonard Woods (Sacred Theology, 1808-1846), Moses Stuart (Sacred Literature, 1810-1848), Ebenezer Porter (Sacred Rhetoric, 1812-1832), and Edwards A. Park (Sacred Rhetoric, 1832-1847, and Sacred Theology, 1847-1881)— formed the character and the minds of a vast number of men on their way to subdue America to God's rule.

Princeton Seminary, second in the order of founding, con-

[36] Donald G. Tewksbury, *The Founding of American Colleges and Universities before the Civil War* (New York, 1932), pp. 91-128.

tributed substantially toward the same goal, as did the other eighteen seminaries organized before 1830.[37] Their efforts at offering an effective curriculum of studies was ably undergirded by the theocrats who in their pulpit, periodicals, and other media, did not cease to publicize the need for the recruitment of ministers.[38]

Andover Seminary, however, is by far the most important for our investigation, because of its close connection with the birth of the major benevolent societies, which represented the most distinctive feature of the strategy of the theocrats. Indeed, the creation of, and participation in, these voluntary associations was more characteristic of the theocrats than any theological idiosyncrasy. It was by means of these societies, rather than by any other method, that these clergymen attempted to realize their pattern for an American theocracy.

It is now taken for granted that the United States is the "clubbiest" nation in the world, having an organization for every purpose. The contradiction between the proverbial individualism of Americans and the prevalence of voluntary associations is only apparent. In the United States individualism has not meant "the individual's independence of other individuals, but his and their freedom from governmental restraint. . . . This conception of a political authority too weak to interfere with men's ordinary pursuits actually created the necessity for self-constituted associations to do things beyond the capacity of a single person, and by reverse effect the suc-

---

[37] *American Quarterly Register*, II (1830), 247. Enrollment figures for this year include Andover, 138, Princeton, 124, Hamilton (Baptist, N.Y.), 76, Auburn (Presby., N.Y.) 58, Yale, 49, Harvard (Unit.) 42, Union (Presby., Va.) 35, Dutch Reformed (N.J.), 24, South and West (Presby., Tenn.), 22, General (Epis., N.Y.) 20.

[38] Cf. John Holt Rice, "Ministerial Character and Preparation Best Adapted to the Wants of the United States and of the World in the Nineteenth Century," *Am. Quart. Reg.*, I (1829), 209-216; John Clark Young, "The Destiny of Our Country Demands a Numerous, Holy, and Efficient Ministry," *Annual of the Presbyterian Board of Education* (Philadelphia, 1835), pp. 166-178; James Waddell Alexander, *An Address to Christians on the Importance and Means of an Increase in the Number of Gospel Ministers* (New York: American Tract Society, n.d.).

cess of such endeavors proved a continuing argument against the growth of a stronger government."[39]

In a real sense, the churches themselves were the pioneer voluntary associations in America. In the colonial era, the dissenting groups were willing to pay the tax for the support of the established church, so long as they were permitted to maintain "societies" of their own persuasion on a voluntary basis. After 1787 the voluntary system went into effect in all the states of the Union, with the exception of three New England States where the Congregational establishment lingered for another generation. In the meantime, a beginning had been made within Congregationalism itself toward chartering church-sponsored voluntary societies for specific objects,[40] and one interdenominational society, combining foreign and home missions in its objectives, had been founded in New York City.[41] But the beginning of national societies dates from the founding of the American Board of Commissioners for Foreign Missions in 1810.

Two tendencies inherent in the strategy of the theocrats can be traced at once from the example of the American Board: a friendly rivalry with British societies, and the desire to rise from sectional to truly national representation and influence.

British societies in most cases antedated their American counterparts. The work of missions, Sunday schools, the printing and distribution of Bibles and tracts, took organizational form in England between 1790 and 1805; the attempt at African colonization was a generation old before the American Colonization Society was formed. The theocrats, largely friendly

[39] Arthur M. Schlesinger, "Biography of a Nation of Joiners," *AHR*, L (1944), 1-25. Quoting from page 1.

[40] The "Society for Propagating the Gospel among the Indians and Others in North America," Massachusetts, 1787; the "Connecticut Missionary Society," 1794. Cf. D. Dorchester, *Christianity in the United States* (New York, 1888), pp. 400-401.

[41] *ibid.* Samuel Miller of Princeton Seminary was active in the founding of this society, together with two other Presbyterian, four Dutch Reformed, one Associate Reformed, and one Baptist minister. "Foreign missions" in these early days referred to the Indians, while "home missions" applied to the emigrants heading West.

toward England in spite of the tensions inherited from Revolutionary days, seized upon these British examples in a spirit of Christian competition. "Great Britain is engaged in a conflict for her existence with a power which threatens to subjugate the civilized world; yet, beside all the expenses of this unexampled conflict . . . Great Britain spends *hundreds of thousand of dollars* annually in distributing the Bible, employing Missionaries, translating the Scriptures, and other extraordinary methods of dispensing the Gospel to mankind. . . . We are accustomed to hear many encomiums on the liberality of Christians in England; let it be remembered that these very encomiums will condemn us, unless we *go and do likewise.*"[42]

In Britain, however, there did not seem to be any motivation other than religious behind these societies. They were organized to evangelize unreached people and areas at home and abroad by various means, but they were neither conceived nor promoted in patriotic terms. The reason is obvious: Britain had been a nation and an empire for centuries, whereas the United States had just become a nation.

The other tendency of the American societies which was early exemplified in the American Board was the desire to be truly national in representation and influence. The American Board was founded by theocrats from Massachusetts and Connecticut; its policy-making Prudential Committee consisted of New England men or men of New England stamp throughout our era; but as early as 1819 a corresponding membership was established, including Congregational and Presbyterian clergymen and laymen from nearly all the states of the Union,[43] and the Annual Report of 1820 gloried in the national character of the organization. "The A.B.C.F.M. is not limited to any section of the country or to any denomination of Christians. Its members, chartered or corresponding, and its patrons, auxilia-

[42] American Board, "First Annual Report," in *The First Ten Annual Reports of the A. B. C. F. M.* (Boston, 1834), p. 29. Composed by the Prudential Committee: Jedidiah Morse, Samuel Worcester, and Jeremiah Evarts.

[43] Report for 1819, *ibid.*, pp. 261-262.

ries, and agents, are in all the States of the Union, and of nearly all considerable religious communions. In its form and spirit . . . it is a NATIONAL INSTITUTION."[44]

The same tendency can be traced in the development of the American Education Society (1815), the American Bible Society (1816), the American Colonization Society (1817), the American Tract Society (1824), the American Sunday School Union (1824), the American Temperance Society (1826), the American Sabbath Union (1828), and the American Home Missionary Society (1828). The membership of these national societies was largely Congregational and Presbyterian but the theocratic pattern was far from being confined to these two denominations. To be sure, it was first conceived by Congregational and Presbyterian clergymen, but as time went on, their societies grew more and more inclusive; or else they served as models to other major denominations which preferred to organize their own national societies for missions, education, or moral reform.[45] However, even these denominational societies were patriotically motivated and operated with the destiny of the nation in view.

An interesting sidelight on the societies is the prominence of laymen among their leaders. Many of these were undoubtedly figureheads, but the personality of some of them and their intense devotion to the causes promoted by the societies proves beyond a doubt that the theocratic pattern had a firm grip on some of the best lay minds of the nation. Jeremiah Evarts, for instance, was a successful Boston lawyer as well as editor of the *Panoplist*, later *Missionary Herald*, the pioneer journal of the theocrats, founded in 1805; he was also treasurer of the American Board from 1811 to 1821 and corresponding secretary—the most important policy-making position—from 1821 to his death in 1831. He also held offices in the American Education Society and the American Bible Society.[46] Elias

[44] Report for 1820, *ibid.*, pp. 316-317.
[45] For example, the Baptists organized their missions board in 1814, the Methodists in 1819, the Episcopalians in 1820.
[46] E. C. Tracy, *Memoir of Jeremiah Evarts, Esq.* (Boston, 1845), *passim.*

Boudinot, prominent in New Jersey politics and renowned for his philanthropy, contributed his leadership to several of the earlier missionary and other benevolent societies, was the first president of the American Bible Society, and at his death left his considerable fortune to these societies.[47] A living monument to the theocratic pattern was Theodore Frelinghuysen, lawyer and Senator from New Jersey, whose offices in the societies at different times included the presidency of the American Board, the Bible Society, and the Sunday School Union, as well as important posts in the Tract Society and the Colonization Society. In 1835 he even contemplated entering the ministry, but Gardiner Spring dissuaded him.[48]

The theocrats did not from the first have a detailed plan for the implementation of their pattern for the nation. Far from it. They had the two basic component parts—Christian commitment and patriotism—which produced the imperative to make the United States a Christian nation in the theocratic mould. The characteristic method—organization of societies for specific purposes—was adopted at the beginning of our era. But their founding proceeded only as rapidly as the specific needs of the nation and of the world came into view, so that the whole structure was not completed until about 1830, and even after that new societies kept springing up. Nor did the theocrats have any doubt concerning the supreme efficacy of these societies. As early as 1819, Lyman Beecher noted that the societies were the most powerful instrument at the service of the churches, with which, in turn, the welfare of the nation rested. "Whoever shakes the corner-stone of this system," he exclaimed, "will bring to dust the noblest edifice ever reared by divine and human cooperation!"[49] The *Address to the Christian Public* of the American Tract Society emphasized

[47] *American Quarterly Register*, I (1829), 118.
[48] T. W. Chambers, *Memoir of the Life and Character of the Late Hon. Theodore Frelinghuysen* (New York, 1863), p. 173.
[49] Lyman Beecher, *The Design, Rights, and Duties of Local Churches* (1819). *Works*, II, 219. (Sermon preached at the ordination of Elias Cornelius, for many years Secretary of the Education Society.)

the influence of the societies on national unity. "Every new institution . . . of such a character exerts a happy influence on our national union, and is a new accession to the best and strongest affections of the human heart, gathered from the remotest parts of the land, to 'lengthen the cords and strengthen the stakes,' to bind together the body politic; so that, while public opinion maintains its existing ascendancy, every new accession of diffusive benevolence will render it more and more difficult for the spirit of faction or usurpation to sever this cemented country."[50]

When one of the leading Baptist theocrats, John Mason Peck, cast a backward look over the previous half century, he discerned two great changes for the good of the United States: the achievement of nationhood, and the rise of the benevolent societies, whose growth led him to exclaim that "Jesus Christ is about to possess the whole land."[51] And three years after Peck's optimistic comment, James P. Milnor, Rector of St. George's Episcopal Church in New York City, and indefatigable promoter of the societies, publicly expressed his gratitude to God for "that grand moral machinery which the Spirit of Jehovah has put into operation, and his Providence is carrying throughout the land . . . and for sending to the most distant nations of the earth, the light of that blessed faith, on which are staked the immortal interests of man."[52]

So extensive were the operations of this "grand moral machinery" that in the year of the advent of Jacksonian democracy the American Board showed an income of $102,009, while the Home Missionary Society, then in its first year, listed receipts of $26,997.[53]

Thus far we have reviewed the ideological foundations of the pattern for an American theocracy and the distinctive strategy by means of which the Protestant clergy wished to

[50] New York, 1824. Quoting p. 5.
[51] John M. Peck, *Fifty Year's Retrospect* (St. Louis, 1825).
[52] James P. Milnor, *Sermon Occasioned by the Death of his Excellence, DeWitt Clinton . . . Governor of New York* (New York, 1828), p. 10.
[53] *American Quarterly Register*, II (1829), 51.

impose it on the nation. Was there any organized opposition to their plans, any pattern to offset or replace their pattern?

The theocrats were opposed, in the first place, by the Unitarians. The direct cause of the founding of Andover was the defection of Harvard to Unitarianism. Though the split within Congregationalism did not occur until 1820, the lines between Trinitarians and Unitarians were clearly drawn as early as 1808. Basically, Unitarianism was a protest against authoritarianism in religion. Just as the Reformation had transferred the seat of authority from the Pope to the Bible, so Unitarianism transferred it from the Bible to the individual. This, of course, is a broad generalization. The pre-Reformation church recognized the Bible as God's Word, but would have it interpreted only by the hierarchy of the church. The Reformers would let the Bible act as its own interpreter, illumined for the believer by the Holy Spirit. But they had a realistic view of man, and therefore continued to formulate creeds and to establish churchly discipline. Unitarianism rebelled against discipline and creeds in the name of the individual. By advocating complete toleration of opinions, it tended to dilute the historic faith of the church to the point where it became a mere ethic, based on the Sermon on the Mount. "Our leading principle in interpreting Scripture," asserted William Ellery Channing, "is that the Bible is a book written for men, in the language of men, and that its meaning is to be sought in the same manner as that of other books."[54] The "idolatry of the Old Testament is passing," exulted Theodore Parker. So is the belief that the writers of the New Testament were "infallible and miraculously inspired." Only the "plain words of Jesus of Nazareth," which are "absolute, pure morality, and absolute, pure religion," will remain.[55]

It is evident that the Unitarians, rejecting the orthodox view

[54] W. E. Channing, *Unitarian Christianity* (1819). *Works* (Boston, 1877), pp. 367-384. Quoting pp. 367-368.
[55] Theodore Parker, *A Discourse on the Transient and Permanent in Christianity* (1841). In *Works* (10 vols., London, 1864), VIII, 1-30. Quoting pp. 13, 22.

of the Bible, refused to accept the theocratic view of America, which was so plainly built upon the Old Testament. But in their rejection of the Old Testament they were making common cause with other Christian groups, with whom, at first glance, they seemed to have little in common. What two men could be farther apart than William Ellery Channing, ministering to the nation's most sophisticated city, and the famous frontier preacher, Alexander Campbell? Yet Campbell's protest against the Old Testament norm was simultaneous with Channing's. As a matter of fact, the founding of the "Christian Association of Washington" (Pa.) antedated the founding of the American Unitarian Association by ten years.

Campbell asserted that the Law "could not give righteousness and eternal life," nor "exhibit the malignity and demerit of sin," nor yet "be a suitable rule of life to mankind in this imperfect state. . . . It was given to the Jewish nation and to none else. As the inscription on a letter identifies to whom it belongs; as the preamble to a proclamation distinguishes who is addressed; so the preface to the law points out and determines to whom it was given. . . . How unjust and inconsistent would it be to convey the contents of a letter to a person to whom it was not directed—how inconsistent to enjoin the items of a proclamation made by the President of the United States, on the subjects of the French government. As inconsistent it would be to extend the law of Moses beyond the limits of the Jewish nation."[56]

Note the absolute contrast with Lyman Beecher's view of the Bible as a "code of laws" particularly suited for man in his fallen state. The Mosaic Law, according to Campbell, as well as according to Channing and Parker, had been superseded by the Gospel, defined largely as the spoken words of Christ. Consequently there was no "American Israel" by divine decree, nor any God-given pattern for the national life, only

[56] Alexander Campbell, *A Sermon on the Law* (1816). Reprinted in *The Millenial Messenger*, published at Bethany, Va., Ser. III, Vol. III (1846), pp. 494-521. Quoting from pp. 497-502.

individual acceptance of Christ "as the Lord, our righteousness," and "punctilious regard to all his precepts and ordinances."[57]

These expressions of Campbell clearly indicate the trend of the movement which he had begun. It was intended to liberate Christians from the bondage of the Law, but it merely replaced an Old Testament legalism by a New Testament legalism. At one with the Unitarians in one of his basic premises, Campbell's protest led to a wholly different extreme, and found its following in a wholly different class: the vigorous, primitive frontier element. The logical outgrowth of Channing's conservative Unitarianism was, on the one hand, Parker's crusading humanitarianism, particularly his rabid, uncritical abolitionism; and, on the other hand, the aloof "transcendentalism" of Emerson. The logical outgrowth of Campbell's initiative was the "anti-mission" movement of the frontier, headed by such fanatics as John Taylor and Daniel Parker. So rapid was the growth of these frontier groups that by the half-century their numbers were estimated at more than a quarter million.[58]

But in addition to these two major types—the Channing type and the Campbell type—there was a third group which opposed the theocratic pattern: the politicians of the Republican and Democratic parties. Many of them, including Andrew Jackson himself, were church-going men, whose personal piety was obviously sincere. Some of them, like the historian Bancroft, were even convinced of the historic mission of the United States, and held the Puritan fathers in the greatest reverence. But their interpretation of America's destiny was radically opposed to theocratic doctrine, and they resisted all the attempts of the theocrats to enlist the government, no matter how indirectly, in the realization of their pattern.

What, then, did these three "anti-theocratic" elements have

[57] *ibid.*, p. 520.
[58] This estimate includes the Campbellites or Disciples of Christ, the Old School or Anti-Mission Baptists, and a number of other small groups. Cf. E. Lansing Burrows, ed., *The American Baptist Register* (Philadelphia, 1853), p. 495.

in common? Was there any pattern of thought and belief uniting such disparate individuals as Channing, Campbell, Bancroft, William Lloyd Garrison, Daniel Parker, Richard M. Johnson, Theodore Parker, and Adin Ballou? All these men and their followers were *individualists*. They believed that the highest source of truth resided in the individual and that the liberty of the individual was the chief end of all political institutions. They held that the individual was the ultimate criterion in religion, which made them reject all "ecclesiasticism," so characteristic of the theocratic pattern.

Underlying their belief in the normative value of the individual was their view of man, whom they regarded as either innately good or, at least, perfectible, whether through the influence of the Holy Spirit (Campbell, "anti-mission" groups) or through the cultivation of his ethical nature (Unitarians, Universalists, "come-outer" groups). All that man needed for the achievement of the fullness of his moral stature was liberty; hence "the less government we have, the better" and the less organized religion we have, the better; hence also the rejection of any uniform pattern for the United States as a nation. If they believed in any national destiny at all, they defined it not as a mandate to conform to God's will but as a providential experiment "to organize the rights of man . . . a problem hitherto unattempted on a national scale in human history."[59]

It appears, then, that insofar as the "anti-theocrats" had any pattern at all for the nation, it consisted in the studied absence of any pattern, due to their transcendent respect for the individual, their optimistic view of man, and their uncritical devotion to personal freedom. All these elements of belief came into sharp focus in their hostility to the clergy and, far more forcefully, against the clergy's chief weapon in the battle for an American theocracy—the benevolent associations.

The grounds of opposition to the clergy were various. For instance, the Anti-Mission Baptists with their literal reading

[59] Theodore Parker, *The Political Destination of America* (1848). In *Works*, IV, 77-110. Quoting p. 82.

of the apostolic commission, insisted that any ministry "dependent on the church to give them a call or seminaries of learning to qualify them to preach" was of the Devil.[60] Channing, on the other hand, was not ashamed of his excellent professional education, but resolutely opposed the "system of exclusion and denunciation" which the orthodox clergy as a class seemed to embody.[61] The politicians of the popular parties attacked the clergy insofar as clergymen or clerical groups showed any desire to "meddle with politics," that is, to exert pressure and enlist public opinion on behalf of such legislation as would further their ends. Over the Sunday School Union's petition for incorporation in Pennsylvania, a debate arose, in the course of which a Senator branded the Union's program as "the casuistical workings of priest craft . . . in a crusade for political power . . . to establish ecclesiastical domination—the rites of baptism—the orthodox faith throughout the land."[62]

It was evident that the benevolent associations should become the special targets of the "anti-theocratic" elements. Here again the grounds of opposition varied with the opponents. The frontier groups condemned the societies chiefly because they were "unscriptural," bureaucratic, and wasteful,[63] and because they were trespassing on God's prerogative to save men by means of his own choosing. One Alabama Baptist preacher went so far as to declare: "Sinners, I have no Gospel for *you*, I am only sent to preach to God's people, to

[60] Daniel Parker, *A Public Address to the Baptist Society . . . on the Principals [sic] of the Baptist Board of Foreign Missions etc.* (Vincennes, 1820), p. 12.
[61] William Ellery Channing, *The System of Exclusion and Denunciation in Religion Considered* (1815). *Works*, pp. 478-486, *passim*.
[62] Senator J. Hare Powell, quoted in Appendix to Ezra S. Ely's sermon, *The Duty of Christian Freemen to Elect Christian Rulers* (Philadelphia, 1828). The statement of the Sunday School Union is no more than a characteristic theocratic warning. It reads: "All the political power in the country within ten or twenty years shall be in the hands of persons whose characters have been formed at Sunday Schools."
[63] John Leland, *Missionary Societies* (1818). In *Writings* (New York, 1845), pp. 471-472. Leland combined the religious and political bias against the theocrats. Though a resident of New England, he was a Baptist of the frontier type as well as an ardent Jeffersonian and Jacksonian.

feed his sheep and lambs. God will save his elect in despite of men and devils—means or no means—no difference, God will save them."[64]

Channing's criticism of the societies was naturally far more discriminating and therefore more charitable. He recognized the worthiness of their objects, though he felt that "an individual who thinks that he is doing a more religious act in contributing to a missionary society than in doing a needful act of kindness to a relative, friend, or neighbor, is leaving a society of God's institution for one of man's making."[65]

But his basic criticism was frankly in the name of individualism and its concomitants: human liberty and perfectibility. The greatest danger inherent in the approach, he argued, is not "that we shall acquire a positive character of vice, but that it will impose on us a negative character . . . that we shall substitute the consciences of others for our own, that we shall paralyze our faculties through dependence on foreign guides, and that we shall be moulded from abroad instead of determining ourselves."[66]

Suggestive criticism came also from Calvin Colton, a clergyman turned politician. His *Protestant Jesuitism*[67] is a poorly organized, repetitious tirade against the theocrats and their societies, particularly against the American Temperance Society, but it is his analysis which first reveals the parallels between the Roman Catholic Counter-Reformation and the pattern for an American theocracy, which he defined as a "combined attempt to establish a spiritual supremacy over the mind of this country," having made its "leading and most forcible demonstration under the guise of the Temperance Reformation."[68] Jesuitism, Colton argues, is not confined to the Roman Church. The theocratic societies embody com-

---

[64] Quoted in Hosea Holcombe, *A History of the Rise and Progress of the Baptists in Alabama* (Philadelphia, 1840), p. 96.

[65] W. E. Channing, *Remarks on Associations* (1830). *Works*, pp. 138-158. Quotation from pp. 147-148.

[66] *ibid.*, p. 142.   [67] New York, 1836.

[68] Colton, *op.cit.*, Preface.

mendable intentions. They have proved the "overwhelming efficiency of a widespread association for any great public design," but they are "jesuitical," for through them "the priesthood . . . have taken advantage of their spiritual influence to serve themselves instead of the public, to gratify ambition and to obtain power. . . ."[69] Discerning the comprehensive nature of the pattern far more clearly than any of its other opponents, Colton concludes: "It is a remarkable fact that in less than the period that belongs to a single generation, the economy of society in this country, in all that pertains to moral reform and religious enterprise, has been formed on a model entirely new to ourselves, but not without type in history. It is the assumption of a controlling influence by a few, who stand at the head of moral and religious organizations of various names. The public, generally, are simple, honest, confiding; and do not note operations of this kind. That is, they do not understand when and how the whole frame of society is getting a new structure, leaving the great mass in subjection to the will and control of select, and often self-elected individuals. They do not even suspect, that societies formed for such good purposes, could have in them the leaven of ambition; and they allow themselves to be formed into minor and subsidiary organizations, comprehending the whole mass of the community, to uphold these supervisory establishments by contributions drawn from every source and from every hand."[70]

It is difficult to deny the basic validity of Colton's criticism, though it may be pointed out that the same would be true of political parties, and that he was merely discerning the dangers of power concentrated in a few hands. However, a cursory examination of the personnel of the benevolent associations, with its multiple overlapping of offices, would convince anyone that Colton's criticism was at least relevant.

There is, then, a basic agreement among the critics and opponents of the theocratic pattern, in spite of their own politi-

[69] *ibid.*, pp. 21, 24.   [70] *ibid.*, p. 107.

cal, social, and religious diversity, so that, for the purposes of our investigation, it may be permissible to draw from their writings indiscriminately, in order to illustrate the nature of their opposition to specific aspects of the pattern. They were all representatives of a changing, dynamic community, upon which the theocrats attempted to impose a more or less static pattern. Their thinking was individualistic, whereas the theocrats thought in terms of society, particularly in terms of the nation, of its divine mission and destiny.

Having thus sketched the ideological foundations of the pattern for an American theocracy both positively and negatively, we may now examine its specific application to various public issues of the period.

CHAPTER II

THE THEOCRATS AND THE STATE

Disestablishment

THE First Amendment to the Constitution provided that Congress should "make no law respecting an establishment of religion, or prohibiting the free exercise thereof." To be sure, this federal law had to await implementation by the states. In the Southern and Middle States the Anglican establishment collapsed at once. In the North, however, the Congregational establishment was in a more favorable position to resist the trend toward complete separation of church and state and managed to survive for more than a generation.

The Congregational clergy had been ardent champions of the American Revolution, but they were distrustful of the spirit of liberty which threatened to carry its effects too far. After the outbreak of the French Revolution they became more and more fearful of the radical changes which were sweeping across the world and which threatened to sweep the Standing Order in New England out of power. One of the most eloquent exponents of theocratic views, Nathanael Emmons, insisted that the leaders of the American Revolution had not meant to modify the colonial political system, which satisfactorily embodied the "principles of a mixed and duly balanced government," that they had "meant only to dissolve the connection between Great Britain and the colonies, and leave the latter in the full enjoyment of the same liberty and order, which they had long before enjoyed."[1] As matter of fact, Emmons continued, "nothing was farther from their intention, than to introduce a loose, wild, frantic democracy, which should free the people from all restraint, and set them all upon a level."[2]

---

[1] Nathanael Emmons, *American Independence* (1802). In *Works* (6 vols., Boston, 1842), II, 224.
[2] *ibid.*, p. 225.

Fearing the consequences of the growing democratization of the federal government under Jefferson and Madison, Congregational theocrats like Emmons, Dwight, and Morse, fought desperately to preserve the establishment in the New England States.[3] Unfortunately they were fighting a losing battle. The defection of the Unitarian element, which began with Henry Ware's election to the Hollis Professorship at Harvard in 1805, seriously weakened their position. The unprecedented decision of the court in the Dedham Case of 1820 further undermined their power. Nevertheless the Massachusetts State Constitutional Convention of 1820-1821 retained the Establishment, although abolishing religious tests for civil office. The complete separation of church and state was thus postponed. Yet belief in the desirability of an established church was rapidly passing even among the theocrats. Lyman Beecher, writing about the election of 1817 which sealed the fate of the Establishment in Connecticut, reminisces: "It was as dark a day as I ever saw. The odium thrown upon the ministry was inconceivable. The injury done to the cause of Christ, as we then supposed, was irreparable. For several days I suffered what no tongue can tell, *for the best thing that ever happened to the State of Connecticut.*"[4]

Nor is this a case of projecting later conclusions into the past. As early as 1826 Beecher saw the benefits of separation quite clearly. Speaking to the Connecticut legislature, he exulted because Christianity did not appear weakened by being cut off from government support, but had actually grown stronger, thanks to the voluntary associations which "make it their business, instead of Select-Men, to see that every family has a Bible, every church a pastor, and every child a catechism."[5]

[3] The writer has traced this struggle in *The History of the Separation of Church and State in America up to 1833* (Thesis, Princeton Theological Seminary, 1943), *passim.*
[4] Lyman Beecher, *Autobiography*, edited by Charles Beecher (2 vols., New York, 1864), I, 344.
[5] Lyman Beecher, *The Memory of our Fathers* (New Haven, 1826), p. 12.

THEOCRATS AND THE STATE

The distinguished theocratic historian of American Protestantism, Robert Baird, organized his whole history around the "voluntary principle." Writing for a European audience he affirmed that "on no point are the evangelical clergy of the United States, of all churches, more fully agreed than in holding that a union of Church and State would prove one of the greatest calamities that could be inflicted upon us, whatever it may prove in other countries."[6]

Actually, the major battles for religious liberty had been fought and won during the Revolutionary Era. At the triumph of the Revolution the Anglican clergy of the Southern and Middle States, depleted by the flight of hundreds of Loyalists, were in no position to resist any longer. Only in New England was there still some fighting to be done, and the leader was a veteran of the struggle for disestablishment in Virginia, Elder John Leland, who spent the last fifty years of his patriarchal life as minister of the Baptist congregation in Cheshire, Massachusetts. Writing in the heat of the battle for constitutional revision in 1820, Leland suggested that Christianity's decline after the fourth century was the direct result of its union with the state; nor did it exert any markedly sanctifying influence on the state.[7]

The same reasoning, however, appears in the works of other contemporary New England ministers who, unlike Leland, were ardent theocrats, but whose denominations resented the continuation of the Congregational establishment in their states. Daniel Sharp, a Baptist theocrat of Boston, told the

---

[6] Robert Baird, *Religion in America* (New York, 1844), p. 116. This work was first published in 1835 in England. The 1844 edition was much the same as the first. In 1856 Baird published a much enlarged final edition which was translated into a number of European languages and achieved wide acclaim.

[7] John Leland, *Short Essays on Government, etc.* (1820) *Writings* (New York, 1843), p. 475. Leland appears as a perfect counterfoil for the theocrats. If all the writings of the theocrats were lost, their pattern could still be retraced with considerable accuracy from his works. Whatever they advocated, he opposed.

Massachusetts legislature that the lack of an "established priesthood" in the United States was a "subject of congratulations, because this circumstance is favorable to the permanency of our government."[8] Wilbur Fisk, Methodist theocrat from Connecticut, underlined the essential dichotomy between church and state. "Christ's kingdom is distinguished from all others, in that its principles and operations tend to the perfection and permanency of all good governments; but the principles and operations of worldly governments tend to deterioration and dissolution."[9]

Thus the separation of church and state, one of America's most original gifts to the world, was rather promptly accepted by the theocrats (except for the Congregationalists), although they continued to view with alarm the relaxing of time-honored political and moral restraints. No longer able or willing to fight for the *status quo ante*, they endeavored to Christianize American government and politics by every means short of a reunion of church and state. Their objective had been fully outlined for them two hundred years earlier by John Cotton whose words they might well have adopted as their battle cry: "It is better that the commonwealth be fashioned to the setting forth of Gods house, which is his church; than to accomodate the church frame to the civil state. Democracy, I do not conceive that ever God did ordeyne as a fitt government eyther for church or commonwealth. If the people be governors, who shall be governed? As for monarchy and aristocracy, they are both clearly directed and approved in scripture, yet so as referreth the soveraigntie to himself, and setteth up Theocracy in both, as the best forme of government in the commonwealth as well as in the church."[10]

[8] Daniel Sharp, *A Discourse . . . before . . . the Legislature of Massachusetts* (Boston, 1826), pp. 12-13.
[9] Wilbur Fisk "Christ's Kingdom Not Of This World," *Methodist Magazine*, x (1827), 209-210.
[10] John Cotton, *Letter to Lord Say and Seal* (1636). Reprinted in Perry Miller and Thomas H. Johnson, *The Puritans* (New York, etc., 1938), pp. 209-210.

THEOCRATS AND THE STATE
The National Government

The first aim of the theocrats was to make certain that the separation of church and state would not be interpreted to mean that America was no longer a Christian nation. "Perfect religious liberty," wrote an Andover Seminary professor, "does not imply that the government of the country is not a Christian government." There is a "real, though indirect connection between the State and Christianity."[11]

Having this concept of the government, the theocrats naturally sought to find some evidence of its Christian character in the persons of its leading figures. The President and members of Congress came in for particularly sharp scrutiny. Samuel Fisher, a Presbyterian minister, scourged President Madison in a sermon entitled *Much Good Destroyed by One Sinner*, and followed his indictment of the President's alleged "infidelity" with a blistering attack on Congress. "A view of our national Council must . . . convince every unprejudiced person that, as a nation, we are practically infidel. If we were to separate from the number of those, whom we have placed over us as rulers, the professed infidel, the openly vicious and impure, the Sabbath-breaker, the profane swearer, the gambler, the intemperate, the duellist, the murderer, and all those who uphold and countenance persons of this description, we have reason to fear that a small minority would be left behind."[12]

Another criticism the theocrats leveled at the national government concerned the content of presidential messages. "From the close of General Washington's administration in 1797, to the inauguration of General Harrison, there was not more than one message to Congress, or inaugural address, in which the Christian religion was distinctly recognized. Most of the annual messages during that period . . . expressed little or nothing to which a Deist might not assent."[13]

---

[11] Bela Bates Edwards, *The Influence of the United States on Other Nations* (1848). In *Writings* (2 vols., New York, 1852), II, 489.

[12] Samuel Fisher, *Two Sermons Delivered at Morris-Town, New Jersey* (Morristown, 1814), pp. 1-37, 41.

[13] Henry A. Boardman, *A Sermon . . . occasioned by the death of William Henry Harrison* (Philadelphia, 1841), pp. 20-21.

The most obvious link between the national government and Christianity was the chaplaincy to Congress, instituted in 1801. The committees in charge of securing the services of a chaplain, both for the House and the Senate, were always at pains to distribute the honors fairly among the various denominations, but even a quick perusal of the roster during the first half of the nineteenth century reveals that the choice was often rather casual. For instance, a Baptist preacher, Spencer H. Cone, who began his career as an actor—then a despised profession—changed to a military vocation, fought in the War of 1812, and who did not even profess Christianity until 1813, was appointed chaplain to the House for the term of 1815-1816, thanks to the good offices of a member of his congregation, a widow who boarded some influential Representatives.[14] The chaplaincy to Congress was a part-time job, which therefore had to be filled by clergymen residing in Washington. The remuneration, however, was desirable. Cone's biographers record with pride that Henry Clay intervened personally to have their father's emolument raised to five hundred dollars a year, which was then rather a large sum.[15]

As to the influence which the services of the chaplains exerted upon the government, there is no gauge to measure it. We may surmise that the existence of the office was little more than a gesture on the part of Congress. However, even this minor Christian institution did not go unchallenged by the opponents of the theocrats. For instance, President Madison expressed his objections in an essay which was not published until a century after its writing. He regarded these chaplaincies as a "violation of both the Constitution and the pure principle of religious freedom," and suggested that Army and Navy chaplaincies should also be forbidden on the same grounds.[16]

[14] E. W. Cone and S. W. Cone, *The Life of Spencer H. Cone* (New York, 1857), p. 140.
[15] *ibid.*, p. 142.
[16] Reprinted in *Harper's Magazine*, March, 1914, cf., W. A. Blakely, *American State Papers on Freedom in Religion* (Washington, 1943), pp. 164-172.

John Leland did not object to the institution itself, but suggested that chaplains should serve without remuneration, since the people had no voice in electing them; "why, then should they be taxed, where they are not represented?"[17]

National Holidays

The next endeavor of the theocrats in their attempt to keep the United States a Christian nation was to secure and safeguard Christian national holidays. During the first half of the nineteenth century Washington's Birthday and the Fourth of July were the only nationwide patriotic observances. President Madison's proclamation of a day of fasting and prayer at the outbreak of the War of 1812 and his appointment of a day of thanksgiving at the close of the war were the last such presidential decrees during the period. Madison himself questioned the validity of this practice and left no doubt as to his conscientious scruples. "Whilst I was honored with the Executive Trust," he confided to a friend, "I found it necessary on more than one occasion to follow the example of predecessors. But I was always careful to make the Proclamations absolutely indiscriminate, and merely recommendatory. . . . In this sense I presume you reserve to the government a right to *appoint* particular days for religious worship . . . without any penal sanction *enforcing* the worship."[18]

This fairly represented the policy of the government. The theocrats, on the other hand, having been reared in the New England tradition,[19] would have liked at least one annual day of thanksgiving on a national scale. Many of them voiced such a desire, but, interestingly enough, the strongest plea came from Samuel S. Schmucker, the only outstanding Lutheran

[17] John Leland, "Letter to Col. R. M. Johnson" (1830), *Writings*, p. 563.
[18] "Letter to Edward Livingston, dated July 10, 1822," in Blakely, *op.cit.*, pp. 173-175.
[19] See W. DeLoss Love, *The Fast and Thanksgiving days of New England* (Boston and New York, 1895), for the number and history of such days.

theocrat.[20] However, no national thanksgiving was appointed until the middle of the Civil War.

More widespread and more successful was the effort of the theocrats for making the Fourth of July a Christian as well as a patriotic holiday. From the beginning patriotism and religion had been intimately connected in the observance of the day. Upon attending the Fourth of July services in Lyman Beecher's church at Cincinnati, a visiting British clergyman recorded his bafflement "at the extraordinary mixture of the secular and the spiritual.... It was a question, whether the tendency was not to make religion worldly rather than the worldly religious."[21]

As long as the program of the day centered in a church service, the theocrats had an excellent opportunity to reach a wide audience with their more critical and discriminating brand of patriotism which differed considerably from that of the average lay orator. The growing secularization of American society, however, took the celebration more and more frequently out of the sanctuary, adding gaiety and even considerable rowdiness to its traditional solemnity. Remarking upon this regrettable change, George Potts, Presbyterian theocrat from Natchez, Mississippi, submitted his Fourth of July sermon for publication, in the hope that it "may be useful in promoting a *religious* observance of our national festival, instead of that merely noisy, intemperate and profane celebration, which has too often been witnessed."[22]

By contrast, some anti-theocrats like Alexander Campbell had only contempt for mixing the sacred with the secular and urged their followers to withdraw from the celebration altogether in order to observe the day in a distinctly Christian way. "While the mere politicians of the land and the children

---

[20] Samuel S. Schmucker, *The Christian Pulpit, the Rightful Guardian of Morals, etc.* (Gettysburg, 1846), p. 5.

[21] J. Matheson, in A. Reed and J. Matheson, *A Narrative of the Visit to the American Churches by the Deputation from the Congregational Union of England and Wales* (New York, 1835), I, 115.

[22] George Potts, *An Address delivered in Philadelphia . . . July 4th, 1826* (Philadelphia, 1826), p. 3.

of the flesh are rejoicing together around their festive boards . . . we ought to glory in the Lord, . . . and sing a loftier song of purer joy than they. And while with them we remember with gratitude the achievements of the patriots of the land, we ought to rejoice in the Christian Chief, . . . who has made us free, indeed, and given us rank and dignity, not of citizens of earthly states, but of heaven."[23]

This attitude was characteristic of those antitheocrats who sought the Christian life by withdrawing from society rather than by trying to cast the whole nation into a Christian mold. At the same time the theocrats continued to bend every effort at Christianizing the institutions of the expanding country. In the political arena their greatest battle was to be the Sabbath controversy.

The Sabbath Controversy

In 1810, Congress passed *An Act Regulating the Post Office Establishment*, providing that post offices should be open and that mail should be carried every day of the week, including Sunday. It is unlikely that any affront to the Christian community was intended, but the repercussions were immediate. Again it was Lyman Beecher who embraced the cause most fervently. The historic flood of petitions against the Sunday mails began with one which he wrote on behalf of the Congregational Association of Connecticut in 1814.[24] That the violation of the Sabbath, even at the service of the public, constituted a serious offense, did not admit of any doubt in the minds of the theocrats. In their eyes the recognition of Sunday as a national holiday furnished one of the strongest proofs that the United States was truly a Christian nation.

The sternness of the "New England Sabbath" in colonial days is well remembered. It was rigorously enforced by law

---

[23] Alexander Campbell, *An Oration in Honor of the Fourth of July* (1830). *In Popular Lectures and Addresses* (St. Louis, 1861), pp. 377-378.

[24] Lyman Beecher, *Autobiography*, I, 268-269.

and continued to be subject to protective legislation until the final downfall of the Establishment.[25] Oddly enough, similar laws existed in Georgia, Alabama, and Kentucky, as well as in the new Northwest as late as 1830.[26] In view of the prevalence of these laws, Beecher and his fellow theocrats felt certain that a return to stricter Sabbath observance was only a matter of recalling the civil authorities to a stricter enforcement of the laws. The Sunday mails statute served them as a test case and they were confident of winning. They did not reckon with the strength of the opposition which needed only such a challenge to become fully articulate.

The earliest protest came, once again, from the indefatigable Leland. "If the observance of the Sabbath is sure to cease without legal enforcement, how did it survive in the first three centuries? Or how is it surviving in New York, New Jersey, and Pennsylvania?"[27]

But Leland's protest was only a token beginning. Large-scale opposition did not arise until the theocrats themselves had organized their campaign and begun to press their cause by political means. During the lull between 1815 and 1828, references to the Sabbath multiplied in the sermons of the theocrats, who placed more and more emphasis on the civil power's duty to enforce the existing laws and to repeal such as may be obstructive to a Christian observance of the day. In 1828 they determined that the time was ripe for an overall attack on the obnoxious statute.

On May the 9th, 1828, the *General Union for Promoting the Observance of the Christian Sabbath* was formed in New York City, with General Stephen Van Rensselaer as President and Arthur Tappan as Treasurer. The Union's efforts were aimed against Sunday travel in all forms, encouraging the

[25] *The Sabbath in Puritan New England* by Alice Morse Earle (New York, 1891) portrays not only its well-known rigors, but also some of its more winsome features.

[26] Edward Channing, *A History of the United States* (7 vols., New York, 1938), v, 231.

[27] John Leland, "On Sabbatical Laws," *Writings*, p. 441. This essay is dated 1815, less than a year after the Beecher petition.

patronage of companies which did not operate on Sunday, and advocating the boycott of those which did.[28] The specific target, however, was the Sunday mails statute, and within a few months the Union's initiative bore fruit in a flood of petitions. One document reported 467 of them, of which 441 were addressed to the House and 26 to the Senate. Most of these petitions came from New England and New York State, with only a handful from other parts of the country. Equally significant was the absence of the names of any clergymen. As usual, the theocrats were conspicuously refraining from direct participation in the political consequences of an issue which they had brought to the attention of the American public.[29]

The Union's activity, however, prompted the opposition to organize and to act. Counterpetitions began to reach the House and Senate by the score, denying that the Sunday mails involved any religious issue, let alone a desecration of the Sabbath, and denouncing the theocrats for their attempt to breach the wall between church and state. John Leland, as vigorous as he had been fifteen years earlier, voiced this apprehension in picturesque terms. If Congress granted the wish of the theocrats, he argued, it would be "a nest egg for themselves and others. . . . The deadly pill, at first, will always be rolled in honey. The honor of religion, the spread of the gospel, the piety and research of the reformers, the good of society, the safety of the state, and the salvation of souls, form the syrup in which the poisonous pill is hidden."[30]

A prominent Unitarian clergyman joined the opposition by suggesting that the opponents of the theocrats might be just as intent as they upon the proper observance of the Lord's day, but that they resisted because they feared the ultimate consequences.[31]

[28] *Missionary Herald*, XXIV (July, 1828), 222-224.
[29] *An Account of Memorials Presented to Congress, etc.* (New York, 1829), *passim*.
[30] John Leland, "Extract from a letter to Col. Richard M. Johnson . . . March 29, 1830," in *Writings*, pp. 561-562.
[31] Bernard Whitman, *National Defence* (Cambridge, 1829), p. 20.

Even some of the theocrats became perturbed lest their political action should be so completely misconstrued and arouse so much hostility that in the end one small victory would lead to several serious setbacks. "There is too much bustle and noise in our religious enterprise," noted John Holt Rice, a distinguished Presbyterian theocrat from Virginia. "The greater union and cooperation now manifest among the enemies of religion is, I believe, to a considerable extent owing to this very cause."[32] Three months later he added in the same vein: "I fear that the Sabbath cause is losing ground. Is it wise, when we know that the world has the majority, to push matters to a vote? Is it wise to push men until they commit themselves against the cause of holiness?"[33]

So widespread was the reaction against the theocrats in the Sunday mails issue, that when Congress finally took notice of the controversy, its decision spelled the immediate doom of their cause. The Johnson Report to the Senate remains to this day a classical defense of the American system of separation of church and state. The Report states emphatically that the precedents of the Jewish theocracy do not apply to America, and that "it is not the legitimate province of the legislature to determine what religion is true, or what false." Then, noting that "extensive religious combinations to effect a political object are . . . always dangerous, and that, when such influences begin to operate upon the political institutions of a country, the civil power soon bends under it," the Report emphasizes again the principle of complete noninterference in religious matters and the equality of all religions, including irreligion, under the American government.[34]

When John Leland read the Report, he hailed it as a milestone in the history of religious liberty, boasting "the language of John Milton, Roger Williams, William Penn, and

[32] John Holt Rice, "Letter to Archibald Alexander, January 8, 1830," in *Memoirs*, edited by William Maxwell (Richmond, Va., 1835), p. 366.
[33] "Letter to Mr. Knowles Taylor, March 2, 1830," *ibid.*, p. 368.
[34] Condensed from W. A. Blakely, *American State Papers on Freedom in Religion* (Washington, 1943), pp. 190-196.

Thomas Jefferson. . . ."³⁵ On the other hand, a theocratic chronicler of this turbulent era affirmed that "Satan never accomplished a greater temporary victory over the Sabbath, through any agency, in any country, than was accomplished by this report, if we except the abolition of the Sabbath in France during the reign of infidelity."³⁶

Thus the Sabbath controversy ended in the defeat of the theocrats, but they never ceased to denounce any slight of the day. A prominent New York theocrat, for instance, found the "most disgraceful form of such profanation" in the "Sabbath sale of polluted and polluting journals," and urged legislative action to end it.³⁷ Others selected some other instance of the popular disregard for the Sabbath, since such disregard grew apace with the influx of European immigrants and their concept of Sunday as a day of amusement, the "continental Sabbath." The Sabbath Union was reorganized in the forties, but its program remained much the same. It still managed to arouse sufficient interest to bring into being an "American Anti-Sunday-Law Convention" in 1848, which was addressed by the country's most notorious abolitionist and one of the fiercest antitheocrats, William Lloyd Garrison. In his speech to the Convention, Garrison reiterated all the arguments of the Johnson Report of 1830 in terms which were more incendiary as well as less rational.³⁸ It may be noted that there exists to this day a "Lord's Day Alliance," with headquarters in Washington and a token staff of ministers and laymen, who continue to press for more rigorous Sunday laws wherever the public is willing to be influenced along these lines.

[35] John Leland, "Letter to Col. Richard M. Johnson, March 29, 1830," *Writings*, pp. 567-568. The Report was largely the work of a Baptist minister.
[36] Emerson Davis, *The Half Century* (Boston, 1851), p. 137.
[37] George B. Cheever, *The Elements of National Greatness* (New York, 1843), p. 23.
[38] Extracts from the work of this Convention and from Garrison's address are printed in Blakely, *op.cit.*, pp. 208-217.

THEOCRATS AND THE STATE
The Clergy in Politics

The Sabbath controversy furnishes an excellent illustration of the conflict in which the theocrats were engaged for the Christianization of the American government and American politics. It revealed that they were unable to treat any departure from their pattern according to its real significance. Rather they treated everything as a matter of principle. Nor were their opponents any less zealous. They too were unable to keep a sense of proportion about even minor issues, because in every controversy the basic question cropped up at once: Should the clergy be active in politics? The theocrats claimed that they should. The antitheocrats denied them the right, except insofar as they would act as unrelated individual citizens.

Hostility to clerical participation in politics dated back to the post-revolutionary era. For a time clergymen could not even hold public office in various states, notably in the South where so many Anglican rectors had been engaged in Loyalist activities. The biography of a Baptist minister in Georgia tells of his successful opposition, in 1798, to a motion aimed at excluding ministers from public office. Yet he himself, when running for the Georgia Senate in 1816 and being defeated, "seemed ever afterwards grateful for his defeat," because, while upholding the clergy's rights as citizens, he still believed that as a group they should stay out of the political arena and confine themselves to their distinctive mission.[39] This was generally the attitude of the antitheocratic ministers, though some of the theocrats themselves preferred the clergy refrain from personal activity in politics. John Holt Rice, for instance, went so far as to approve of the exclusion of clergymen from public office in the revised Constitution of Virginia.[40]

Well aware of this aversion to direct clerical participation

[39] C. D. Mallary, *Memoir of Jesse Mercer* (New York, 1844), pp. 99-102.

[40] John Holt Rice, *Historical and Philosophical Considerations of Religion* (Richmond, 1832), p. 87.

in politics, the theocrats made it a matter of policy to stay in the background. They did not run for office. They did not sign any of the petitions in the Sabbath controversy. They found it more effective to throw their weight behind the election of Christian officials, which they could do on the strength of their own democratic privileges. However, while no one contested their right to electioneer as private citizens, they often exposed themselves to violent criticism when they used their pulpits to "preach politics." The problem was: "Where should the line be drawn between such concern for political morality as they were fully expected to show, and party politics which they themselves loudly repudiated as lying beyond their authority as ministers of the Gospel?

"To treat of the moral character and conduct, either of governments, or rulers, is not politics," asserted Samuel Fisher.[41] Most of the theocrats would have heartily endorsed this statement. Prejudice against so-called "political sermons," observed Robert Little of Washington, is a result of people's failure to distinguish "between what is really essential to the Body-Politic, and what only concerns the parties into which that body is sometimes unhappily divided."[42] George Potts agreed that the clergy should not enter party politics, but emphasized their duty to preach "on questions of political morality."[43] Samuel S. Schmucker went even further by urging his fellow theocrats to inculcate into their congregations specifically "the recognition of God as Supreme Ruler of all nations, and the precedence of his claims over those of Caesar"; the recognition of the "universal brotherhood and equality of men in civil rights"; and "the obligation of the moral law of God in all legislative, judicial, and executive business of our public offices and all political action of private citizens."[44]

Such general statements from the pulpit would not have

[41] Fisher, *op.cit.*, Appendix, p. 52.
[42] Robert Little, *The National Anniversary. In Two Sermons* . . . (Washington, 1822), p. 3.
[43] George Potts, *op.cit.*, p. 5.
[44] Schmucker, *op.cit.*, pp. 18, 23, 26.

given rise to any real objections. Opposition arose, however, when the theocrats demanded action in specific political situations. The clearest and most notorious call to such action came from Ezra Stiles Ely, Pastor of the Third Presbyterian Church of Philadelphia.[45]

It is hard to believe that Ely was motivated by party aims. In the presidential campaign which was then being waged he preferred Andrew Jackson to John Quincy Adams, in spite of Jackson's popularity with the common people, because Jackson was a churchgoing man and a fellow Presbyterian. He could not fail to see that Jackson would bring into power the very elements he wished to prevent from achieving political power.

"Every ruler should be an avowed and sincere friend of Christianity," Ely begins. This does not mean that there should be a religious establishment, but simply that "none of our rulers have the consent of their Maker that they should be Pagans, Socinians, Mussulmen, Deists, the opponents of Christianity; and a religious people should never think of giving them permission, as public officers, to be and to do, what they might not lawfully be and do, as private individuals."[46]

It is the duty of Christian citizens to elect and support as public officials, "the friends of the blessed Savior"; hence there should be "a new sort of union, . . . a *Christian party in politics,* which . . . all good men in our country should join. . . ."[47] This would not necessitate organization, but merely the application of Christian principles to the exercise of the suffrage, viz., "never wittingly to support for any public office" anyone possessing "a bad moral character," which includes not only "confirmed sots and persons judicially convicted of high crimes," but also "all profane swearers, notorious Sabbath-breakers, seducers, slanderers, prodigals, and riotous persons, as well as the advocates of duelling."[48]

Furthermore, he recommended never to support any man as

---

[45] Ezra S. Ely, *The Duty of Christian Freemen to Elect Christian Rulers* (Philadelphia, 1827).
[46] *ibid.,* p. 6.   [47] *ibid.,* p. 8.   [48] *ibid.,* p. 10.

a candidate "who is not professedly friendly to Christianity and a believer in divine Revelation." This again does not mean "that Christianity shall be made a constitutional test of admission to office...."[49] It simply affirms the right of Christians to prefer being ruled by Christians.

The use of the phrase, "a Christian party in politics," would have sufficed to cause serious repercussions. Ely, however, went even further by suggesting that the major denominations, notably the Presbyterians, Baptists, Methodists, Congregationalists, and Episcopalians, could marshal an electorate of decisive strength, since "the Presbyterians alone could bring half a million electors into the field, in opposition to any known advocate of Deism, Socinianism, or any species of avowed hostility to the truth of Christianity."[50]

This threat of bringing the clergy's influence directly into politics aroused a storm of protest from the antitheocrats. "It is lamentable," wrote a Unitarian minister, "that Christians cannot learn to do unto others as they would have others do unto them.... Should the pious Jew erect his synagogue on the side of my door, he should worship the God of his fathers in peace. And should the devout Mussulman build his mosque on the other side, he should be protected in his conscientious worship... But I should look upon every man who would control the consciences and opinions and votes of others, either by force or fear, ... as an enemy to the rights of man, as an enemy to his country, and as disgrace to his professed Master."[51]

John Leland condemned Ely's scheme as a "nightmare," in which every denomination would have "to sacrifice its peculiar characteristics, and all unite to form a Christian Phalanx, to be established by Congress as the religion of the United States."[52] So widespread and so adverse was the reaction to Ely's utterance, that John Holt Rice once again found some-

---

[49] *ibid.* [50] *ibid.*, p. 12.
[51] Bernard Whitman, *op.cit.*, p. 22.
[52] John Leland, "The Mosaic Dispensation" (1832), in *Writings*, p. 670.

thing to criticize which most of his fellow theocrats endorsed. Noting that Ely had brought particular odium upon the Presbyterians, Rice wrote to Archibald Alexander: "Although our strength is overrated, we are strong enough to excite fear.... The *mobocracy* of the age hates us, because we are not liberal enough to suit their taste . . . and from every quarter there is a hideous outcry against us."[53]

It is now apparent that Ely's idea of a Christian party in politics was more visionary than dangerous. There was too much rivalry even between those denominations which he had named as being able to marshal a formidable Christian voting bloc. Large-scale, concerted political action by Protestants was out of the question, except on certain limited issues such as Sunday legislation, and even there the theocrats were opposed rather than aided by fellow ministers of other denominations who did not share the theocratic viewpoint.

The Pitfall of Party Politics

It may seem that the primary reason for the opposition encountered by the theocrats in their attempt to secure Christian officials was the lingering anticlerical feeling which revived considerably during the Jacksonian era. But this was not so. Anticlericalism played a part, to be sure, but the major cause was the obvious inability of the theocrats to live up to their claim and keep political preaching completely nonpartisan.

The Congregational clergy, after supporting the American Revolution to a man, had become fearful lest the infiltration of French ideas should push the quest for liberty too far. They had neither the historical perspective nor the desire to realize that "the American colonies revolted, not because they were oppressed, but because they were free, and because their freedom carried the promise of still greater freedom, one unrealizable in the more settled and static conditions of old society, but beckoning as a possibility in the new continent."[54]

[53] Rice, *Memoirs*, pp. 370-371.
[54] Hans Kohn, *The Idea of Nationalism* (New York, 1944), p. 272.

The French Revolution acted as a potent stimulus upon the yet disfranchised and inarticulate masses of the young nation in their growing demand for "still greater freedom." The Republican leaders, advocating a wider distribution of political power, were thoroughly familiar with French revolutionary thought, and some of them were infected with the dread virus of "infidelity." Hence, the radicalism and the agnosticism of the French and of their American disciples were instantly and vehemently denounced by the theocrats of the day,—by Timothy Dwight, Nathanael Emmons, and Jedidiah Morse.

But in denouncing Republicanism of the Jeffersonian brand, they could not and did not steer clear of a virtually open alliance with the Federalist party. Few were as blunt as Emmons who declared in a Fourth of July sermon that "this anniversary properly belongs to the Federalists," that the Republicans were "apostates from the true principles of the revolution, and, of consequence, apostates from our federal government," and that hence "it is absurd in the extreme of their orators, on this day consecrated to commemorate the best moral, religious, and political principles, to trumpet the corrupt principles of anarchy, infidelity, and atheism, through our enlightened and well-indoctrinated nation."[55]

Most of the theocrats were less outspoken, but they did support the Federalists to a man, and their opposition to the War of 1812 made them appear in the eyes of the nation not only as party-bound but as downright unpatriotic.

On the other hand, the dissenting clergy of New England usually supported the Republican party. The biography of a New Hampshire Baptist minister, for instance, notes that he sided with the Federalists in their opposition to the War of 1812, which was "so rare a thing among the Baptists that it created alienation among his people and finally led to his dismissal."[56]

[55] Natanael Emmons, "American Independence" (1802), in *Works* (6 vols., Boston, 1842), II, 229-230.
[56] Erastus Andrews, "Elisha Andrews," in Sprague, *Annals of the American Pulpit*, IV (*Baptists*), 272.

Naturally most theocrats disclaimed any party preference and insisted that they were merely fulfilling their prophetic office. It was difficult, indeed, to find fault with Samuel Fisher's defense upon being dismissed from his church for "preaching politics." "I know," he wrote, "that the wealthy and the great are too often disposed to claim an exemption from the censures of those whose business it is to reprove iniquity . . . but the Minister who will hesitate to do it, through fear of losing his popularity, his place, or even his life, not only dishonors God, but is wholly unworthy of the sacred office."[57] Yet the reason for his dismissal appeared in quite a different light to the Republican members of his congregation, who bitterly resented what they considered an unjust and unpatriotic attack upon President Madison and his administration. How could they be sure that their pastor had, indeed, a "word from the Lord," rather than a whole set of Federalist prejudices invested with the sanctity of the pulpit?

The Federalist party became defunct in 1819, but the conservative temper which it represented did not disappear. After the precarious "Era of Good Feelings" the party lines were redrawn between Jacksonian Democrats and Whigs. Naturally the theocrats transferred their sympathies to the Whigs. Once again they faced the problem of how to speak prophetically on the political questions of the day above the din of party strife while being thoroughly biased in favor of one of the existing parties. "Federalism had valued the clergy . . . as a great stabilizing influence in society, hoping thus to identify the malcontent as the foe of both God and the law. In the next quarter century conservatism, in collaboration with the pulpit, worked out a systematic view of America as essentially and legally a religious nation, in which the church should assist the state in preserving the existing social order. Jacksonian democracy ran up sharply against these conceptions, both of religion and government."[58]

[57] Samuel Fisher, *op.cit.*, Appendix, pp. 55-56.
[58] Arthur M. Schlesinger, Jr., *The Age of Jackson* (Boston, 1946), p. 350.

THEOCRATS AND THE STATE

Theocratic criticism of the growing democratization of American politics was directed largely at the most obvious and spectacular abuses: the frequent disorders at the polls, the frantic scramble for offices, and the generally low tone of political controversy. "Put the exercise of the elective franchise into the hands of an ignorant and vicious population, and how fatally it will be used as an engine of destruction and death!" exclaimed J. P. K. Henshaw, later Episcopal bishop of New York. "Even now . . . how often are scenes of drunkenness exhibited at the polls, permitted to disgrace our boasted birthright, and mingle their polluting influence with the exercise of the highest privilege of freemen!"[59]

The "spoils system" came in for its share of biting prophetic castigation. Horace Bushnell called it "a spectacle of baseness and rapacity such as was never seen before," adding that "no preaching of the Gospel in our land, no parental discipline, no schools, not all the machinery of virtue together, can long be a match for the corrupting influence of our political strifes actuated by such a law as this. It will make us a nation of apostates at the foot of Sinai."[60]

The fathers of the nation, suggested John W. Nevin, the outstanding theocrat of the German Reformed Church, would be ashamed of the prevailing political practices. "Sympathy with the mind of Washington," he went on to say, "would be a most excellent antidote to the vile Spirit of Party."[61] However, most of the theocrats would rather have agreed with George D. Peck, who averred that not even the mind of Washington but Christianity alone would be an adequate "corrective of our political corruption."[62]

In none of these sermons or other printed sources of the

[59] J. P. K. Henshaw, *The Usefulness of Sunday Schools* (Philadelphia, 1833), pp. 21, 22.

[60] "American Politics—A Sermon," (1840) in *Life and Letters of Horace Bushnell*, edited by Mary C. Bushnell (New York, 1880), pp. 94-95.

[61] John W. Nevin, "Party Spirit," (1840) in *Works*, edited by Theodore Appel (Philadelphia, 1889), p. 123.

[62] *Methodist Magazine and Quarterly Review*, xi (1837), p. 448.

theocrats do we find any reference, by name, to either one of the great parties, yet the most elementary knowledge of the political struggles of the times makes the implications of their preaching quite plain. For the Whigs represented, by and large, the same classes and the same interests which had been embodied in the Federalist party. Actually the theocrats identified themselves with the Whigs even more closely than they had with the Federalists. Theocratic support of the Federalists was confined largely to the Congregational clergy fighting for the survival of their Establishment. Support of the Whigs was not confined to any one denomination. Both times the theocrats sided with the party which seemed ready to acknowledge orthodox Protestantism as at least the titular national religion, while accusing the other party not only of social radicalism but of infidelity.[63]

The Real Roots of the Pattern

In fairness to the theocrats, however, it is impossible to conceive of their pattern for American government and politics solely in terms of political partisanship. Nor was their attitude toward the changing political order motivated by conscious self-interest. It was rather a well-articulated plan to remold the nation in the likeness of the Massachusetts theocracy of the seventeenth century while taking into account the changed conditions, especially the separation of the church from the state.

First among the roots of this pattern was, of course, their pessimistic view of man and the consequent profound distrust of the common people. "It cannot be denied that human nature lusteth to envy," wrote Lyman Beecher. "No passions in men are more powerful than selfishness and pride, and inordinate desire, and discontent. There were the origins of the contest between the patricians and the plebeians in Rome, which

[63] Schlesinger, *op.cit.*, chapter 27, reaches substantially the same conclusion. So does Henry F. May, *The Protestant Churches and Industrial America* (New York, 1949), Part I, "The Conservative Mold."

continually agitated and at length destroyed the republic."[64]

This estimate of human nature and of the designs of the rising masses seemed more conducive to alarm in the United States than in Europe, because, as another theocrat put it: "In no part of the world has so little depended on the Ruler and so much on the people. Never was it of so little consequence, what the Government is, and of so much consequence what the people are. Never before has the experiment been made to determine, with how little power the ends of society may be attained,—how little we must submit to be controlled, and how far we are capable of governing ourselves."[65]

The theocrats agreed wholeheartedly with this analysis and they feared the risk inherent in the experiment. Anything might happen as a result of this rapid extension of freedom to an untutored, undisciplined people. "In despotic and arbitrary governments the absence of this moral principle is to some degree compensated by what are termed the five strong points of monarchy,—a hereditary monarch, a nobility, a standing army, an established church, and a strong police. But in a republic, whose cardinal features are the direct antithesis of these points, in which all power is ultimately wielded by the *people*, it is evident that the destiny of the government is indissolubly linked to the character of the people. . . ."[66]

Like all the theocrats, Gardiner Spring was watching with grave concern the political changes all over the world, but he concluded that the dangers were most serious in the United States, because, "though it is almost an anomaly in the history of the world, the American people, in a high sense, constitute the American government."[67]

[64] Lyman Beecher, "The Perils of Political Atheism," *Works* (3 vols., Boston, 1852), I, 117-118. Lecture dated 1832.
[65] Charles B. Hadduck, *The Patriot Citizen* (Hanover, N.H., 1842), p. 11. The writer was a professor at Dartmouth College.
[66] Samuel S. Schmucker, *The Happy Adaptation of Sunday Schools to the Peculiar Wants of Our Age and Country* (Philadelphia, 1839), p. 7.
[67] Gardiner Spring, *Dangers and Hope of the American People* (New York, 1843), p. 4.

"The sovereignty of the people is a fact," cautioned George W. Bethune, "and over the results for good or evil you have no control, beyond your individual vote, except, by diffusing the leaven of truth through the mighty, heaving mass, you persuade them to rule well; or, by neglecting your opportunities, you leave them, so far as your agency is concerned, to moral corruption, self-tyranny, and national suicide."[68]

The theocrats repeatedly asserted that they were not opposed to political freedom, but only to its abuse. As a matter of fact, they seized every opportunity to claim that the "republican liberties" of Americans were derived directly from Scripture, notably from the Old Testament. Lyman Beecher went so far as to suggest that the Jewish theocracy was a perfect prototype of the American government. "The Mosaic institute," he affirmed, "comprehends, in a high degree, all the elements and outlines of a federal national republic, more resembling our own than any government on earth ever did. . . ."[69]

Yet, while claiming to cherish the political liberties of the American people, derived from "that republican book, the Bible,"[70] the theocrats endorsed the extension of political freedom only insofar as it was possible simultaneously to educate the people in the moral principles of Christianity. This was the political mission of the voluntary societies. Indeed, "the restraints of a religious education constitute the most effectual police that can be imagined," affirmed Samuel G. Winchester. Therefore, "as patriots, if from no other motive, we should labor to disseminate the principles of the Bible and strengthen the influence and restraints of religion."[71]

If the theocrats considered this restraining influence of Christianity as indispensable to the stability of the American government, they also considered themselves as eminently

---

[68] George W. Bethune, *The Relation of the Sunday School System to Our Christian Patriotism* (Philadelphia, 1847), pp. 4-5.

[69] Lyman Beecher, "The Republican Elements of the Old Testament" (1833), *Works*, I, 176.

[70] Schmucker, *op.cit.*, p. 21.   [71] Winchester, *op.cit.*, p. 37.

THEOCRATS AND THE STATE

qualified to generate and spread it. Hence they confidently expected the government to give them special recognition by "supporting religious institutions," "suppressing public vices," and in general "guarding with great care the interests of religion."[72] "Here are Moses and Aaron united in counsel and in labour for the common good. Here is the true American union, of which no Christian and no patriot need be ashamed ... the only union of religion and civil government which we desire or consent to. . . ."[73] In these words the President of Amherst College came near to expressing the essence of the theocratic pattern for American government and politics. The theocrats wanted more than government approval for certain specifically Christian institutions; they wanted more than the right to influence the political life of the nation; they wanted the government and the Christian community to endorse and support the program of the voluntary societies as the primary agent for the Christianization of America. "When we were colonies," wrote Lyman Beecher, "the law could make provision for the creation and application of moral powers. But these means of moral influence the law can no longer apply; and there is no substitute but the voluntary energies of the nation itself, in associations, patronized by all . . . who love their country."[74]

The Real Causes of Opposition

No matter how quickly the theocrats called, "Infidelity!" when their pattern was being opposed, it must have been apparent even to some of them that all the antitheocrats were by no means infidels. John Leland had given a lifetime to the service of God. The historian Bancroft was nearly as ardent a Christian as he was a Jacksonian. President Jackson himself attended church regularly, though he did not become a com-

[72] William B. Sprague, *The Claims of Past and Future Generations on Civil Rulers* (Boston, 1825), pp. 27-28.
[73] Heman Humphrey, *The Way to Bless and Save Our Country* (Philadelphia, 1831), pp. 16-17.
[74] Lyman Beecher, *The Memory of Our Fathers*, p. 17.

55

municant until the middle of his second term. Even James K. Polk, whom the theocrats disliked and distrusted even more than Jackson, never missed worship on Sunday. True, there were also many influential Democrats who had little or no regard for Christianity and there were erratic Christian radicals like Adin Ballou, William Lloyd Garrison, or Orestes Brownson, who professed respect for Christ but held no brief for the church. It cannot be said that the antitheocrats were all infidels, or even that they were all identified with the program of the Democratic party. Their opposition to the theocratic pattern was rather grounded in certain common convictions of a positive nature.

For one thing, insofar as they acknowledged the desirability of the application of Christian principles to the political order, they accepted only the New Testament as a normative source for such principles. The Old Testament, they held, had force of law only for the Jews. "The king of Israel gave that people their laws and orders," wrote John Leland, "but Christ has given laws for the regulation of Christianity." Therefore, "if the sacred code in the New Testament is not sufficient to govern Christians . . . either the wisdom or the goodness of Christ is deficient."[75]

In the same vein, a humble Baptist preacher on the New York frontier indicted the theocrats for holding that "the Jewish Church . . . at the coming of Christ only underwent some change in its appearance, but nothing in reality," and for "looking into the Old Testament for a form of civil government. . . . An illustration of this sentiment may be clearly seen in the government of Great Britain, where the chief magistrate is styled, 'King by the grace of God,' 'His most Christian Majesty,' 'Defender of the Faith,' etc., whether he be a *saint* or an *infidel*."[76]

Again, the antitheocrats had an optimistic view of human nature, which led them to believe that even an untutored peo-

[75] John Leland, "On Sabbatical Laws" (1815), in *Writings*, p. 441.
[76] Alfred Bennett, *The Kingdom of Christ, distinguished from the Kingdom of Caesar* (Utica, 1830), pp. 7-8.

ple could act with a degree of political maturity far in excess of their formal preparation. A Baptist preacher on the northwestern frontier of New England rejoiced in the fact that "on a recent extensive journey our *Chief Magistrate* found his person most affectionately embraced by all classes of citizens. . . . Notwithstanding the contempt republicanism has been held in, by the courts of Princes, as being too imbecile to afford security to the state and too levelling in titles and distinctions to insure its rulers sufficient awe and respect, yet none of our venerable Presidents have had their lives menaced, or their persons insulted in any circle whatever, although they come and go and mingle with thousands without an armed cavalcade."[77]

A prominent Unitarian minister echoed the same feelings when reviewing the struggle for constitutional revision in Massachusetts. "There is probably no other country on earth where the same experiment could have been made with safety," he exulted.[78]

Leland went so far as to affirm that while "individuals often break over the bounds of moral honesty to injure their neighbors," yet, "this is not more frequent than it is for legislative bodies to overleap their legitimate domain," and that therefore "the liberty of the native of the woods, with proper restraints for overt acts, should be the goal of the political life."[79]

"The less government, the better," might have been the watchword of all the antitheocrats, but only a tiny minority of them advocated withdrawal from all active participation in politics. Representative of such an extreme view was Adin Ballou's *Standard of Practical Christianity* (1838), which he wrote for the Hopedale Community. He stated: "Placing unlimited confidence in our Heavenly Father, we distrust all other

[77] Kendrick Clark, *A sermon, delivered . . . before the honorable Legislature of Vermont* (Montpelier, 1818), pp. 31-32.

[78] Henry Ware, *A Sermon, delivered before . . . the Legislature of Massachusetts, etc.* (Boston, 1821), p. 22.

[79] John Leland, Extract from a letter to the Hon. R. M. Johnson," (1830), in *Writings*, p. 568.

guidance. We cannot be governed by the will of man, however formally and solemnly declared, nor put our trust in an arm of flesh. Hence we voluntarily withdraw from all interference with the governments of this world. We can take no part in politics, the administration of the defence of those governments, either by voting at their polls, holding their offices, aiding in the execution of their legal vengeance, fighting under their banners, claiming protection in their courts, petitioning their legislatures to enact laws, or obeying unrighteous requirements."[80]

The only concession which Ballou and other consistent "comeouters," were willing to make was to promise peaceable demeanor and patient endurance for whatever penalties their nonparticipation might entail.

The majority of the antitheocrats, however, held that the proper attitude of the Christian as a citizen consisted in "rendering to Caesar the things that are his," in other words, in "honoring, obeying, and supporting civil government . . . prepared to serve his own generation *by the will of God* and to obey the calls of his country in war or in peace, in the cabinet or in the field." In so doing, the Christian citizen "gives entire satisfaction . . . to the claims of his country; and the rest of his time may and *ought* to be devoted to the interests of the church of God."[81]

Beyond this individual participation in the government and politics of his country the antitheocrats expected nothing of the Christian citizen, except, of course, acquiescence in the democratic process, wherever it might lead. John Leland himself, in spite of his devotion first to Jeffersonian republicanism and then to Jacksonian democracy, paid a strange tribute to this principle during the last year of his long and eventful life. When, with the election of Harrison, the hated Whigs came into power, Leland managed to discipline his disappointment

[80] Reprinted in W. S. Heywood, *The Autobiography of Adin Ballou, 1803-1890* (Lowell, Mass., 1896), p. 310.
[81] Bennett, *op.cit.*, p. 12.

and to write in his diary: "Jan. 6, 1841. Gen. Harrison comes into the presidency by an overwhelming majority; of course, the greatest part of the people are pleased. If, as many men believe, the means made use of for his promotion, have been ridiculous, false, and deceptive, degrading to any country that looks for respectability, still he is the *chosen one*. *I* will acknowledge him. For him will I pray. But whether he is exalted to be the scourge to the United States, or a blessing to the people, I leave for the future historian to say. I am no prophet."[82]

The antitheocrats considered the American Revolution not as the end of a historical process, but as a beginning, as the first step toward the attainment of complete political liberty for the people. "A more glorious work is reserved for this generation," wrote Alexander Campbell, "a work of as much greater moment, compared with the Revolution of '76, as immortality is to the present span of human life: the emancipation of the human mind from the shackles of superstition, and the introduction of human beings into the full fruition of the reign of heaven."[83]

Summary

From the vantage-point of the mid-twentieth century we tend to look upon such utterances with mingled wistfulness and contempt. History seems to have proved the naïveté of the antitheocrats, the folly of their excessive faith in man and of their abstract, visionary idea of freedom. To be sure, American democracy was growing. The last vestiges of the old order were giving way to the new. But the new order, in turn, was to be composed of unregenerate human beings, stumbling— both wilfully and blindly—toward the Civil War, and toward all the other well-known and tragic events of subsequent American history. The folly of the antitheocrats consisted

---
[82] Note in Leland's *Writings*, p. 741.
[83] Alexander Campbell, *op.cit.*, p. 375.

primarily in leaving God out of the *corporate* life of the race, as if he were content to work with individuals only.

The theocrats, on the other hand, with their more realistic view of man and their recognition of God's presence in, and judgment over, society, were guilty, paradoxically, of lack of faith. They claimed to trust in God, because of what he had done for the nation in the past, but they acted as if he had lately withdrawn from the scene, leaving the entire work for them to do. They made much of the God who had been America's "help in ages past," but unconsciously belittled his power as America's "hope for years to come." They hoped to bring back an idealized past which had probably never existed, rather than confidently to face the future with its inevitable changes. They had much to say about America's destiny under God, but claimed to be sole agents of God, of an absentee God. Hence their struggle filled them with a sense of deep discouragement. Nathan Lord might as well have been speaking at the funeral of the theocratic pattern, when he exclaimed over the body of John Quincy Adams: "Are Church and State, in our country, right, each in itself, and both in their reciprocal relations? Are we becoming the true theocracy, the end of promise? Or, as man affects self-government, does he not, practically, become more independent of the government of God? . . . The history is not yet written. Our country is still a problem. Who shall solve it?"[84]

[84] Nathan Lord, *Eulogy on the Honorable John Quincy Adams* (Hanover, Mass., 1848), p. 22.

CHAPTER III

THE THEOCRATS AND THE CATHOLIC PROBLEM

Anti-Catholicism in America

"The Lord has been pleased to form us for his peculiar service, by making us, from the beginning, a religious people. The Israelites were more eminently the people of God on account of religion than on any other account; yea, in that respect they were the only people of God in the world. They were separated from the rest of mankind for the great purpose of preserving and propagating the true religion, in opposition to the attempts of all other nations, to spread superstition and idolatry over the face of the earth."[1]

These were some of the glowing words with which one of New England's staunchest theocrats greeted the opening of a new century. His terminology was characteristic of his day. He could refer to Americans as a "religious people" and to the "superstition and idolatry" of other nations without the need of being more specific. His hearers were accustomed to using the words "religious," "Christian," "Protestant," and "Puritan," interchangeably. They also knew that "superstition" and "idolatry" designated the Church of Rome. "Christianity" was identical with "Protestantism," and "Popery" was regarded as the Church of the Antichrist, or, at best, as a hopeless travesty upon the true church.

Nearly half a century later we find the same thoughts and almost the same words on the lips of a Presbyterian minister, speaking in one of the capital cities of the old West. "Puritanism," he declared, "is at least eighteen hundred years old. It is but another name for Apostolic Christianity. Puritanism,

---

[1] Nathanael Emmons, *God Never Forsakes His People* (1800) in *Works* (6 vols., Boston, 1842), II, 172.

Protestantism, and True Americanism are only different terms to designate the same set of principles."[2]

The half century which had elapsed between Emmons' "Century Sermon" and Boynton's patriotic discourse, had witnessed the beginnings of significant changes in America's population. The numerical growth itself was extraordinary. In 1800 there were 5,308,483 inhabitants. By 1850 their number had swelled to 23,191,876, nearly a five-fold increase.[3] But even more startling was the difference in America's religious complexion. The 40,000 Roman Catholics of 1800 had increased to 1,606,000 by 1850, a forty-fold growth.[4] Their numbers grew considerably by the annexation of Louisiana, the Floridas, Texas, New Mexico, and California, with their Catholic population of French and Spanish stock. But the main source of growth was, of course, immigration from Europe, particularly from Germany and Ireland. A slowly broadening stream in the twenties, it became a flood in the thirties, received an added impulse by the Irish famine in the middle forties and the revolutions of 1848, and rolled on unchecked until the outbreak of the Civil War. It was inevitable that the coming of hordes of Catholics, nursed in the "superstition and idolatry" of Rome, should profoundly alarm the theocrats who conceived of the United States as a Protestant nation, and had taken her for granted as such.

The Colonial Background

The heritage of anti-Catholic feeling had been handed down from the time of New England's first settlement. The Puritan settlers, it is true, had broken away from the Church of England rather than from the Roman Church, and therefore we rightly expect to find them more vocal in their condemnation of the English Church. But they always took care to in-

[2] Charles B. Boynton, *Oration Delivered on the Fifth of July, 1847 . . . in Cincinnati* (Cincinnati, 1847), p. 10.
[3] Gerald Shaughnessy, *Has the Immigrant Kept the Faith* (New York, 1925), pp. 73, 134. This figure excludes Negroes.
[4] *ibid.*

sist that the Church of England was a true Christian church, whereas they considered the Church of Rome as the Antichrist.[5]

Moreover, the Church of England itself had no fondness for Rome. The Society for the Propagation of the Gospel in Foreign Parts, founded in 1701, was the missionary financing agency of the Anglican clergy in the colonies. Its charter of incorporation contained a direct reference to "Divers, Romish Priests and Jesuits" whose work it proposed to counteract.[6]

Roman Catholics were subjected to civil disabilities in all the colonies where the Church of England was established. Even in Maryland, where the Catholic authorities had secured a broad toleration by the Act of 1649, mainly because of the presence of a Protestant majority,[7] restrictions were applied to the practice of Romanism as soon as the colony became a royal province and Anglicanism the established religion.[8]

In New England the same sentiments prevailed, but they were more marked insofar as the Congregational clergy were more articulate and aggressive. Typical of anti-Catholic feeling was the inauguration at Harvard in 1750 of a lectureship, endowed by a judge, Paul Dudley, whose intent was to perpetuate the Puritan hatred of Rome. The Dudleian lectures, every third of which had to be used "for the detecting and convicting and exposing the Idolatry of the Romish Church,"[9] continued, with one major interruption, until the end of the nineteenth century. Civil disabilities inflicted upon Catholics in colonial New England were much the same as the Anglican colonies. Only Rhode Island never discriminated against them.[10]

[5] Perry Miller and Thomas H. Johnson, *The Puritans* (New York, 1938), pp. 9-10.
[6] Quoted in Mary A. Ray, *American Opinion of Roman Catholicism in the Eighteenth Century* (New York, 1936), p. 64.
[7] Josiah F. Polk, *The Claim of the Church of Rome to the Exercise of religious toleration during the proprietary government in Maryland, examined* (Washington, 1846), *passim*.
[8] Sanford H. Cobb, *The Rise of Religious Liberty in America* (New York, 1902), p. 387.
[9] Quoted in Ray, *op.cit.*, p. 128.
[10] Cobb, *op.cit.*, pp. 437-438.

CATHOLIC PROBLEM

The Peaceful Twenties

Such, then, was the colonial heritage of anti-Catholic sentiment and anti-Catholic legislation. However, there was hardly any physical persecution of Catholics. Their numbers were so small that they scarcely drew attention to themselves, and as long as they obeyed the law they were left unmolested. Nor was there any anti-Catholic motivation in the early efforts of the theocrats. The immediate object of their attention was the rising West, where thousands of emigrants from New England and the Middle States began to settle during the depression which followed the War of 1812. Uprooted from their homes, freed from the restraints of an organized community, cut off from the benefits of stated worship and religious teaching, these settlers caused the theocrats increasing concern. They had to be provided with Bibles, with Christian literature, with an educated ministry, lest they should lapse, within a generation or two, into infidelity. This at least, was the tenor of two famous missionary reports, based on extended travels through the area.[11] The only encounter of these missionaries with Roman Catholics took place in New Orleans and gave rise to friendly rather than hostile reflection. Attempting to distribute Bibles among the French Catholics, Schermerhorn and Mills not only obtained the Bishop's consent, but even received a donation from him, much to their surprise. Two years later the Bishop was no longer willing to endorse the project, but observed nevertheless "that he should prefer to have the present version of the Testament in the possession of the people, rather than have them remain entirely ignorant of the sacred Scriptures."[12] In view of the tremendous controversy which the use of the Protestant Bible in the public schools of New York aroused in the forties, this tolerant attitude on the part of a

[11] John F. Schermerhorn and Samuel J. Mills, *A Correct View of that Part of the United States, which lies West of the Allegany* [sic] *mountains* ... (Hartford, 1814).
Samuel J. Mills and Daniel Smith, *Report of a Missionary Tour* ... (Andover, 1815).
[12] Mills and Smith, *op.cit.*, p. 37.

Catholic bishop is curious indeed. It leads us to conclude—and the absence of any mention of Roman Catholics in the constitutions of the early benevolent societies[13] corroborates our conclusion—that because of the small number of Catholics in the United States, the theocrats were not yet aware of any Catholic threat, but were directing their efforts at the prevention of infidelity, of which the turbulent frontier was giving a great deal of evidence.

The Dudleian lecture of 1821 lightly shrugs off the power of Rome. "The claims of this proud hierarchy, as they have in a great measure ceased to terrify, have accordingly lost much of their former interest. Blessed be God, the alarms, which agitated the breasts of our venerable and scrupulous ancestors, and which had not subsided at the establishment of this Lecture, are now known only in history. The thunders of the Vatican have long since spent their rage; and, even in its neighboring atmosphere, they are regarded as artificial and harmless attempts to imitate the war of the elements."[14]

Written apparently under the impact of the news from the Papal States that Pius VII had barely been able to subdue the revolt of the *Carbonari*,[15] these words reveal how little was thought of any threat to the United States from that quarter even as late as 1821. Nor did Protestant feeling change until the middle twenties, though occasional anti-Catholic articles appeared in some religious magazines such as the *Boston Recorder*, the *Christian Watchman* and the *New York Observer*.[16]

Protestant feeling about the growth of the Catholic church in the United States did not crystallize at once. In the late

[13] *Constitution and Address of the American Society for Educating Pious Youth* (Boston, 1815). *Constitution and Address of the American Bible Society* (New York, 1816). Even the early issues of *The Home Missionary* (New York, 1828) lack any reference to Rome.
[14] John Pierce, *The Right of Private Judgment Vindicated Against the Claims of the Romish Church . . . A Dudleian Lecture . . .* (Cambridge, 1821), p. 4.
[15] MacCaffrey, *History of the Catholic Church in the Nineteenth Century* (2 vols., Dublin & St. Louis, 1910), I, 212.
[16] Ray Allen Billington, *The Protestant Crusade, 1800-1860* (New York, 1938), pp. 43-44.

twenties it took the form of concern over Catholic competition, to which Protestants could oppose nothing except greater missionary exertions of their own. The right of Catholics to propagate their own faith was nowhere denied, since such denial would have been contrary to the American principle of complete religious freedom. The sudden awareness of Catholic growth struck Protestants as strange, and made them feel uneasy, but there was not yet any distinct apprehension of a menace to the nation.[17]

Reports from the West, however, soon began to change this tolerant outlook. The "Correspondence" in *The Home Missionary*, which in its early issues had not paid any attention to Catholics, began to print notices of Catholic growth with increasing frequency. "The Jesuits are making rapid strides here in their usual way, building chapels, schoolhouses, and establishing nunneries," noted a "highly valued correspondent" writing from Missouri on March 9, 1829. "Large contributions, by Protestant people, or those who have been educated as such, are made to erect these buildings, and many are sending their children to these schools...."[18]

Protestant support of Catholic expansion and Protestant patronage of Catholic schools became the chief targets of anti-Catholic writers for the next five years. It seems that the laity, far less imbued with anti-Catholic feeling than the clergy, and naturally curious about anything "different," particularly on the frontier where any diversion was welcome, were not so much alarmed as intrigued by Catholic activity. The reports of American Catholic leaders, such as Bishop Fenwick of Cincinnati, to the "Society for Propagating the Faith" of Lyons, France, frequently referred to some modest wooden chapel in the West, the scene of Catholic preaching, which "could not contain the Protestants who crowded it."[19] These

[17] "Notices of the Papal Church in the United States," *American Quarterly Register*, II (1830), 189-190.
[18] *The Home Missionary*, II (1829), 11.
[19] "Notices of the Papal Church in the United States," *American Quarterly Register*, III (1830), 90.

Protestants, "or those who have been educated as such," hailed anything that took them out of their hard and humdrum existence. The progress of Catholic schools in the West, and their appeal to Protestants, may also be accounted for by the absence of any other schools, Protestant or public, in large areas. It was inevitable that these Catholic schools should become potent instruments for the creation of pro-Catholic feeling, and that in many cases they should lead to the conversion of Protestant pupils to Catholicism. Proselytism was, of course, not the avowed object of these schools. Often they would pledge in their prospectus that no attempt would be made to convert non-Catholic pupils.[20] These pledges need not be interpreted cynically, but the fact remains that by merely allowing things to take their natural course, many pupils of nominally Protestant background adopted the faith of their school.

During the late twenties and the early thirties, the Protestant community was becoming more and more conscious of Catholic growth in the United States, and the strangeness of Catholic worship and Catholic methods provoked reactions ranging from friendly curiosity to apprehension. A hitherto unnoticed aspect of the Catholic church in the United States appeared in the "trusteeism controversy" in Philadelphia and New York. The bishops finally established their right to have church property vested in their own person rather than in a board or lay trustees. During the course of these debates, however, the autocratic organization of the Catholic church became apparent to the American public.[21]

The impression created by the First Provincial Council of Baltimore, held in November, 1829, confirmed the impression that Catholicism was foreign to American institutions. The imposing ceremonies sharply contrasted with the simplicity of Protestant worship to which Americans were accustomed.[22]

[20] *Biblical Repertory*, III (1831), 261-262.
[21] Billington, *op.cit.*, pp. 38-41.
[22] *American Quarterly Register*, III (1830), pp. 93-96.

But the foreign nature of Catholicism did not arouse any real alarm until the coming of the Irish Catholic immigrants and their priests.

Conditions in Ireland in the middle twenties were appalling. Failure of crops led the landlords to evict masses of tenant farmers, who overnight became public charges. Emigration seemed the only solution offering immediate relief. Thousands, therefore, embarked for Canada or the United States, carrying little more than a bag of potatoes.[23] From this beginning the Irish immigration continued to furnish the main source of Catholic growth in the United States for a quarter century. Statistics of arrivals for this early period are not always clear, since they usually lump Great Britain and Ireland together. Neither are there any reliable figures as to the religious affiliation of the immigrants. However, it seems safe to say that between 1825 and 1834 at least five thousand Irish Catholic immigrants entered the United States each year, the number increasing with the years.[24] Catholic immigrants from other European countries, notably Germany and France, also began to arrive in growing numbers. Their coming was noted with satisfaction by the Baltimore Council, but care was taken to point out the need for their gradual "Americanization." "The convulsions of Europe," stated the *Pastoral Letter*, "have not been without advantage to us. . . . As our congregations have in a great measure been hitherto an emigrant population, so has our ministry been to a considerable extent composed of adopted citizens. But the children of the former, and the successors of the latter have for some time past assumed more of our native character, and must necessarily become chiefly, if not altogether national, henceforth."[25]

[23] "Emigration Conditions in Ireland, 1824-26." Edith Abbott, *Historical Aspects of the Immigration Problem* (Chicago, 1926), pp. 68-72.
[24] W. J. Bromwell, *History of Immigration to the United States . . . from September 30, 1819, to December 31, 1855* (New York, 1856), pp. 44-84.
[25] "Pastoral Letter to the Laity" (1829). Peter Guilday (ed.), *The National Pastorals of the American Hierarchy, 1792-1919* (Washington, 1923), p. 22.

But such a statement from the American hierarchy, reassuring though it was meant to be, did little to allay the growing apprehensions of the Protestant clergy as to the foreign nature and foreign connections of the Catholic church.

The "Foreign Conspiracy" and Nativism

Foreign interest in the Catholic church in the United States centered around the work of three Catholic missionary societies: The Society for Propagating the Faith, founded at Lyons in 1822; the Leopold Foundation, organized in Vienna in 1828; and the Ludwig Mission, established by Louis I of Bavaria in 1838.[26] The reports of the French society furnished Protestants with the earliest statistics on Catholic growth in the United States. The Bavarian society never received much notice, because by the time of its founding the Nativist movement was well under way, owing to the tremendous publicity accorded to the activities of the Austrian society. Samuel F. B. Morse was acquainted with the work of the Society at Lyons, but considered it insignificant compared with the political significance of the designs of the Leopold Foundation. In his *Foreign Conspiracy Against the Liberties of the United States*, which provided most of the ammunition for the anti-Catholic argument of the thirties and forties, he affirmed that Austria was both the power behind the Papacy and the originator of a subversive design on American democratic institutions by means of Catholic infiltration.[27] We can date the beginnings of the Protestant offensive from the publication of this work, in the form of a series of articles in *The New York Observer* early in 1834.

Morse's anti-Catholic bias has not been satisfactorily accounted for. Billington traces it to a single incident in which Morse had his hat knocked off by a soldier while watching a procession in Rome during the Holy Year of 1830.[28] He fur-

---

[26] B. J. Blied, *Austrian Aid to American Catholics, 1830-1860* (Milwaukee, 1944), pp. 17-34.

[27] Chapters I, II, and *passim*.   [28] Billington, *op.cit.*, pp. 122-123.

ther states that Morse "remained an ardent nativist throughout his life,"[29] though his anti-Catholic activity subsided after 1837. Another historian, after referring briefly to Morse's "lapse into anti-Catholic Native American agitation" goes on to say that "he had come home from Italy with a strong aversion to Catholicism; he fell an easy victim to the Maria Monk imposture and was inveigled into writing and sponsoring several widely circulated anti-Catholic Native-American tracts." However, "in his riper years he disentangled his facts and grew more tolerant."[30]

Aside from the obvious contradiction concerning Morse's later attitude, the latter statement contains another error: Morse could not have been influenced by the Maria Monk story in writing his *Foreign Conspiracy*, because the *Awful Disclosures* of the alleged escaped nun did not appear until more than eighteen months after Morse's series of articles. One gains the impression that an attempt has been made to discredit Morse without due regard to facts.

But Morse's character and motivation are not nearly as important as his influence. The anti-Catholic literature following upon the publication of the *Foreign Conspiracy* did little more than quote Morse's work and elaborate on his statements, adding more emotion than substance to them. How plausible was the evidence of a "foreign conspiracy" against the United States? On the answer to this question depends the historical appraisal of the crusade to keep the United States a Protestant nation.

Morse's first argument was that the Catholic Church was not merely a religious but a political organization. "I have nothing to do," he wrote, "with the *purely religious* character of the Roman Catholic sect."[31] But Catholic dogma postulated certain political doctrines which were manifestly contrary to republican principles. Foremost among them was the doctrine

[29] *ibid.*, p. 138.
[30] George H. Genzmer, "Samuel F. B. Morse," *Dictionary of American Biography* (New York, 1934), xiii, 248.
[31] Morse, *op.cit.*, p. 33.

of the temporal supremacy of the Pope, evidenced not only in the existence of the Papal States but also in the explicit statements and practices of the Popes from Innocent the III to Gregory the XVI.[32] The exercise of this supremacy had consistently led to the persecution of "heretics" and to the suppression of civil liberty as well. Catholics in the United States insisted that the Roman church had changed since the Inquisition; but the reading of the *Encyclical Letter* of Gregory XVI, dated September 1832, could make anyone wonder. In this encyclical the Pope called liberty of conscience a "most pestilential error," excoriated "that pest, of all others most to be dreaded in a state, unbridled liberty of opinion," with its adjunct, "that worst and never sufficiently to be execrated and detested liberty of the press," and urged again the proscription and annihilation of "bad books," which could never be "otherwise destroyed than by the flames...."[33] Such words from the Head of the Catholic church brought it home to even the most tolerant Protestant that the Roman church, while she might have altered some of her methods, had not abandoned her claims to political control, and continued to be the sworn enemy of liberty, both religious and civil.

Contemporary events in Europe further corroborated this impression. "We do not doubt," wrote the *Biblical Repertory*, "that in a Protestant country like this, where there is an overwhelming majority of anti-popish population ... they find it convenient to make disclaimers, to employ glosses, and to pursue a course adapted and intended to turn away the public mind from the most odious parts of their system. But the question is, what aspects does the Papal system wear *at this hour* in Spain, in Portugal, in Italy, in Austria ... where it is at full liberty to enforce its claims and to act out its spirit, without fear or restraint?"[34]

By proving that the Roman church had been consistently

[32] W. C. Brownlee, *Popery an Enemy to Civil and Religious Liberty*... (New York, 1835), Part II, chapters 2-6.
[33] Quoted in Morse, *op.cit.*, pp. 41-42.
[34] VIII (1836), 194.

hostile to political and religious liberty, and by offering evidence of her unchanged character, Morse and the Protestant clergy who adopted his conclusions had advanced a long way toward arousing the American Protestant community. But Morse insisted that there was a definite plot against the United States, by which Austria was fomenting the collapse of the American republican system.[35] The facts which led him to this conclusion were plausible enough: the Leopold Society had been organized upon recommendation of Cardinal Rudolph, brother of Emperor Francis I, and was placed under his protection. The all-powerful Metternich endorsed it, the Emperor assented, and Pope Leo XII blessed it.[36] All this time Austria remained the most powerful member of the Holy Alliance (excluding Russia) and the defender of the Pope against the revolutionary uprisings in Italy. She also took the lead in suppressing all the revolutions which agitated Europe throughout this period. These were the facts, but they alone could not prove the existence of a conspiracy. Neither could the existence of such a conspiracy be deduced from the letters of American Catholic leaders to the Leopold Foundation, but that did not deter Morse, who wrote: "In documents thus prepared by Jesuits, (the most wary order of ecclesiastics,) to draw forth more liberal supplies of money from abroad, and then submitted to the revision of the most cautious cabinet of Europe . . . we must expect to find great care to avoid any unnecessary exposure of covert political design."[37]

In fact, the existence of a conspiracy, as such, could not be proved because it did not exist. Whether Morse himself believed in its reality, or whether he merely used it as a device to attract attention, we cannot tell. But by "exposing" it he achieved two things: he reminded the Protestant community forcefully of the political principles of Roman Catholicism, and he challenged them to rise to the defense of those republican principles which they regarded as Protestantism's gift to America.

[35] Morse, *op.cit.*, pp. 21-23.   [36] Blied, *op.cit.*, pp. 19-24.
[37] Morse, *op.cit.*, p. 25.

CATHOLIC PROBLEM

The influence of these Protestant republican principles, Morse assumed, had so alarmed Europe's Catholic despots that they had resolved, by means of the immigrant plot, to subvert American institutions. "The example alone of our prosperity which we exhibit in such strong contrast to the enslaved, priest-ridden, tax-burdened despotisms of the old world, is sufficient to keep those countries in perpetual agitation. . . . Every revolution that has occurred in Europe for the last half a century, has been in a greater or less degree the consequence of our own glorious revolution."[38]

It seems strange, of course, that the European despots should attempt the political conquest of the United States by using their most oppressed and discontented subjects as the instruments of their design, but viewed from America there was a certain plausibility in the argument. For one thing, the character of the majority of the immigrants—their poverty, their ignorance, the high rate of sickness and crime among them—led American Protestants to think that Catholic Europe was using the United States as a dumping ground for her paupers and criminals. Rules of admission to the United States were very lax indeed. As early as 1819, Congress had passed a law limiting ships to two persons for every five tons of their registry.[39] This, however, was a purely sanitary measure and had no bearing on the physical, mental, or moral fitness of immigrants. The influx of large groups of immigrants during the years between 1827 and 1832 created such a burden for the charities of Baltimore, that the legislature was petitioned to devise some means of control.[40] The report of a committee investigating the almshouses of New York, Philadelphia, Baltimore, and Boston during 1834, showed that for 4,786 Americans in their care there were 5,308 foreigners, of whom the majority hailed from Ireland.[41] While all these paupers were

[38] Morse, op.cit., pp. 19-20.
[39] Marcus L. Hansen, *The Atlantic Migration, 1607-1860* (Cambridge, 1940), p. 102.
[40] Edith Abbott, *Historical Aspects of the Immigration Problem* (Chicago, 1926), pp. 565-566.
[41] ibid., pp. 572-574.

not Catholics, the Protestant community could not fail to see that most of them were of that faith, which in turn made Morse's indictment more acceptable to them.

But the character of the immigrants was not the most impressive evidence of a "foreign conspiracy." More significant was their direct political activity, which took anti-Catholic feeling out of the confines of the religious community and made it a national issue, giving rise to the Native American party. This was, indeed, the strongest argument in support of the alleged "foreign conspiracy" against the United States. The same immigrants who in Europe might make trouble for the despotic regimes were being dumped on this country to make trouble for our republican institutions. In Europe, any attempt at rebellion would be speedily drowned in blood. But in America there was no need to rebel, since the very government of the nation was open to them through the exercise of the elective franchise. Unaccustomed to American institutions and the democratic process, who would influence and direct their votes? The priests, of course. And what are these priests? "They are Jesuits, in the pay and employ of a despotic government, who are at work on the ignorance and passions of our community; they are foreigners, who have been schooled in foreign seminaries in the doctrine of passive obedience; they are foreigners under vows of perpetual celibacy, and having, therefore, no deep and permanent interest in this country; they are foreigners, bound by the strong ties of pecuniary interest and ambition to the service of a foreign despot."[42]

Again, just as in the case of the letters of the American hierarchy to the Leopold Society, disloyalty could not be established by documentary evidence; neither Morse nor the later Nativists could link any Catholic priest in the United States to any concrete instance of political chicanery. But nothing as obvious was required, since the power of the priests over their people was well known. The confessional gave them access to the people's innermost thoughts and enabled them to

[42] Morse, *op.cit.*, p. 47.

sway their actions at will. Among immigrants to the United States the ascendancy of the priests was even greater, since the church was the only institution which had accompanied them from the fatherland to their new home. The ignorance of the immigrants, their utter dependence on the priests, and the foreign character of the Catholic priesthood, combined to justify the direst apprehensions of the Protestants. "If it be true," warned George B. Cheever, "that Roman Catholics in this country will move at the Pope's bidding, then, since it is true that the phalanx of such voters is strong enough to sway the balance between parties, there may be some probability in the assertion that ten years will not pass away, before the President of these United States will be nominated in the Vatican!"[43]

Whether the political abuses resulting from the large influx of immigrants and their speedy admission to the franchise were part of a foreign plot is more than doubtful, but the fact remains that in the turbulent party struggles of the thirties and forties the presence of the immigrant loomed large. According to one authority, both major parties made good use of the immigrant's ignorance through "immigrant bosses."[44] It is well known that the Irish crowded into the democratic party, but the Whigs, too, exploited the immigrants, since all the foreign-born could never be induced to vote the same way, if for no other reason, at least because of the antipathies which they brought with them from Europe. The more discriminating among the Protetsant clergy soon realized that the immigrants themselves did not instigate the political abuses, that the "putrid dregs from the sinks of Europe" were being "bought at a price" and "ravenously snatched at by the Spirit of Party."[45]

The ravages of the party spirit had gone so far with the immigrants that many Protestant leaders despaired of ever suc-

[43] *The Elements of National Greatness* (New York, 1843), p. 39.
[44] Oscar Handlin, "The Immigrant and American Politics," in D. F. Bowers, *Foreign Influence in American Life* (Princeton, 1944), pp. 86-90.
[45] Cheever, *op.cit.*, p. 32.

CATHOLIC PROBLEM

cessfully attacking the root of the evil: the naturalization laws. A Methodist pastor in Boston warned as early as 1834: "The time has gone by in which your laws of naturalization might have been amended. Your ballot box is now under the control of too much foreign influence and domestic ambition to allow of such an amendment as would affect the evil. Nothing remains for us but the more indirect operation of moral *means*."[46] But upon the organization of the American Republican party in 1843, the demand for such a change of the naturalization laws became the main plank of the Nativist platform, and the adoption of a residence requirement of twenty-one years was urged upon the legislatures, "as long as the native citizen is obliged to spend from birth, before he can enjoy this privilege of voting."[47]

Concern of the theocrats over the influx of Catholic immigrants found a distinctive emphasis in their interest in the growing West. Catholic growth in the cities was not viewed with nearly as much alarm as the reports of Catholic growth on the frontier. When Lyman Beecher determined to accept the presidency of the newly-founded Lane Seminary in Cincinnati, he took a strategic view of the importance of the West which was to set the tone for all the efforts of the theocrats to save the West for Protestantism. "While at Philadelphia and since," he wrote in 1830, "my interest in the majestic West has been greatly excited and increased. . . . The moral destiny of our nation, and all our institutions and hopes, and the world's hopes, turns on the character of the West, and the competition now is for that of preoccupancy in the education of the rising generation, in which Catholics and infidels have got the start of us. I have thought seriously of going over to Cincinnati . . . to spend the remnant of my days in that great conflict. . . . If we gain the West, all is safe; if we lose it, all is lost."[48]

[46] A. Stevens, *An Alarm to American Patriots* (Boston, 1835), pp. 17-18.
[47] Cheever, *op.cit.*, p. 34.
[48] *Autobiography*, edited by Charles Beecher (two vols., New York, 1865), II, 224.

It was also Lyman Beecher who did the most to popularize Morse's disclosure of a "foreign conspiracy" by applying it directly to the disputed territory, the Mississippi valley, in his flaming *Plea for the West*.[49] Using all the arguments and "evidences" of Morse almost to a word, Beecher skillfully employed them for the promotion of Protestant effort to counteract Catholic growth in the West. One of the best means of prevention was to inform the public of the nature of Catholicism. The American Tract Society had faced this fact early by publishing the first popular anti-Catholic pamphlet.[50] After the publication of Morse's *Foreign Conspiracy* and Beecher's *Plea*, the Society sponsored a special printing of *Thoughts on Popery* by William Nevins, a systematic exposition of Catholic errors and superstitions, which achieved a startlingly wide sale.[51]

Another means of prevention was to discredit the sincerity of Catholic educational efforts by pointing to the ignorance of Catholics and the hierarchy's apparent unconcern for their condition. "These seminaries and colleges in the West . . . are sustained by foreign funds. . . . Why are not these funds sent to Canada, where Popery has such extensive prevalence, and where 78,000 out of its 87,000 adults write their signatures with their mark, and of the remaining 9,000 many can write only their names?"[52]

The more belligerent among the theocrats soon began to feel that organization was required to launch a full-fledged counteroffensive. The year that saw Nativism enter politics in the form of the American Republican party also witnessed the birth of the American Protestant Association, interdenominational in nature, and pledged to encourage "the union . . . of Protestant ministers . . . to give their several congregations instruction on the difference between Protestantism and Popery" and in general "to awaken the attention of the community to

[49] Cincinnati and New York, 1835.
[50] Tract No. 32. *Romanism Contradictory to the Bible*.
[51] Billington, *op.cit.*, pp. 61, 351.
[52] Stevens, *op.cit.*, p. 12.

the dangers which threaten the liberties . . . of these United States from the assaults of Romanism."[53] The *Address*, drawn up by a committee consisting of clergymen from eight leading denominations,[54] gave a panoramic view of the Catholic menace, which it described, by way of summary, as a grand scheme "for the purpose of securing the controlling influence in the Valley of the Mississippi and, thereby, a political predominance in the country at large. . . ."[55]

This association and several others which followed in its wake encouraged the use of that type of anti-Catholic literature which has done more than any other factor to bring the "Protestant Crusade" into disrepute, entirely apart from the actual merit of its arguments and insights. Beginning with Maria Monk's *Awful Disclosures* in 1836, unscrupulous merchants of sensationalism succeeded in selling tons of scurrilous literature to a gullible, thrill-seeking public. So deep was the impression created by these wild stories of escaped nuns and priestly crime, that several of the leading theocrats gave them credence,[56] while others went further and sought adventure at first hand around the strongholds of the enemy.[57] It was largely through the influence of this infamous literature that the few atrocities against Catholic persons and property during this period were committed. Yet, so widespread was the belief in Catholic "secrets" and "immorality" that even such a distinguished clergyman as Robert Baird could justify the burning of the Charlestown convent (1834) by saying that it "was not destroyed because it was a Roman Catholic institution . . .

[53] *Constitution and Address of the American Protestant Association* (Philadelphia, 1843), pp. 7, 8.
[54] *ibid.*, p. 23. The outstanding names were those of Henry Boardman, Old School Presbyterian; Stephen H. Tyng, Episcopalian; John Kennaday, Methodist; and A. D. Gillette, Baptist.
[55] *ibid.*, p. 18.
[56] Samuel S. Schmucker, for example, in his widely circulated *Discourse in Commemoration of the Glorious Reformation* (New York, 1838), makes a great deal of the Maria Monk story.
[57] Robert J. Breckinridge was convinced of the existence of a dungeon underneath the Baltimore Cathedral, cf. *Papism in the Nineteenth Century in the United States* (Baltimore, 1841), pp. 61-65.

had it been a Protestant one it would, under the same circumstances, have shared the same fate."[58]

These extreme anti-Catholic elements unfortunately set the tone for the whole controversy after 1835, but their flamboyant writings and vociferous speeches could not wholly drown out the voice of the theocrats who were also deeply apprehensive of the threat of Catholic growth to the United States, but preferred a more generous defense. They rejected the boundless optimism of Channing, who, after noting the various advantages of Catholicism over Protestantism, went on to assert that "with all these advantages, Catholicism is still not very formidable. It has something more to do than to fight with sects; its great foe is the progress of society. The creation of dark times, it cannot stand before the light. In this country in particular, it finds no coadjutors in any circumstances, passions, or institutions."[59]

Neither did they share John Leland's implicit faith in the rightness of the democratic process. Noting that the Catholics could not adopt any coercive measures for proselyting as long as they remained in the minority, Leland remarked, "Should they by fair persuasion . . . increase their number above all other sects collectively, in that case they must of right have the rule; for no man who has the soul of an American will deny the maxim, that 'the voice of the majority is the voice of the whole.' "[60]

Such optimism was unacceptable to the theocrats, who believed in the depravity of human nature and the interest of Satan in human society. They preferred to continue to combat the Catholic church in a spirit of holy competition, while keeping a watchful eye on her political doings, and working for the enlightenment and the conversion of both Catholics and infidels.[61]

[58] *Religion in America* (New York, 1844), p. 271.
[59] "Letter on Catholicism," 1836. *Works* (Boston, 1877), p. 471.
[60] "Free Thoughts on Times and Things," 1836. *Writings* (New York, 1845), pp. 671-672.
[61] James B. Taylor, *The Exigencies and Responsibilities of the Present Age* (Philadelphia, 1836), pp. 7-8.

Millennial faith among the theocrats occasionally led to some wishful speculations. For instance, a clergyman of the Reformed Presbyterian denomination, who identified the Pope with the Anti-Christ, calculated that the twelve hundred and sixty years allotted for his reign upon earth would be over before he could harm the United States. "And when the mystical Babylon falls, it is not to be rebuilt in some other portion of the globe, but to rise no more forever...."[62]

A more plausible daydream caused a New England minister to exult over the "marvelous defection" of Catholics and the great success of Protestant evangelization, which together would bring to an end the threat of Catholic growth through immigration. "When the third generation comes," he asserted, "it is only here and there that a family remains in the Catholic communion. The state of Maryland, colonized by Catholics, is an example which speaks volumes."[63]

Such sanguine hopes were unwarranted. A Catholic monograph conclusively disproves them from a statistical point of view.[64] Conversions took place in both directions but neither side could claim a decided advantage over the other. The most that can be said is that all Protestants did not show an unmitigated fear of the immigrant influx, but rather saw in it a God-given opportunity to do missionary work.

This was actually the greatest difference between the attitude of the theocrats toward immigrants and the attitude of the American Republican party or other Nativist groups. The Nativists made use of the religious argument, but their motive was political and economic self-interest. The theocrats, on the other hand, objected to the immigrants as Catholics rather than as foreigners,[65] but even their concern for the West did not make them follow blindly the lead of the extreme Nativists.

[62] McLeod, *op.cit.*, p. 23.
[63] S. M. Worcester, *Our Country and Our Work* (Salem, 1843), p. 24.
[64] Shaughnessey, *op.cit.*, Conclusion.
[65] Cf. the incident related by Billington, *op.cit.*, pp. 245-246, in which a village in Illinois literally adopted a group of Protestant converts from Madeira.

CATHOLIC PROBLEM

In 1847, at the height of the immigrant influx from Ireland and the apex of Nativist agitation, a Presbyterian minister in the West had the courage openly to question the existence of a "foreign conspiracy," to recall his hearers to America's tradition as "the home of the homeless," and to conclude: "Our country is safe enough, if we instruct the whole people, and especially the immigrant portion of them . . . in the true principles of government, teach them the difference between intelligent liberty and mere licentiousness, place in their hands the Bible and the constitution of the Republic. . . ."[66]

There may not have been any "marvelous defection" from Catholicism to Protestantism among the immigrants, but there was a steady "americanization," for, Morse's suspicion notwithstanding, "the European of 1815 or 1914 left the Old World and settled in the New usually as an individual . . . he felt no conscious mission or urge to reproduce any but the most personal features of his life to which he was habituated. . . . To be sure he brought with him germs of institutions. . . . But in time the chemistry of the new scene dissolved even such Old World attachments."[67]

After the victory over Mexico and the new vast extension of the nation's territory, the belief in America as the refuge of the emigrant was linked with the belief in her role as the evangelist of the world, and the theocrats could share the vision expressed in the statement of two devoted secretaries of the American Home Missionary Society. "As physical barriers are now so generally removed, and the whole world is coming into a condition of preparedness for receiving a Christian civilization, is it not probable that a race will be raised up for this world-mission, whose character shall contain those selected elements which are most needful to make a complete

[66] W. C. Anderson, *The Republic and the Duties of its Citizens* (Dayton, Ohio, 1847), pp. 10-14. See also John W. Nevin, "Pseudo-Protestantism," in *Life and Work of John W. Nevin* by T. Appel (Philadelphia, 1889), pp. 228-241, and George Peck, "The Reformation the Source of American Liberty," *Methodist Quarterly Review*, xxviii (1846), 5-24.
[67] Hansen, *op.cit.*, pp. 11-12.

missionary people? Let there be a mixture of the peculiarities of different races." Thus the coming of large numbers of immigrants will turn out to have been a blessing, the distinction between home and foreign missions will disappear, and "the enterprise of evangelizing this land will become in effect, and on a grand scale, a Mission to all Mankind."[68] So far did the accent of theocratic strategy shift from the defensive to the offensive, from the strategy of exclusion to the strategy of missionary conquest, that they even launched a society with the express purpose of weaning Italy from the Pope.[69] As for political Nativism, it spent its force by the mid-fifties, giving way to the far more absorbing issues of slavery and the maintenance of national unity.

Summary

It remains for us briefly to appraise the "Protestant Crusade." Billington's monograph does not offer such an appraisal. There is a careful introduction on "The Roots of Anti-Catholic Prejudice," but no concluding chapter. The very last sentence of the final chapter, however, gives a clue to the writer's own stand. Only sectional controversy and civil war writes Billington "proved strong enough to break the hold that the Monks, the Breckinridges, the Beechers, the Brownlees, and the Gavazzis had on overzealous American Protestants."[70] But is this the last word? Is it legitimate to lump "the Beechers" and "the Monks?" Was the struggle to keep the United States a Protestant nation merely an outburst of "overzealousness"?

It does not seem so. The basic insights of the Protestant "crusaders" were altogether correct. Allowing for the fictitious

[68] Badger and Hall, "Correspondence," *The Home Missionary*, XXII (1849), p. 46.
[69] Cf. Edward N. Kirk and Leonard Bacon, *The Christian Alliance* (New York, 1845), *passim*. Charter members included Lyman Beecher (President), Nathan Bangs, Robert J. Breckinridge, Horace Bushnell, Spencer H. Cone, Thomas DeWitt, John M. Krebs, Samuel Miller, John W. Nevin, George Peck, Samuel S. Schmucker, Nathaniel W. Taylor, Stephen Tyng, William R. Williams, etc.
[70] Billington, *op.cit.*, p. 430.

CATHOLIC PROBLEM

nature of Morse's "foreign conspiracy," and condemning unreservedly the perpetrators of the Maria Monk hoax and all similar excrescences, we are left with several indictments whose validity has been proved by the subsequent history of our country.

For one thing, the Protestant "crusaders" were right in asserting that the Roman Catholic church had not changed and could not change, because of her own dogmatic structure. Again, they were right in calling attention to the traditional alliance between Roman Catholicism and political reaction, whether it be called monarchy, despotism, or fascism. The indictment of the Roman Catholic church as being hostile to religious and civil liberty was also well-founded. The success of Paul Blanshard's *American Freedom and Catholic Power*,[71] documented solely from Catholic sources, furnishes proof of a new awareness among Protestants of an old fact, which these men a century ago discerned so clearly. Even the comparison between Catholic and Protestant countries in regard to religious and political liberty, popular education and material progress is just as valid today as it was in 1812 or in 1848.

Thus the Protestant "crusaders" had every reason to look upon the coming of large numbers of Catholics with alarm. From their study of history and from contemporary evidence they knew that the Catholic church's strategy varied with her status: whether she was in the minority or in the majority. Hence the immigrants were viewed as living tokens of a fateful alteration of America's religious complexion which would inevitably bring about an alteration of her political structure as well. The arguments used against the Catholic immigrants contained a mixture of truth and fancy. Many of them were paupers or even criminals, but their background in European society accounted for that. They settled in the cities because there they found a more familiar environment and were able to stay together. In the corrupt party politics of the age, however, they were victims rather than instigators. Neither did

[71] Boston, 1950.

they have any sinister design on the West. They simply moved on from the cities when living conditions became intolerable; or else they had from the beginning a preference for farming. As for their churches receiving support from Lyons, Vienna, or Bavaria, that did not necessarily mean anything more than the interest the American Board was showing in the remote Sandwich Islands. Yet, the Protestant "crusaders" were not wholly wrong even with regard to the immigrants, for inasmuch as they were Roman Catholics they could not help appearing as a threat to the United States, if the United States was to continue as a Protestant nation.

CHAPTER IV

THE THEOCRATS AND THE INDIAN PROBLEM

THE theocrats of the first half of the nineteenth century inherited the conviction that America was the rightful possession of the white race. The colonists had not been able to conceive of the Indian as a potential member of their communities. He was a savage whose inferiority in everything except war admitted of no argument. He also fancied himself to be the owner of lands which, according to the colonists, belonged to the British Crown and had been secured for them by special charters. The colonists, with a few exceptions, despised the Indian because he stood in their way and because they feared him.

The Missionary Impulse

But the theocrats also fell heir to the noble feelings and self-sacrificing efforts of the pioneer missionaries of the seventeenth and eighteenth centuries. The American colonies had been projected partly as a missionary venture,[1] but this motive came to be so far subordinated to economic considerations that it might have been forgotten except for the heroic endeavors of the Mayhews, John Eliot, David Brainerd, the Moravians and the Society of Friends.[2] The memory of their exertions on behalf of the Indians served as a constant challenge and stimulus to the theocrats when at last their gaze began to turn to the red men, who at this time were no longer merely foes to be conquered or held at bay, nor yet individual lost souls to be saved by individual consecration, but a problem well *within*

---

[1] "The principal and main ends are first to preach and baptize into the Christian Religion and . . . to recover out of the arms of the Devil a number of poor and miserable souls. . . ." Promotional leaflet of the Virginia Company (1610), quoted in Garrison and DeGroot, *The Disciples of Christ* (St. Louis, 1948), p. 63.

[2] A concise chronology of Protestant missions among Indians may be found in G. E. E. Lindquist, *The Indian in American Life* (New York, 1944), pp. 164-167.

INDIAN PROBLEM

the expanding frontiers of the young nation, particularly in the Southwest. In colonial times the Indian had constituted a problem of security for the governments of the colonies. Shortly after the birth of the United States when emigration crossed the Alleghenies and new states were being formed rapidly, the Indian suddenly became a racial problem for the infant national community.

It was the newly awakened missionary spirit of Protestantism which directed the attention of the theocrats to the condition of the Indians. Preaching to the Society for Propagating the Gospel among the Indians, the oldest missionary society in America, founded in 1787, Joshua Bates declared that "Christianity is designed to become the religion of mankind," noting with exultation that "within a few years much has been done in the glorious work of *evangelizing* the world."[3] But missionary interest in the Indians based on Bible prophecy arose with the publication of *A Star in the West; or, A Humble Attempt to Discover the Long Lost Ten Tribes of Israel* by the aged revolutionary statesman, Elias Boudinot,[4] who had retired from public life in 1805 to devote himself wholly to the study of Scripture.

By inquiring into the languages, character, customs, traditions, religious beliefs and observances, and moral standards of the Indians, Boudinot managed to detect all sorts of similarities between them and the ancient Hebrews. Though he himself did not consider his evidence by any means conclusive,[5] he still maintained that "even if we should be mistaken in all our conjectures . . . would any people have reason to repent acts of humanity and mercy to these wretched outcasts of

[3] *A sermon . . . before the Society for Propagating the Gospel among the Indians . . . November 4, 1813* (Boston, 1813).
[4] Trenton, 1816.
[5] An illustration of Boudinot dilettantism can be seen in his tables comparing Hebrew, Indian, and English words of similar sound, cf. *op.cit.*, pp. 102-103. Even so great a friend of the Indian as Isaac McCoy could not detect any resemblance between "Hallelujah" and the "unmeaning whooping" at certain festivals where Boudinot discovered it.

INDIAN PROBLEM

society?"[6] and his arguments continued to fuel the imagination of the theocrats intent upon extending the benefits of Christianity and civilization to the Indians.[7] It is characteristic of the Biblical literalism of the age that such a fanciful interpretation of Scripture could be so eagerly advocated and received by so many well-educated clergymen and laymen.[8]

The missionary impulse toward the Indians was powerful enough (at least in the East where the memories of Indian warfare were faintest and where there were few or no Indians left), but it was by no means unanimous. The first *Address* of the American Board for Foreign Missions presented the Christian public with the project of a mission to the Iroquois along with the mission to Burma,[9] but many theocrats remained to be convinced of the practicality and strategic value of Indian missions compared with all the opportunity beckon-

---

[6] Boudinot, *op.cit.*, p. 300.

[7] An anonymous pamphlet entitled *The Indian's Advocate; being an answer to an objection against sending missionaries to the Indians* (Geneva, N.Y., 1817), written by someone affiliated with the American Board draws nearly all its ammunition from *A Star in the West*.

[8] Boudinot's interest in the Jews was not confined to the "ten lost tribes." He was the first President of the American Society for Ameliorating the Condition of the Jews, cf. *Constitution and Address* (New York, 1820). The society planned to "invite and receive from any part of the world, such Jews as do already profess the Christian religion, or are desirous to receive Christian instruction, to form them into a settlement, and to furnish them with the ordinances of the Gospel and with such employment as shall be assigned to them. . . ." This society continued to exist until 1852, but the project of a settlement never materialized, though there were many individual conversions, chiefly through the agency of an English convert, Samuel F. C. Frey, cf. A. E. Thompson, *A Century of Jewish Missions* (New York, 1902), chapter xv. Simultaneously the American Board had launched a "Palestine Mission," consisting of two clergymen, Pliny Fisk and Levi Parson, cf. *Sermons at the Ordination of the Rev. Levi Parson and the Rev. Pliny Fisk . . . November 31, 1819* (Boston, 1820), but their efforts soon came to naught. Though the results of the work of the American Society were slight, interest among the churches had been thoroughly aroused, so that in 1824 there were "at least one hundred and fifty auxiliary institutions" embracing its goal, cf. Aaron Bancroft, *A Discourse before the Worcester Auxiliary Society for Meliorating the Condition of the Jews* (Worcester, Mass., 1824), p. 18. The question arises why a settlement of converted Jews was regarded as necessary, if Judaism was only a religion. Or were the theocrats thinking of the Jews as a race?

[9] Boston, 1811.

ing in the East. An outstanding Presbyterian missionary, on the eve of his own departure for India, suggested that the East rated an unquestionable priority,

"1st. Because a mission to the west on a plan promising success, would be attended with greater expense than a mission to the East.

"2nd. Because, from the situation of the Indian tribes a mission among them would be attended with greater perils and sufferings. . . .

"3rdly. Because the acquisition of the language would require a greater expense of time and labor in the west than in the east.

"4thly. Because in the west, when the language is obtained, it is spoken by a few hundred only, who are in no situation to receive necessary instruction because they are uncivilized, while in the east the same language is spoken by many million who have every advantage for attending to the gospel. And

"5thly. Because in the east, Providence seems to have set an open door rather than in the west."[10]

The missionary's conviction notwithstanding, however, the United States was destined, within half a century to encompass all the remaining Indian tribes, whereas American and European missions to India and China were still barely making a dent on the teeming multitudes of the East. Meanwhile, with the founding of the American Board in 1810 the theocrats had definitely accepted the responsibility for the redemption of the conquered race which was fast coming within the confines of the expanding nation. After an exploratory tour in 1816, conducted by Samuel J. Mills, William Goodell, and Cyrus Kingsbury, the American Board established its first station in the Cherokee country in eastern Tennessee, which was followed two years later by another station, called Eliot, among the Choctaws, and a third station, Dwight, among the Cherokees who had moved to the Arkansas territory, until in

[10] Gordon Hall, *The Duty of the American Churches in Respect to Foreign Missions* (Philadelphia, 1812), pp. 17-19.

INDIAN PROBLEM

1820, one half of the missionaries and nearly half of the expenditures of the Board were for work among the Indians.[11] In 1817 a group of Presbyterian, Associate Reformed, and Reformed Dutch clergymen in New York founded the United Foreign Missionary Society to "spread the Gospel among the Indians of North America, the inhabitants of Mexico and South America, and in other portions of the heathen and anti-Christian world."[12] Stephen Van Rensselaer, a politician and philanthropist from New York State, wholly devoted to the theocratic ideal, became its first president, and Philip Milledoler, President of Rutgers College, its corresponding secretary. The society established missions in western New York and in the Missouri and Michigan territories as well as a station "among American emigrants," i.e. Negro freemen, on Haiti,[13] but in 1826 it merged into the American Board which thus became the most powerful Indian missionary agency.

The father of Baptist Indian missions was Isaac McCoy, who received a one-year commission to work among the natives of Indiana and Illinois in 1817. "It was on the 27th of October, 1818," he wrote, "that we set out for our mission premises, . . . With my wife and seven small children I went into the wilderness, to seek an opportunity of preaching Christ to the Indians. . . ."[14]

The Methodist Church did not have a missionary society until 1819, and then it did not distinguish between home and foreign missions, but simply stated that its efforts would not be "restricted to our own nation or colour; we hope that the aborigenes of our country, the Spaniards of South America, the French of Louisiana and Canada, and every other people

[11] William E. Strong, *The Story of the American Board* (Boston, 1910), p. 41.
[12] *An Address of the United Foreign Missionary Society* (New York, 1817), p. 4.
[13] *Reports of the UFMS* (New York, 1823, 1825).
[14] Isaac McCoy, *History of Baptist Indian Missions* (Washington and New York, 1840), pp. 46-47.

89

INDIAN PROBLEM

... will be comprehended in the field of the labours of our zealous missionaries."[15]

The pioneer Methodist missionary among the Indians was James B. Finlay. His success with the Wyandots of western Ohio brought some of the leading Methodists to the realization that the Indians had "a claim on American Christians paramount to all others," which in turn gave rise to "an honest blush ... that the Methodist should be behind any religious community in a work ... worthy of the zeal of the Apostles."[16]

The beginnings of organized efforts for the Christianization and civilization of the Indians were marked by a dogged optimism on the part of the theocrats. They realized the magnitude of the task, but were ready to counter all objections. "The Indians have been abused by white people and thus prejudiced against the Christian religion," wrote an anonymous missionary.[17] It is no wonder that earlier missions among them had not been more successful. In all the colonial wars, the Revolutionary War, and the War of 1812, the Indians were employed by both sides and exposed to the hatred of both sides, until bloodshed and depredations offset all missionary progress. "I am aware that I am treading upon what some may deem dangerous or forbidden ground," said a Presbyterian clergyman to the newly formed Western Missionary Society in Pittsburgh, where memories of Indian battles were fresh. "The minds of many have been and still may be greatly prejudiced upon this subject, and not without some semblance of reason—many have suffered much, others have lost all through the treachery and cruelty of these heathen tribes. But what then? Ought we not to say, 'Father, forgive them, for they know not what they do'?"[18]

But the ignorance of the Indians was also one of the most potent obstacles to their conversion. Most of the theocrats

[15] *Constitution and Address of the Missionary and Bible Society of the ME Church in America* (New York, 1820), p. 7.
[16] Joshua Soule, "Progress of Religion among the Wyandott Indians at Upper Sandusky," *Methodist Magazine*, v (1822), 31-32.
[17] *The Indian's Advocate* (Geneva, New York, 1817), p. 10.
[18] Obadiah Jennings, *A Missionary Sermon, Preached ... in Pittsburgh ... October 7, 1818* (Steubenville, Ohio, 1818), p. 7.

INDIAN PROBLEM

would have agreed with Edward Dorr Griffin that "immense will be the labour and expense of civilizing and christianizing, (for they must go together,) ... the savages on our borders; to teach every man, woman and child the alphabet; to bring them forward to read the Scriptures; to initiate them in the arts of civilized life; ... to repeat this process with every Indian in the United States."[19]

But not all of them thought that civilization must precede Christianization. "Does not the savage character of the heathen forbid the hope of success, at least until the arts of civilized life shall have prepared the way ... ?" asked Obadiah Jennings, rhetorically, countering at once, "No! The Gospel is the only effectual means whereby they can be truly civilized. All other means ... without this principal ... must necessarily prove ineffectual."[20]

Pleading for missions among the Chickasaws, T. Charlton Henry, Presbyterian pastor at Columbia, S.C., asserted that "these dry bones can live," that it is criminal to say, "Let them perish!", that they are "ripe and ready for instruction" and "susceptible of spiritual and intellectual improvement."[21] Voicing similar sentiments to the missionary society of his denomination in the same state, Stephen Olin castigated the prevalent "infidel discouragement" which assumes "that a fatal decree has already gone forth against this devoted people; that the elements of a nature, so incorrigibly savage, are deposited in their bosoms, as bids defiance to the meliorating influences of civilization" and seems content "to be waiting for the day of their doom."[22]

[19] *Foreign Missions. A Sermon ... preached in New York, May 9, 1819* (New York, 1819), p. 14.
[20] *Op.cit.*, pp. 13-14.
[21] *A Plea for the West. A Sermon preached before the Missionary Society of the Synod of South Carolina and Georgia, in Augusta, November 21, 1824* (Charleston, S.C., 1824), *passim*. Henry cites the example of an Indian "female missionary society" in an unnamed tribe, whose members had collected some money and decided to use it for missions among a neighboring tribe with whom their own tribe at that time was at war.
[22] "An Address to the S.C. Conference Missionary Society," *Methodist Magazine*, VII (1824), 309.

Wherever they placed the emphasis, whether on Christianization or civilization, the theocrats realized that the two were indissolubly linked, and they were eager to extend their joint benefits to the Indians. But in carrying out their benevolent design, the theocrats had to reckon with the government of the United States and with the growing population of the border states, whose power in Congress increased every time a new state was formed, and whose wishes respecting the Indians were diametrically opposed to those of the theocrats.

The Indians had been "wards" of the federal government ever since its formation. Their status was not clearly defined. The colonial governments had made solemn treaties with the various tribes, which implied their recognition as sovereign nations. The government of the United States continued this policy, allowing self-government to the Indians within the limits of the states, but promising the states to extinguish the Indian titles in their favor just as soon as would be practicable. The Indians within the states were thus under the protection of the federal government, but their removal to the West was contemplated by Jefferson as early as 1802, and after the Louisiana purchase, in 1805, the government began to negotiate with several tribes about exchanging their lands for new lands beyond the Mississippi. A few Choctaws actually left in 1808 and a few Cherokees in 1809, but the bulk of them remained.[23]

After the War of 1812 the great westward migration precipitated the events which Jefferson had foreseen. The emigrants surrounded the Indian territories, exploited the Indians in trade by plying them with whiskey, and at the same time organized to gain possession of their lands by pressuring the government to remove them. The reports of missionaries among the Indians during the twenties are tediously unanimous on this point: that the major obstacle to constructive work with the Indian is not his savagery or ignorance, but

[23] Laurence F. Schmeckebier, *The Office of Indian Affairs* (Baltimore, 1927), pp. 12-26.

INDIAN PROBLEM

the immorality of the white man, with his "ardent spirits," his trickery, and his lust for the Indian lands.[24]

Jedidiah Morse's Master Plan

Thus removal of the Indians beyond the Mississippi became the insistent demand of the whites in the border states, but the New England theocrats had another remedy to offer: not exclusion from the American community, but Christianization, civilization, and assimilation. Their master-plan was submitted to the War Department, charged with Indian affairs ever since 1789, by the venerable Jedidiah Morse, who had been pastor of the First Congregational Church of Charlestown, Massachusetts, for nearly forty years, and who, from his resignation in 1818 to his death in 1826, concentrated his best efforts on the promotion of the plan.

Commissioned by two independent missionary societies to make an exploratory tour of the Indian tribes of the Northwest, Morse applied to the Secretary of War, John C. Calhoun, for a government commission to the same effect, extending the field to include the southwestern tribes. Calhoun granted him five hundred dollars, plus additional expenses, if the results should warrant it. On May 10, 1820, Morse set out on his northern tour, accompanied by his youngest son, Richard. "We passed in Steam-Boats to New York and Albany; thence to Utica in the stage; to Montezuma, ninety-six miles, on the new Canal; thence to Buffalo by stage; thence across Lake Eerie to Detroit, and thence to Mackinaw, in the Steam-Boat Walk-in-the-water; thence to L'Arbre Croche, thirty-six miles, in birch canoes; thence to Green Bay, in the U.S. Cutter Dallas, Capt. Knapp; and returned home to New Haven on nearly the same route; where we arrived on August the 30th, after an absence of nearly four months."[25]

[24] See the sections on "Indians," more often listed under the names of the various tribes, in *The Missionary Herald* (Boston, 1804), *The Methodist Magazine* (New York, 1817-), *The American Baptist Magazine* (Boston, 1820), *The Christian Advocate* (Philadelphia, 1822-), *passim*.
[25] Jedidiah Morse, *A Report to the Secretary of War of the United States, on Indian Affairs* (New Haven, 1822), p. 13.

INDIAN PROBLEM

Within six months the vigorous sexagenarian set out on his southern tour, covering a similar distance by conveyances just as primitive. Within two years after receiving his commission, his report, including an Appendix of four hundred pages, was in the hands of Calhoun and appeared in print, presumably at the author's expense. It is difficult to conceive of a more thorough and more sweeping project.

Morse's sincerity was matched only by his naïveté. He indicted the current "mixed plan" applied to the Indian trade, whereby both the government and private interests had dealings with the Indians. He advised that the government should take over the entire Indian trade, for the protection of the Indian's interest. He failed to see the strength of the private trading companies, which had been applying ceaseless pressure on the government ever since it had entered the field by creating the office of Superintendent of Indian Trade in 1806 and giving him charge over the trading houses established under Washington's administration. About the time Morse's report was published, the private interests, and the Missouri Fur Company in particular, actually succeeded in forcing the government out of the Indian trade.[26]

Morse aimed at nothing less than to have the government scrap all previous approaches to the Indian problem and adopt the strategy of the missionary societies, notably of the American Board.[27] The heart of the plan was to send "education families" to live among the Indians in order to teach them the way of life and the religion of the white man. "I give this name to those bodies which have been commonly denominated *Mission Families*, because it seems better to describe their character, and may less offend the opposers of missions."[28]

Such "families" consisted of ministers, teachers, mechanics, farmers, etc. They formed the nucleus of a Christian community, and combined the functions of church, school, workshop, and farm. They were rapidly becoming the accepted mis-

[26] Schmeckebier, *op.cit.*, pp. 23-24.
[27] Morse, *op.cit.*, p. 82.   [28] *ibid.*, p. 78.

sionary approach to the Indian, and the government had taken favorable notice of their educational efforts and had set aside, as early as 1819, a "Civilization Fund" of $10,000 a year, which for the next fifty years continued to be used "in aid of religious organizations undertaking the education of the Indians, sometimes increasing the amount to as much as $60,-000 for buildings and maintenance."[29] This, of course, was still a pittance, considering that up to the Civil War it constituted the government's only direct contribution to the uplifting of the red man.

Morse's next suggestion concerned the need "for the exercise of a suitable government and control" over the Indians. "This government . . . should be in its nature *paternal — absolute, kind,* and *mild,* such as may be created by a wise union of a well-selected military establishment and an Education Family. The one possessing the power, the other the softening and qualifying influence. . . ."[30] It would have to prevent the "introduction of spiritous liquors" and protect the Indians against "unprincipled white people." It would therefore have to be composed "*exclusively* . . . of men of principle," since "example, in the case before us, *peculiarly*, must accompany instruction and precept."[31]

To insure the Indians such a government, "Indian superintendents, agents, sub-agents, and all other officers . . . should either be members of one or other of these Education Families . . . or so intimately connected with, or friendly to them, as shall bring all official influence and authority over the Indians, to aid them in all their operations."[32] Furthermore, "At every military post in the Indian country there should be an Education Family. . . . In this way, at the same time, would be imparted to the soldiery, that moral and religious instruction, which is necessary to prepare them for wholesome and exemplary intercourse with the Indians."[33]

With regard to the education of the Indians, Morse could

[29] Hinman, *op.cit.,* pp. 94-95.
[30] *ibid.,* p. 85.   [31] *ibid.,* p. 86.   [32] *ibid.,* p. 87.   [33] *ibid.,* p. 88.

point with justifiable pride to the Cherokee tribe among whom the efforts of the American Board had borne impressive fruit. The schools of the Board in this tribe were too young to show any great results, but they were building on the foundations laid by the Moravians, particularly by John and Anna Gambold.[34] From their little school, founded as far back as 1805, nine Cherokee youths journeyed to Cornwall, Connecticut, in 1818, to become members of the first class of the American Board's Foreign Mission School, "the product of Puritanism galvanized by missionary zeal."[35]

Morse included a detailed report on the progress of the Foreign Mission School. It listed the "English names, native names, and countries of the members . . ." twenty-eight in all, of whom three were "Anglo-Americans" [sic], one from the Sandwich Islands, and twenty-three American Indians.[36] He also enclosed a letter from the Principal, Herman Daggett, as well as letters from three young Indians (two Cherokees and a Choctaw) to President Monroe.

It is likely that these letters, written "by permission of my instructor," were requested by Daggett, of whom, in turn, Morse had solicited them to bolster his case for the adoption of the school by the government as its "Indian College," though he advised that it should continue to "be open, as it now is, for heathen youths from all parts of the world." "In what way," he asked, "can we, with so little expense, raise and extend the reputation of our country, so effectually promote peace and good will among men, and diffuse blessings throughout the world?"[37]

But Morse's plan for the education of the Indians proposed also another method, with admittedly far-reaching consequences. Writing under the title, "The education of Indian

[34] J. Taylor Hamilton, *A History of the Moravian Church During the Eighteenth and Nineteenth Centuries* (Bethlehem, Pa., 1902), pp. 322-323.
[35] Ralph H. Gabriel, *Elias Boudinot, Cherokee, and his America* (Norman, Oklahoma, 1941), p. 51.
[36] Morse, *op.cit.*, p. 265.   [37] *ibid.*, pp. 76-78.

INDIAN PROBLEM

females and intermarriages between Indians and white people," Morse expounded an idea just as idealistic as it was advanced. "I connect these subjects," he explained, "because, in contemplating the latter, the former should be kept in view. While Indians remain in their present state, the minds of civilized people must revolt at the idea of intermarrying with them. It is natural and decent that it should be so. Intermarriages, however ... have taken place to a great extent, and this too by many men of respectable talents and standing in society. More than half the Cherokee nation, a large part of the Choctaws and the Chickasaws, and, I may add indeed, of all other tribes with whom the whites have had intercourse, are of mixed blood."[38]

For this reason Indian girls and women should be the primary object of education, that they may "become prepared, in turn, to educate their own children," until the Indians "gradually attain their proper standing and influence in society. Then let intermarriage with them become general and the end which the government has in view will be completely attained. They would then be literally of one blood with us, be merged into the nation, and saved from extinction."[39]

We have no record of how Morse's bold suggestion was received by Calhoun and the government, but we do have a most interesting record of an instance of Indian-white intermarriage, which involved the New England theocrats far more deeply than even they cared to be involved, and proved beyond a doubt that Morse's ideal of the Indian absorption into the American population was little more than a vision, compounded of sordid reality and a noble dream.

The Story of Elias Boudinot

The story of *Elias Boudinot, Cherokee*[40] is the story of one of the "graduates" of Sister Gambold's school who came to

[38] *ibid.*, pp. 33.   [39] *ibid.*, pp. 73-75.
[40] Ralph A. Gabriel, *Elias Boudinot, Cherokee, and his America* (Norman, Oklahoma, 1941). The outline of the story of Elias Boudinot's marriage is taken from this work.

INDIAN PROBLEM

Cornwall for further education, was adopted by the community and sent to Andover Seminary, where he received the stamp of the theocrats, from whom he no longer differed except for his loyalty to his own people and his copper skin. Shortly after his return to the Cherokee country, a Cornwall girl named Harriet Gold, daughter of a deacon of the Cornwall Church who was also an agent of the Foreign Mission School, asked her father's permission to marry the young Indian. The reaction of the Connecticut village was violently adverse. Harriet's image was burned in effigy on the village green of Cornwall and her own brother took part in the proceedings. The agents of the Foreign Mission School, realizing that public opinion was about to deal the death blow to the school, tried to save it by registering their "unequivocal disapprobation of such connexion," and by affirming that they regarded "those who have engaged in or been accessory to this transaction as criminal; as offering insult to the known feelings of the Christian community; and as sporting with the sacred interests of this charitable institution. . . ."[41]

Lyman Beecher was the first signer of this document, which also bore the signatures of three other prominent Congregational clergymen as Agents of the School.[42] It is a pity that Morse's reaction to the incident is not known, but he was in his last illness when it occurred. It would undoubtedly have been a great blow to him. Here was an Indian, converted to Christianity, educated in the best Christian schools; an Indian who had certainly reached the stage where his marriage to an "Anglo-American" Christian would not be not only excusable, but a positive gain to the strength of the American race; but the Christian people of Connecticut—not of Georgia, but of Puritan Connecticut!—who had pampered him as a promising "heathen youth," refused to have anything more to do with him. As for Lyman Beecher and the other clergymen, it is difficult to ascertain to what extent they held any

---
[41] ibid., p. 76.
[42] They were Timothy Stone, Joseph Harvey, and Philo Swift; cf. ibid., p. 77.

race prejudice and to what extent their action was motivated by their concern for the Foreign Mission School. In any case, they did not save the school. The banns for Elias Boudinot and Harriet Gold were published on June 17, 1825. At its Annual Meeting, held in September, the American Board appointed a committee "to take the whole subject of this school into consideration." The following March the couple were married without further incidents at the home of Benjamin Gold at Cornwall, but in September the investigating committee of the American Board reported "that the interests of the missionary cause do not require the continuance of the school...."[43]

The committee argued that "heathen youths" could now be cared for adequately in their own countries, and that, where this was not the case, they could be placed individually in various American academies, since "young men, brought from the wilderness ... and formed into a little community by themselves ... are apt to receive more marked attentions from persons of all ages and both sexes, than any of our own young men receive, or than we should think it safe and proper that any young person should receive."[44] Whereas, if they are placed individually into different schools, "after a short time, the peculiarity of their situation will have passed away with its novelty, and they will stand, as they ought to stand, on a perfect equality with their fellow-students," than which "there is scarcely anything more important in the preparatory measures with reference to Indian civilization...."[45]

The Foreign Mission School ended on this inconclusive note. Not only the government, but even the Christian community was not ready for the admitted and hoped-for consequences of Morse's scheme. But Morse, had his entire plan been adopted, would have done his best to carry it out. He proposed the forming of a society for promoting the welfare of the Indians,[46]

[43] "Foreign Mission School," *Report of the ABCFM, 1826* (Boston, 1826), pp. 103-111.
[44] *ibid.*   [45] *ibid.*
[46] Morse, *op.cit.*, pp. 75-76.

drafted its *Constitution*[47] and, failing apparently to receive any encouragement from Calhoun, proceeded to organize it on his own initiative and at his own expense.[48] According to its constitution, the society was to be headed by all the living ex-Presidents of the country as Patrons, by the Vice-President as president "ex officio," and by the "heads of Departments, Judges of the Supreme Court, and Governors of the several States and Territories as "ex officio" Vice-Presidents.[49]

Morse had drawn up the whole roster of officers, including special correspondents (mostly missionaries to the Indians as well as two converted Indian chiefs), and had sent letters to them inviting their acceptance of the offices which he had assigned to them. Not only that, but he published their replies in this same report, though most of them did not accept. John Adams remarked tersely that the President and Congress were "the constitutional authorities for conducting all our Foreign Relations."[50] Jefferson wrote a detailed criticism, noting "that the clergy will constitute nineteen twentieths of this association, and, by the law of this majority, may command the 20th part, which, composed of all the high authorities of the U.S., civil and military, may be outvoted and wielded by the 19 parts, with uncontrollable power both as to purpose and process."[51]

James Madison accepted the "honorary relation," though he could offer only "good wishes" as his contribution. All the Justices of the Supreme Court, governors, etc., either declined or failed to reply. On the other hand, many of the clergy and most of the missionaries to the Indians welcomed the founding of the Society enthusiastically. The only prominent public figure who accepted the office assigned to him was the Secretary of War, Calhoun, who could not very well refuse since he had issued Morse's commission. "It will afford me pleasure,"

[47] *ibid.*, pp. 284-290. (First draft.)
[48] *The First Annual Report of the American Society for Promoting the Civilization and General Improvement of the Indian Tribes in the United States* (New Haven, 1824), p. 12.
[49] *ibid.*, p. 4.   [50] *ibid.*, p. 20.   [51] *ibid.*, p. 21.

INDIAN PROBLEM

he wrote with guarded courtesy, "while I hold my present official station, to act with the Society, in so far as it may be consistent with my duties, in effecting the object which it proposes."[52]

These lines were written on March 19th, 1822, but Calhoun's real reply came two years later, when he "created the Bureau of Indian Affairs by order of March 11, 1824, and placed at its head Thomas L. McKenney, who had been Superintendent of Indian trade for some years." What influence, if any, Morse's *Report* had on the government cannot be ascertained, except by conjecture made in the light of subsequent events. It then becomes apparent that the aged theocrat's master plan, which fairly represented the point of view of the American Board and of the rank and file of the New England theocrats, had fallen on deaf ears: the government was determined to force the Indians out of all lands east of the Mississippi. To complicate matters, other theocrats, equally ardent champions of the Indians, had been among the first to advocate their removal, for their own welfare and ultimate gain. Foremost among these advocates of a great Indian state west of the Mississippi was the man whose motives can least be impeached: the Baptist missionary to the Osages, Pawnees, and Potawatomies of the Illinois Territory, Isaac McCoy.

Isaac McCoy, Realist

The disagreement between Morse's plan and McCoy's plan was not as complete as it might appear at first sight. Both men were aware of the existence of two kinds of Indians: the larger tribes of the southwest, well-organized and advancing in civilization, and the smaller tribes and remnants of tribes of the central and northern border area, which persisted in their former way of life as hunters and were rapidly diminishing in numbers. Morse absolutely opposed the removal of the southwestern tribes; McCoy, working among the latter, insisted that removal beyond the reach of the white man was their

[52] *ibid.*, p. 24.

only salvation, though he felt that the southwestern tribes, too, should take advantage of the opportunity to flee from the white man and to settle in a new land of their own.[53]

Following President Monroe's Annual Message to Congress which openly endorsed their organized removal, the government continued its rather gentle policy of persuasion, reinforced by bribery. The advent of Andrew Jackson, however, marked the beginning of a policy of force, though his administration never ceased to protest that the "exchange of lands" proposed to the Indians would be fairly compensated for, that their removal would be attended with all possible comforts, and that, above all, it was clearly meant for their own welfare.

Writing to the Creeks on March 23, 1829, in the best Indian style, Jackson explained: "Where you now are you and my white children are too near each other to live in harmony and peace. . . . Beyond the great river Mississippi, where a part of your nation has gone, your father has provided a country large enough for all of you, and he advises you to remove to it. There your white brothers will not trouble you; they will have no claim to the land, and you can live upon it, you and all your children, *as long as the grass grows and the water runs*, in peace and plenty. For the improvements in the country where you now live, and for the stock which you cannot take with you, your father will pay you a fair price."[54]

The Secretary of War, John H. Eaton, echoed the same sentiments.[55] So did the Superintendent of Indian Affairs, Colonel Thomas L. McKenney, "in whom" McCoy "always found a *friend*, while he continued in office,"[56] but who seems rather to deserve the judgment passed upon him by a later historian, viz., that he was "lavish in defence of his own motives and

[53] Morse, *A Report to the Secretary of War*, pp. 82-83. McCoy, *op.cit.*, pp. 41, 196-197, 200-201.
[54] *Documents and Proceedings relating to the Formation and Progress of a Board, in New York, for the emigration, preservation, and improvement of the Aborigenes of America* (New York, 1829), p. 5.
[55] *ibid.*, p. 9. This "Indian Board" consisted chiefly of clergymen.
[56] McCoy, *op.cit.*, p. 327.

actions . . . constantly prating about Indian betterment, yet siding eagerly with the politicians in their argument of state rights, and in their desire to move the natives westward."[57] McCoy himself, though advocating removal, was not deceived by Jacksonian hypocrisy. He accepted a government appointment to make an exploratory tour of the territory intended for the Indians, but not without misgivings, since he found out in Washington (December, 1827) that "while many were willing to make the experiment from motives of humanity towards the Indians, they doubted the possibility of rescuing the aboriginal race from extermination . . . and frankly told me that they believed the Indian race was destined to become extinct."[58]

Nevertheless, a little over a year later he submitted the report of his tour to Congress, pointing out that he had found "the country under consideration" to be "adequate to the purposes of a permanent and comfortable home for the Indians," but urging that nothing should be done toward their removal which would not be "in strict accordance with justice and humanity."[59]

Jeremiah Evarts, Idealist

It was at this time, when submitting the report of his tour, that he met Jedidiah Morse's successor as champion of the plan to absorb the Indians, particularly the Cherokees, into the American population, "J. Evarts, Esq., Corresponding Secretary of the American Board, a worthy gentleman and Christian."[60]

Like Morse, Evarts was a New England theocrat who thought in terms of absolute justice, and cherished a vision of the world-wide dominion of Christianity. He was, however, not a clergyman but a lawyer, and it fell to his lot to take up the defense of the threatened Cherokees and their brothers before the bar of the American public. As Editor of the *Missionary*

[57] Dorothy A. Doudore, "Thomas L. McKenney," *DAB*.
[58] McCoy, *op.cit.*, p. 323.   [59] *ibid.*, p. 375.   [60] *ibid.*, p. 377.

Herald since 1821, he had printed with pride the reports of missionary progress among these tribes, and had insisted that the attainment of the white man's civilization would make them acceptable members of the white man's community as well as citizens of the American nation. Anticipating legislation for the forced removal of the Indians, Evarts published in the fall of 1829, a series of articles in the *National Intelligencer* under the pseudonym of William Penn, in which he gave a masterful summary of the treaties which the United States had concluded with the Indians, exposing the fallacy of Georgia's argument that the Cherokees owned their lands as "possessory tenants" only and had therefore violated the law of the state when they had formed a constitution of their own in 1827.[61] His argument, which Chief Justice Marshall called "the most conclusive argument that he ever read on any subject whatever,"[62] commanded wide attention in the religious press as well as the Whig papers, and also furnished the ammunition for Theodore Freylinghuysen's six-hour speech in the Senate (April 7, 1830) on the strength of which the speaker attained national reputation.

Evarts argued that the plan represented "the wishes and supposed interests of the whites, and not the benefit of the Indians"; that "its advocates talk much of future generosity and kindness, but say nothing of the present obligations of honor, truth, and justice"; that the southwestern tribes, contrary to the northern Indians, "are unwilling to remove"; that "there is not a sufficient quantity of good land in the contemplated tract . . . to say nothing of the other tribes to be thrust into their company"; "that the Government cannot fulfil its promises to emigrating Indians."[63] "Twenty years hence, Texas, whether it shall belong to the United States or not, will have been settled by the descendants of Anglo-Ameri-

[61] *Essays on the Present Crisis in the Condition of the American Indians* (Boston, 1829), pp. 5-94.
[62] E. C. Tracy, *Memoir of Jeremiah Evarts, Esq., 1781-1831* (Boston, 1845), p. 339.
[63] Evarts: Wm. Penn, *op.cit.*, pp. 95-98.

INDIAN PROBLEM

cans. The State of Missouri will then be populous. There will be great roads through the Indian country and caravans will be passing and repassing in many directions. The emigrant Indians will be *denationalized* and will have no common bond of union. Will it be possible, under such circumstances, to enforce the laws against intruders?"[64]

Thus, Evarts concluded, any guarantee to the Indians would be of dubious value. What is more, "the constrained migration of 60,000 souls . . . must be attended with much suffering," and the first removal would not be the last. "If the emigrants become poor, and are transformed into vagabonds, it will be evidence enough, that no benevolent treatment can save them, and it will be said that they may as well be driven beyond the Rocky Mountains at once."[65]

History has shown how right he was. It is not necessary to doubt the good faith of the Baptist theocrats like McCoy, or of those Dutch Reformed theocrats who were so fully persuaded of the administration's rightness as to assert in the Preamble of the Constitution of their "Indian Board" that "the harmony of these United States, the preservation of the Indians from total extinction, and consequently the cause of humanity, require . . . the final and speedy removal of the scattered remains of the Indian tribes. . . ."[66]

They were simply at one with the majority of the American people in that they did not see far enough. Who, in effect, could have forecast the lightning speed of the settlement of the West?

Evarts did not cease to agitate against the removal of the Indians. His *Memoir* lists seventeen publications on behalf of their cause, which kept him occupied literally until his dying day, January 10, 1831.[67] His arguments were taken up by others, embodied in memorials to Congress, and preached from hundreds of pulpits, but not many even among the New Eng-

[64] *ibid.*, p. 99. [65] *ibid.*, p. 100.
[66] *Documents and Proceedings*, 1829, pp. 21-22.
[67] Tracy, *op.cit.*, pp. 431-432.

land theocrats were as clear-sighted as Heman Humphrey who was the first to call the proposed removal by its real name —a flagrant instance of racial prejudice. "What if only ten poor families in a remote corner of Maine or Missouri were threatened with a similar outrage? Every man in the nation would rise up and blow the trumpet with all his might! . . . In the case supposed there are *ten* families, and in that of the Indians . . . there are *ten or fifteen thousand*. Where is the difference? Ah, the ten are *white* men and the ten thousand are *red* men!"[68]

The missionaries in the Cherokee nation assembled at the capital, New Echota, on December 29, 1830, to protest against the removal of the Indians. Their feelings, based upon a firsthand knowledge of the Cherokees, were so strong that they even made light of the argument which was most frequently voiced in favor of removal, because it contained the most truth. "The proximity of whites," they wrote, "also is by no means injurious in every respect. The evil which they have brought upon the Indians by the introduction of ardent spirits, and of vices unknown before them, is indeed great. On the other hand, however, the gradual assimilation of the tribe, thus surrounded by civilized people, to the customs and manners which constantly invite their imitation, and the facility thus afforded for procuring the comforts of life, are benefits of no little value. To deprive them of these advantages, while in their present state, would be an incalculable evil."[69]

This statement was penned by a missionary of the American Board, Samuel Austin Worcester, who was soon to attain national fame as plaintiff in *Worcester vs. Georgia*, in which Chief Justice Marshall upheld the Cherokee nation against Georgia.[70] Jackson, however, allowed the state to ignore the

[68] *Indian Rights and our Duties*. A Discourse . . . (Amherst, Mass., 1830), p. 22.
[69] "Resolutions and Statements of the Missionaries, . . ." *Missionary Herald*, xxvii (1831), 82.
[70] Cf. *Opinion of the Supreme Court . . . delivered by Mr. Chief Justice Marshall . . . in the case of S. A. Worcester, plaintiff, in error . . . vs. the State of Georgia* (Washington, 1832), *passim*.

INDIAN PROBLEM

Supreme Court's ruling and to keep Worcester in prison for another eighteen months, together with his colleague, Elizur Butler, who had also signed these resolutions. Among the signers were also four other missionaries of the American Board, two missionaries of the United Brethren, and Evan Jones, a Baptist missionary, author of a moving description of the Cherokee "Trail of Tears."[71]

Expulsion and A New Beginning

These resolutions were passed by the missionaries too late. On May 26, 1830, after a 28 to 20 vote in the Senate and a 102 to 97 vote in the House, Andrew Jackson had signed the act empowering him to proceed with the removal of the Indians.[72] The missionaries among the Cherokees and the Cherokees themselves, as well as all their friends, continued to hope wistfully that the government would not resort to force, should the Indians simply remain in an attitude of passive resistance. Representatives of the majority of the Cherokees, headed by the Principal Chief, John Ross, kept petitioning the government for one reprieve after another, but through the intermediary of the Reverend John F. Schermerhorn, "the sanctimonious glove concealing the iron fist of that uncompromising Indian hater, Andrew Jackson,"[73] a treaty was signed by the representatives of the minority in 1835, and by its terms the Cherokee lands were surrendered. Meanwhile the removal of the Choctaws and the Creeks had been proceeding since 1831, while the Seminoles offered bloody resistance in the Florida swamps and the Chickasaws waited in the hope that the Cherokees might win their case. But in 1837 the Chickasaws began to move westward without waiting for armed coercion. The Cherokees, that is, as many as had remained, were left alone. On May 24, 1838, the ultimatum of the government expired, and General Winfield Scott proceeded against them with his

---

[71] Cf. his correspondence to the *American Baptist Magazine*, XVII (1837) and XVIII (1838), *passim*.
[72] McCoy, *op.cit.*, p. 400. [73] Gabriel, *op.cit.*, p. 145.

troops. They were captured, plundered, and marched off to exile. The missionaries either went before them to the Arkansas Territory, like Samuel A. Worcester, or they went with them, like Evan Jones, sharing their trials.[74] With their removal the theocratic pattern for America's Indian minority collapsed, at least for the time being. It became manifest that the American people refused to assimilate them, in spite of the frequency of intermarriages, and that even the theocratic elements, polarized in the persons of McCoy and Evarts, were divided on the issue. Temporarily, at least, the Indians ceased to be a national, racial problem, and became once more the object of foreign missionary efforts.

Slowly the missionary societies took up afresh the Christianization and civilization of the Indians. Many missionaries had gone along with the expelled tribes to their new homes and had kept their friendship and respect. The American Board even had the foresight to send one of its missionaries on an exploratory tour beyond the Rocky Mountains, remembering what Jeremiah Evarts had said about the probability of future removals.[75]

There was no doubt, however, in anyone's mind that the prospects of Indian missions, even when conceived as a part of the foreign missions enterprise rather than as part of the problem of America's racial complexion, were dark, indeed. David Greene, reporting to the annual meeting of the American Board at Philadelphia, ascribed the decline of Indian missions since 1828 "partly to the breaking up of missions by removal of the tribes . . . and the fact that the large boarding schools and farming establishments were not transferred to the new Indian country; partly to sickness and death in the mission families; and partly to the difficulty of late in obtaining laborers for these missions."[76] The best Greene could do was

[74] Hinman, *op.cit.*, pp. 52-54. The definitive record of the emigration of the "five civilized tribes" is *Indian Removal* by Grant Foreman (Norman, Oklahoma, 1932).
[75] Rev. Samuel Parker, *Journal of An Exploring Tour Beyond the Rocky Mountains . . . 1835, 1836, 1837. . . .* (Ithaca, N.Y., 1838).
[76] *Missionary Herald*, xxxvii (1841), p. 451.

INDIAN PROBLEM

to plead for continued efforts among them, on the ground that their individual souls could be saved, even if they were doomed to extinction as a race.[77] The same spirit of discouragement prevailed in the missionary endeavors of other Christian groups.[78]

Some new missions were launched among the Indians; for instance, the Dakota Mission of the American Board dated as far back as 1834.[79] The Methodists first sent Jason Lee to the Oregon country in 1835, and a year later Whitman and Spalding joined him to take up their work for the American Board near Walla Walla.[80] But, by a peculiar irony of history, the attempt of the theocrats to rescue the American Indian and to make room for him in the national community, already defeated by the removal of the Indians, received an additional blow: it became entangled with the Negro problem. For in addition to alcohol and new diseases, the white man had also introduced to the red man his "peculiar institution,"—black slavery.

Negro slavery among the Indians was not of recent origin. After a first-hand investigation on behalf of the American Board, Selah B. Treat found that it had presumably existed among the Cherokees, Choctaws, and Chickasaws since the middle of the eighteenth century, being introduced through the marriage of Indian women to slaveholding white men.[81] The phenomenon did not receive much notice until after the removal of the southwestern tribes beyond the Mississippi, probably because antislavery agitation had been slight before 1831. One of the earliest instances of Northern missionaries getting into slavery trouble is recorded in connection with the work of Presbyterians, Methodists, and Baptists among the Creeks in their new location. The missionaries were accused

[77] *ibid.*, p. 452.
[78] Cf. *Methodist Quarterly Review*, XXIX (1847), 282.
[79] Hinman, *op.cit.*, pp. 75-77.
[80] *ibid.*, pp. 56-59.
[81] "Slavery among the Cherokees and Choctaws," *Missionary Herald*, XLVI (1848), 346. Treat had just spent three months among the Cherokees and in the "Choctaw Nation," which now included the Chickasaws.

of preaching abolitionism to the Indians and were forced to leave.[82]

Laws forbidding the missionaries to "preach abolition" or even to teach the slaves, had been passed by the Cherokees and the Choctaws. The American Board did not take an unequivocal stand against slavery, but preferred to temporize, in spite of the insistent demand by Northern missionary societies and individual Christians.[83] The events of the year 1845, resulting in the split of two of America's largest denominations, the Baptist and the Methodist, into northern and southern branches, seemed to prove to the leaders of the American Board the wisdom of their policy. Even the creation of a rival missionary society, gathering into its membership many clergymen of abolitionist convictions,[84] did not move them to change their attitude toward slaveholding Indians, whom they refused to bar from membership in the church. All they did, as a result of Treat's report, was to remind the missionaries that the "system of slavery" was sinful, that to condemn it came under the general obligation of preaching the Gospel, that slaveholding converts should be thoroughly investigated as to their treatment of slaves, and that the missions themselves were positively forbidden to employ slave labor, even when purchasing slaves with a view to freeing them.[85]

Summary

The vexatious problem of Negro slavery among the Indians was really just another symptom of the collapse of the theocratic pattern in its application to the red man. Yet the pattern had been, in a sense, far in advance of the times. "Not until 1887 did the nation officially admit that the Indian, long

[82] Grant Foreman, *Advancing the Frontier, 1830-1860* (Norman, Oklahoma, 1933), pp. 142-143.
[83] Strong, *op.cit.*, pp. 52-53.
[84] *A Brief History of the Origin and Growth of the American Missionary Association* (New York, 1876). This society was formed in 1846. "Any person of evangelical sentiments . . . who is not a slaveholder, or in the practice of other immoralities," was invited to join.
[85] *Missionary Herald*, XLVI (1848), 358-362.

INDIAN PROBLEM

hated, long fought, might become a loyal American citizen. Throughout the first three quarters of the nineteenth century only a handful of missionaries and social idealists denied by word and deed the prevalent dogma that he was of an inferior race, incapable of learning the white man's ways or of ever becoming an American."[86]

Granted that Jedidiah Morse's grand scheme came too late, that it was conceived on too vast a scale, and presented with the naïve enthusiasm of an old man no longer able accurately to appraise the social changes of his day, it nevertheless set forth a proposal to solve America's racial problem, at least so far as the Indian was concerned, in the light of the Christian principle of the brotherhood of all men, made of one blood and sharing one fate.

Morse's total scheme was never adopted even by all the New England theocrats. It was rejected outright by many other theocrats, promoters of the benevolent societies, who felt that colonization was the Indian's only hope.[87] But there was one group of men who bore a mute, yet a most eloquent witness to its basic rightness and practicality. They were the missionaries who actually lived among the Indians. "Without definitely formulating a policy, these Christian pioneers in the Indian country were actually practising the policy of Christian assimilation, working out a method by which whites and Indians could live together in harmony, mutually sharing in the benefits of the land and sharing also the obligations of a Christian society."[88]

[86] Curti, *The Roots of American Loyalty* (New York, 1946), pp. 89-90.
[87] This was in basic accord with the attitude of *all* the theocrats toward the Negro problem, which will be discussed fully in the next chapter.
[88] Hinman, *op.cit.*, p. 41.

CHAPTER V

THE THEOCRATS AND THE NEGRO PROBLEM

THE problem of the Negro, though also primarily a racial problem, was quite different from the problem of the Indian. The Indian had been the original owner of the land. He had been conquered and dispossessed. By the middle of the nineteenth century both his friends and his foes agreed that he was doomed to slow extinction. His removal to the West put him temporarily beyond the boundaries of the expanding nation, settling him in more or less self-governing communities, but his significance for the nation ceased and was never regained. The Negro, on the other hand, belonged to a rapidly increasing race, and interest in him grew year by year, until he became, involuntarily, the main underlying cause of the Civil War.

The theocrats agreed on their obligation to evangelize and civilize the Indian, but at first could not agree with regard to his place in American society. The New England theocrats were inclined to adopt Jedidiah Morse's plan, with its hope for ultimate assimilation. The theocrats of the South and of the West preferred his removal from the American community, not out of self-interest but for the sake of his own welfare.

With regard to the Negro, however, there was a remarkable consensus among the theocrats from the very beginning. They believed that there was no room for him in American society except as a slave. They condemned slavery as a regrettable evil, but realized at the same time that freeing the Negro and leaving him in the status of a racial minority, segregated and despised, did not solve the problem either for him or for the country. "Amalgamation" was not even considered except as a threat. The prejudice against the very idea of intermarriage, even as a possibility for the remote future, was as strong then, both South and North, as it is now, more than a century later, though among the underprivileged classes it was a social fact in the early nineteenth century just as it is today. Yet, none of the theocrats dared leave any doubt as to his attitude toward the mixing of the two races. Speaking of the anticipated liberation of the slaves, John C. Young of Kentucky keynoted the feelings of the theocrats in no uncertain terms. "When the servile race was of the same colour with their lords, no difficulty could arise upon their liberation: they could live together as equals and soon amalgamate; for there was no memento of their former degradation stamped upon their brow. But ours will be an utterly dissimilar condition. Amalgamation is impossible, but by a depravation of morals, ruinous to the country—by a promiscuous concubinage, destructive alike to decency and religion. Such is the repugnance of the whites, that they will never unite with the blacks in lawful wedlock. . . . In South America and the West Indies, where religion is a form and virtue a name, the races have mingled, but under conditions to which no patriot, or moralist, would subscribe. Universal profligacy and an open, shameless contempt of the marriage rite, are hard terms on which to purchase the union of two hostile races."[1]

The clerical historian of Liberia justified the long-range aim of the theocrats with respect to the colony in terms of the same belief in the total incompatibility of white and black. "Two races of men . . . differing as much as the whites and the blacks, cannot form one harmonious society in any way other than amalgamation; but the whites and blacks in this country, by no human effort, could be amalgamated into *one homogeneous mass* in a thousand years; and during this long period the state of society would be perpetually disturbed by many contending factions. Either the whites must remove and give up the country to the coloured people, or the coloured people must be removed; *otherwise the latter must remain in subjection to the former.*"[2]

[1] John Clark Young, *Address to the Kentucky Colonization Society* (Frankfort, Kentucky, 1833), p. 26.
[2] Archibald Alexander, *A History of Colonization on the Western Coast of Africa* (Philadelphia, 1849), p. 17.

This, then, was the solution proposed by the theocrats: colonization away from the American mainland. For in spite of the fact that the creation of a Negro colony in the West was occasionally suggested, the overwhelming majority of the theocrats cast their vote for Africa and for the instrument of African colonization, the American Colonization Society. From 1817 and 1832 and, with a few exceptions, until the end of our period, the theocrats adopted and supported the Society as the God-given means of solving the great race problem besetting the young nation.

Early Voices

The very idea of African colonization originated in the mind of a New England theocrat, Samuel Hopkins. His interest in Africa was primarily of a missionary nature, yet, located in the heart of the slave trade at Newport, Rhode Island,[3] he was the first American clergyman to lodge an effective protest against the trade and against slavery itself. His main interest, however, was the evangelization of Africa through Negroes trained in America. Together with Ezra Stiles, the illustrious President of Yale, Hopkins sponsored the education of two slaves for this task. The Revolutionary War intervened, preventing their departure for Africa. Yet, nearly a quarter century after Hopkins' death two other slaves fulfilled their patron's dream. On December 28, 1825, Newport Gardner and Salmar Nubia, with sixteen others, were constituted a church by a group of Boston theocrats, and on January 4, 1826, they set sail for Liberia, then in the sixth year of its existence. The two Negro ministers were too old to endure the Liberian climate, but their very insistence on going, at their age, is a monument to Hopkins' influence.[4]

[3] "Even as recently as 1804, Rhode Island owned 59 of 202 slavers carrying Negroes into the single port of Charleston, South Carolina, and of the 17,048 Africans taken into that port during those four years (1804-1808) by American vessels, Rhode Island slavers took 6,238; and of these the Newport slavers . . . took 3,488." Edwards A. Parks, *Memoir of . . . Samuel Hopkins* (Boston, 1854), p. 115.

[4] *ibid.*, pp. 154-156. The ordaining body included Sereno Edwards Dwight, Benjamin Wisner, and Justin Edwards.

Hopkins brought his views before the public as early as 1776, in his *Dialogue Concerning the Slave Trade and the Slavery of Africans*. After the Revolution he reaffirmed his stand in an address to the Providence Society for Abolishing the Slave Trade,[5] to which he appended a plan for a colony of American Negroes in Africa, drawn on the model of the British experiment at Sierra Leone, then in its fourth year. Anticipating the difficulty of obtaining government aid for the scheme, Hopkins suggested that the antislavery societies might be able to carry it out by themselves.[6] It was private enterprise which brought thousands of Africans across the ocean. Nothing was more natural for Hopkins than to envision private enterprise, motivated this time not by greed but by philanthropy, successfully restoring them to Africa.

Hopkins was not only the first colonizationist but also one of the first antislavery clergymen in America. Before him only one Christian group, the Friends, had borne a collective witness against slavery.[7] The Methodist *Discipline* struck the first antislavery note among the major denominations in 1784, but in the others antislavery sentiment was confined to individual ministers. Spearheaded by Hopkins, Stiles, and Jeremy Belknap, a group of Massachusetts theocrats filed a petition which led to the prohibition of the slave trade in that state in 1788. Jonathan Edwards the Younger and Levi Hart played the same part and attained the same end in Connecticut.[8] Other theocrats also spoke out occasionally against slavery but did not offer any practical remedy.[9]

[5] The first abolition society was organized in Philadelphia in 1775. By 1791 "there were as many as twelve, representing all the states from Massachusetts to Virginia, with the exception of New Jersey, where a society was formed the following year. Mary S. Locke, *Anti-Slavery in America* (Boston, 1901), pp. 97, 99.

[6] Samuel Hopkins, *A Discourse upon the Slave Trade and the Slavery of Africans* (Providence, 1793), pp. 21-25.

[7] *A Brief Statement of the Rise and Progress of the Testimony of the Religious Society of Friends, against Slavery and the Slave Trade* (Philadelphia, 1843), *passim*.

[8] Locke, *op.cit.*, pp. 40-41.

[9] See Jonathan Edwards the Younger, *The Injustice and Impolicy of*

NEGRO PROBLEM

Ideological Background

To understand the theocratic pattern for the Negro in the United States, it is necessary to consider its ideological foundations. The outstanding textbook on Christian ethics which enjoyed uncontested supremacy in the colleges and seminaries of the theocrats for nearly half a century was William Paley's *Principles of Moral and Political Philosophy*.[10] After 1835 it was gradually replaced by Francis Wayland's *Elements of Moral Science*,[11] but its influence lingered to the end of our period.

Slavery, according to the British author's definition, is "an obligation to labour for the benefit of the master, without the contract or consent of the servant." It is morally justifiable in three cases: as a punishment for crimes committed; as a result of capture in war; and in payment of debts.

When the Christian church was formed, Paley argues, slavery existed everywhere in the world, and a direct protest against it would only have led to a "bellum civile . . . the most calamitous of all contests. . . ." "But does it follow from the silence of Scripture that all the civil institutions which then prevailed were right, or that the bad should not be exchanged for the better?"[12]

However, exchanging the bad for the better must be a gradual process, Paley contended, since "Christianity can only operate as an alterative. . . . By the mild diffusion of its light and influence the minds of men are insensibly prepared to perceive and correct the enormities, which folly or wickedness, or accident have introduced into their public establishments. In this way the Greek and Roman slavery, and since these, the feudal tyranny, has declined before it."[13]

---

the *Slave Trade and the Slavery of Africans* (n.p., 1791); Alexander McLeod, *Negro Slavery Unjustifiable* (New York, 1802); Eliphalet Nott, *Address to the Candidates for the Baccalaureate in Union College . . .* (Schenectady, 1811).
  [10] London, 1788, 2 vols.   [11] Boston, 1835.
  [12] Paley, *op.cit.*, I, 239.   [13] *ibid.*, pp. 240-241.

These, then, were the ideological foundations of the theocratic pattern for the Negro, derived largely from Paley: a conservative interpretation of the Biblical view of slavery, and the hope for its ultimate cessation under Christian influence. Jedidiah Morse typifies this attitude in a sermon to freedmen, in which, after indicting the slave trade and noting that "slavery indicates a corrupt state of society and mars the beauty of the body politic," he does not even allude to the possibility of emancipation in the slaveholding states, but passes to safer ground by turning to "a slavery of vastly deeper misery" and "a freedom of infinitely richer value."[14] Concern for the Negro's soul apart from the condition of his body remained characteristic of the theocrats throughout the first half of the nineteenth century. However, the practical alternative offered by the theocrats extended to the Negro's material, as well as to his spiritual, welfare. If Samuel Hopkins conceived of African colonization largely as an evangelistic venture, the theocratic founders of the American Colonization Society added to this motive a sincere desire to improve the Negro's earthly condition while preparing him for heaven.

1812-1831
Founders of the American Colonization Society

Samuel J. Mills, influenced probably by Hopkins' scheme,[15] began to agitate on behalf of colonization as early as the War of 1812. His missionary travels through the West gave him countless opportunities to plead the Negro's cause and to raise funds for a school in which Negro ministers and teachers could be trained as leaders in the colonizing venture. In 1816-1817 he collected over eight hundred dollars, mostly in Baltimore and Washington, noting realistically that "some gave to aid

[14] Jedidiah Morse, *A Discourse delivered at the African Meetinghouse in Boston, July 14th, 1808, in grateful celebration of the abolition of the African Slave Trade* . . . (Boston, 1808), pp. 6-7, 14.
[15] Parks, *op.cit.*, pp. 164-165.

the school as an auxiliary to the colonization effort, who would not have given had not that view been presented."[16]

Mills had been thinking in terms of the entire Negro population of the country, though he knew that the beginning would have to be small. It was Finley who proposed to restrict the experiment to freedmen in order to avoid the suspicion and enlist the cooperation of the slaveholders. As early as February 1815, shortly after meeting Mills, he wrote to a friend in New York, expressing concern over the "free blacks," whose "number increases daily, and their wretchedness, too," and suggesting that a colony like Sierra Leone would yield three distinct benefits: "We would be cleared of them,—we should send to Africa a population partly civilized and Christianized for its benefit; and our blacks themselves would be put in a better situation."[17] The significance of limiting the colonization appeal to freedmen can hardly be overrated. In 1815 there were about 200,000 free Negroes in the United States, nearly half of whom lived in the Upper South, in the states of Maryland, Delaware, Virginia, and North Carolina. In these states they constituted one-tenth of the Negro population.[18] In the Lower South individual manumissions had occurred, but not in large numbers. In the North some of the states, notably New York and New Jersey, still retained slavery, but there were sizable numbers of freedmen. North of Philadelphia, however, the Negro population, whether slave or free, was not numerous enough to cause apprehension.

Thus, when Finley limited his appeal to freedmen, he found an immediate and highly favorable response in the Upper South, where the whites stood to benefit most from the removal of an ignorant, economically underprivileged, and possibly dangerous class. The colonization movement began as a

[16] Gardiner Spring, *Memoirs of the Rev. Samuel J. Mills* (New York, 1820), p. 129.
[17] Robert Finley, "Letter to John P. Mumford, Esq., New York," reprinted in *African Repository*, I (1826), 2.
[18] Alice D. Adams, *The Neglected Period of Anti-Slavery in America* (Boston and London, 1908), pp. 5-6.

venture of the Middle States and continued to receive the major part of its lay support from these states, in which the motive of self-interest reinforced philanthropic considerations. Clerical interest, however, far exceeded that of the laity, both in its geographic extension and in its sustained intensity. From the organization of the American Colonization Society on January 1, 1817, no single group was more devoted to its program than the theocrats.[19] To gauge this support we must note the response of the major denominations, the response of individual clergymen and congregations to the Society's appeal for a special collection on the Fourth of July of each year, and finally the degree of clerical participation in the Society's auxiliaries and in the service of the Society in other capacities.

Official Response of the Major Denominations

The Presbyterian Church was the first officially to endorse the Society. The General Assembly of 1818, after taking the boldest antislavery stand in the history of the denomination, suggested three remedies for that "gross violation of the most precious and sacred rights of human nature ... utterly inconsistent with the law of God ... and as totally irreconcilable with the spirit of the Gospel of Christ," and among these remedies the Society's plan rated the first place. The report, unanimously adopted by the Assembly, stated: "We exceedingly rejoice to have witnessed its origin and organization among the *holders of slaves*, but we hope that others will support it just as fully."[20]

The Methodist General Conference, the Baptist General Convention, and the General Convention of the Protestant Episcopal Church adopted the Society's program within the

[19] As usual, the clergy held few official posts in the leadership of the national Society. This was part of a policy of self-effacement in any cause with political implications. Among the thirteen managers of the Society, only three were ministers: James Laurie of the Associate Reformed Church, Stephen B. Balch of the Baptist Church, and Obadiah B. Brown also of the Baptist Church. See *First Annual Report* (Washington, 1818), p. 4.
[20] "Resolutions on Slavery," *African Repository*, I (1825), 272-276.

first five years.[21] The General Synod of the Reformed Dutch Church followed suit in 1825.[22] The Congregational Churches had no single mouthpiece by which to signify their adherence, but at its annual meeting in 1825 the American Board instructed its Prudential Committee, "in case they think proper, to admit the descendants of Africa into the foreign mission school at Cornwall, Connecticut with a view to their preparation for missionary labors," resolving further, "that it is also recommended to the Prudential Committee to establish a mission in Africa as soon as they shall find it practicable and be able to make the requisite preparations."[23] This was equivalent to unofficial Congregational endorsement, much to the satisfaction of the General Secretary of the Society, Ralph Gurley.[24]

Gurley, a Presbyterian minister, began his work for the Society in 1822 and continued as General Secretary and moving spirit of the Society for eighteen years. According to an authoritative estimate, "he did more than any other single man connected with the Society—and many men thought, as much as almost any half dozen men—to keep open the avenues of thought and sympathy and cooperation between the biggest and best men in every part of the Union. Utterly unlike in their private practices, what Henry Clay was in the Halls of Congress, Gurley was to Colonization, essentially a peacemaker and a lover of the Union."[25]

Adding Gurley's great name to the roster of theocrats who rendered outstanding service to the colonization cause, we might mention two more who made history in the creation and early fortunes of Liberia. One was Samuel Bacon, an Episcopal clergyman educated at Harvard, who acted as government agent on the first emigrant ship, which arrived at Sierra Leone on March 9, 1821, carrying eighty-nine Negroes.[26] Bacon lived

[21] "Letter to the Editor," *ibid.*, pp. 5-7.
[22] "Public Sentiment," *ibid.*, pp. 124-126.
[23] *ibid.*, pp. 248-249.   [24] *ibid.*, pp. 344-345.
[25] Early Lee Fox, *The American Colonization Society, 1817-1840* (Baltimore, The Johns Hopkins Press, 1919), p. 73.
[26] Alexander, *op.cit.*, pp. 112-127.

long enough to see the colonists sheltered in makeshift houses, but the man who saved the tiny colony from extinction during its first two years was a Congregational clergyman, Jehudi Ashmun, Liberia's first colonial agent.

Arriving on August 9, 1822, with another shipload of emigrants, Ashmun lost his wife during the first winter, nearly died of the fever himself, successfully defended the settlement against a vicious attack by neighboring savage tribes, started a colonial journal which gives us a unique insight into the harrowing experiences of the colonists, and administered the colony with unabated vigor until his death in 1828.[27] Thus Liberia was the child of the theocrats, conceived in the mind of Samuel Hopkins, born of the efforts of Mills and Finley, nursed through its infancy by Bacon and Ashmun, and reared to adulthood by the unstinting devotion of Ralph Randolph Gurley.

The Fourth of July Collection

Another impressive token of the Society's adoption by the theocrats was their response to the Society's appeal for a special collection to be received on the national holiday. From the *African Repository*, official organ of the Society, it appears that at least during the twenties the major part of the Society's funds came from Protestant congregations as a result of this special collection. In 1827 alone the *African Repository* acknowledged offerings from thirty-two Presbyterian, ten Methodist, nine Episcopal, nine Congregational, and four Baptist churches. These numbers, however, should be doubled or tripled, since by this time most of the collections were received through traveling "collection agents" and through auxiliary societies affiliated with the national Society. Most of the collection agents were clergymen, many of them outstanding theocrats. For instance, there was William Meade, later Episcopal Bishop of Virginia, one of the earliest and most effective agents as well as one of the most liberal benefactors of the Society. In New England Horace Sessions, a Congregational

[27] *ibid.*, pp. 177-240.

clergyman, collected impressive amounts for the Society. Gurley himself was not only an indefatigable traveler and lecturer but also the most successful "collection agent" of the Society.

Clerical Leadership in the Auxiliary Societies

Even more important was the part played by the theocrats in the auxiliary societies. Twenty-five of these were organized in 1827 alone, covering the whole area between Massachusetts and Georgia, and nearly all of them employed clergymen in positions of leadership. For instance, Leonard Bacon, one of the earliest clerical colonizationists, became Secretary of the Connecticut Colonization Society, which also numbered four ministers among its managers.[28] Robert Baird was elected Secretary of the New Jersey Colonization Society.[29] In the Chillicothe (Ohio) Society five out of the twelve managers were pastors;[30] in the North Carolina Society both Vice-Presidents, Caldwell and McPheeters, were prominent clerics;[31] and a clergyman even succeeded in organizing a society in Jackson County, Georgia, after a delay of two years, because of "ill founded jealousies and fears of the South relative to the *ultimate* designs of the North and the Parent Society. . . ."[32]

During the next five years state societies were formed in Kentucky, New York, Pennsylvania, Indiana, Tennessee, and Mississippi, while the number of local auxiliaries grew apace and clergymen held important posts in all of them. The famed Methodist preacher, Andrew Broaddus, labored as Vice-President in the auxiliary society at King William County, Virginia, and delivered the Fourth of July address to the society in 1826.[33] His distinguished colleague in New York, Nathan Bangs, made the same appeal before the New York City Society the following year.[34] Many of these sermons were printed, providing us with a conspectus of the motives which made

[28] *African Repository*, III (1827), 92.   [29] *ibid.*, p. 122.
[30] *African Repository*, III (1827), 220.   [31] *ibid.*, p. 349.
[32] *ibid.*, p. 370; IV (1828).   [33] *ibid.*, II (1826), 191-192.
[34] *ibid.*, III (1827), 179-183.

the theocrats embrace the colonization scheme as the solution of America's Negro problem.

The Missionary Motive

The primary motive of the theocrats was missionary. It had been uppermost in the mind of Samuel Hopkins. His great disciple, Samuel J. Mills, might justly be called the "father of American Protestant missions." Significantly, he lived to see the Negro's Land of Promise, having been sent on an exploratory journey by the newly-founded American Colonization Society. Unfortunately, he did not live to report his findings. He died aboard ship on the homeward voyage and the report was made on his behalf by his traveling companion, Ebenezer Burgess, a Congregational minister.

Burgess' report breathed the missionary spirit of Mills. "Providence," he wrote to the Society, "will explain its own mysteries. ... The removal of multitudes from the land which gave them birth, to foreign and Christian lands, however effected by the ambition and rapacity of wicked men, gives an opportunity, by the return of some of their descendants, to introduce the useful arts and a knowledge of our holy religion more easily, naturally, and extensively, into the continent of Africa, than could have been done by any other system or means which human wisdom could have devised."[35]

The colonization of the freedmen who had acquired at least the rudiments of Christianity and civilization inspired high hopes for the spiritual conquest of Africa.[36] Many other theocrats expressed this sentiment during the early years of the colonization effort, but the most comprehensive treatment came from the pen of Leonard Bacon.

A charter member of the famous "Andover Society of Inquiry Concerning Missions," Bacon had made a study of the

[35] Ebenezer Burgess, *Address to the American Society for colonizing the free people of colour of the United States* (Washington, 1818), p. 6.
[36] Samuel Miller, *A Sermon, preached at Newark . . . for the benefit of the African School* . . . (Trenton, 1823), p. 21.

Negro in the United States during 1823, and had become convinced of the wrong of slavery.[37] By 1825 he had determined for himself that only colonization could right the wrong. Entering wholeheartedly into the work of the American Colonization Society, he asserted that the removal of the freedman would contribute not only to the redemption of Africa, but also to the uplifting of the slaves who would remain in this country and of the whole Negro race everywhere. To Bacon the four million Negroes in the United States and the fifty million in Africa presented "a continent of misery, a race degraded from the level of humanity."[38] Colonization, however, would bring a twofold remedy. On the one hand, "by civilizing and christianizing the African continent, the degradation of Africans in other countries may be removed."[39] On the other hand, "by elevating the character of Africans in foreign countries, the civilization of their native continent may be greatly and rapidly promoted."[40]

The Philanthropic Motive

The second motive of the theocrats was their desire to elevate the Negro race, both in this country and in Africa. This motive combined effectively with the missionary motive. The processes of "Christianization" and "civilization" were assumed to be complementary, and both, after a period of tutelage, were to be entrusted to the Negroes themselves. In the meantime, however, the theocrats had no glorified, unrealistic vision of America's freedmen. On the contrary, they were unanimous in noting that "the two hundred and fifty thousand free people of colour" constituted "the most ignorant, degraded, and vicious class in the community."[41] This was probably not an exaggeration. At least the incidence of disease and crime among the free Negroes was startlingly high. Yet the theocrats were

[37] Adams, *op.cit.*, p. 66.
[38] Leonard Bacon, *A Plea for Africa* (New Haven, 1825), p. 14.
[39] *ibid.*, p. 15.   [40] *ibid.*, p. 17.
[41] Nathaniel Bouton, *Christian Patriotism* (Concord, N.H., 1825), p. 15.

hopeful about their potentialities and proposed Africa as the setting in which these could be fully developed. Their optimism for the Negroes in Africa was exceeded only by their pessimism for them should they have to remain in the United States. The African School of the Presbyterian Synod of New Jersey was organized in 1816 "for the purpose of educating young men of colour to be teachers and preachers to the people of colour within these States and elsewhere."[42] Edward Dorr Griffin, one of the School's founders and directors, was particularly optimistic. After considerable Biblical research, he rejected the theory of the "curse of Ham"[43] which allegedly rested on the Negro race, concluding that they were descendants not of the cursed Canaan but of Cush, another son of Ham, whose posterity peopled Africa, and that they were responsible for the notable civilization of ancient Ethiopia.[44]

Somehow, in spite of their pessimistic view of man, the theocrats sensed that the Negro's condition was not so much the result of a destiny decreed at the dawn of time, nor yet of an innate inferiority, but rather of the treatment he had received at the hands of professedly Christian nations. For this reason the Presbyterian General Assembly of 1818 cautioned against undue haste in ending slavery in the United States, "lest we add a second injury to the first by emancipating them in such a manner that they will be likely to destroy themselves and others."[45] For one thing seemed obvious: the Negro had no future in the United States. His freedom would never be more than nominal. "You cannot bleach them into the enjoyment of freedom," observed Nathaniel Bouton caustically. By removing them to Africa, on the other hand, "you will confer on them both the name and the reality of freedom."[46]

This view of the Negro's chances was held by all the theocrats, consistently and tenaciously. Even Robert Finley saw

[42] *An Address to the Public on the subject of the African School* . . . (New York, 1816), p. 3.
[43] Genesis 9: 25-27.
[44] Edward D. Griffin, *A Plea for Africa* (New York, 1817), *passim*.
[45] *African Repository* I (1825), 274.
[46] Bouton, *op.cit.*, p. 16.

no other hope for the Negro's latent social and religious potentialities than the "gradual separation of the black from the white population, by providing the former with some suitable situation, where they may enjoy the advantages to which nature and their Creator's will entitles them."[47]

From another standpoint, Samuel Miller pointed to the danger which the presence of the freedmen in the United States might bring to the whites, should their numbers continue to increase at a rapid rate. "Suppose a million and a half of such people scattered through the United States. They could never be trusted as faithful citizens. On the other hand, the whites . . . would seldom think of anything but rendering them subservient to their pleasures, their pride, and their avarice."[48]

Eliphalet Nott carried this apprehension even further by calculating that by the end of the century there would be twenty-four million Negroes in the United States, if their numbers should keep doubling every twenty years. "Twenty-four million slaves! And is the republic so soon to embosom such an appalling amount of ignorant, vicious, degraded and brutal population! What a drawback from our strength! What a tax on our own resources! What a hindrance to our growth! And what an impediment to the fulfilment of our destiny! Could our worst enemies, or the worst enemies of republics, wish us a severer reproach, or a heavier judgment?"[49]

National Security

Thus the third motive of the theocrats in endorsing the colonization scheme was their concern for national security. A man of antislavery convictions might use this argument with

---

[47] Robert Finley, "Thoughts on the Colonization of Free Blacks," in *Memoir of the Rev. Robert Finley* by I. W. Brown (New Brunswick, 1819), p. 83.

[48] Miller, *op.cit.*, p. 13.

[49] Eliphalet Nott, "Address to the New York State Colonization Society," in *African Colonization: Proceedings of the Formation of the New York State Colonization Society* . . . (Albany, 1829), p. 12.

equal persuasiveness on behalf of colonization and abolition, suggesting that there might be a future for truly free Negroes in the United States. Most of the theocrats, however, categorically denied this possibility. They preferred the view, which Gurley himself openly avowed, that national self-interest dictated the removal of the freedmen, and eventually of all Negroes, and that therefore supporting the American Colonization Society was really a patriotic duty.[50]

Most Southern clergymen stressed the "good riddance" view and even suggested, like the unnamed Episcopal rector in North Carolina, that colonization of the freedmen would "increase the usefulness and improve the moral character of those who remain in servitude and with whose labors the country is unable to dispense."[51] Whether such clergymen personally represented the slaveholder's viewpoint, or whether they were using the argument from a sincere concern for the welfare of the freedmen, will never be known. It probably varied with the individual. Whatever their private feelings, however, their situation was delicate. When George Potts, pastor of the First Presbyterian Church of Natchez, spoke in Philadelphia on July the Fourth, 1826, and an offering was received for the Society, he dared not allude to the object of the offering. When the sermon was printed, his hosts—Philadelphia theocrats Ashbel Green, John H. Kennedy, William L. McCalla, and J. J. Janeway—felt called upon to explain to the public that he privately supported the Society, and to urge great sympathy and tact toward Southern colonizationists.[52]

National Unity

The theocrats advocated colonization also because they were tremendously concerned with the preservation of the Union.

[50] Ralph R. Gurley, *A Discourse delivered on the Fourth of July, 1825* . . . (Washington, 1825), p. 20.
[51] "Address delivered before a Society in North Carolina," *African Repository*, III (1827), 67.
[52] George Potts, *An Address delivered in Philadelphia, July 4, 1826* . . . (Philadelphia, 1826), pp. 42-44.

This motive can hardly be overrated. To save the United States from a division into two hostile camps over the problem of the Negro was one of their fondest hopes. For the sake of national union they were willing to make the utmost concessions to the slaveholders. "Let us ever be ready to make allowance for their feelings, to treat them with delicacy and respect, and carefully avoid all language which may tend to excite unkind sentiments, or *to exhibit the appearance of a divided country*.... The evil ... is a *National Evil*; and there ought to be a *National Feeling* and a *National Effort* respecting it."[53]

Thus spoke Samuel Miller. But pleas for patience and tact did not go far enough. The theocrats knew that the North, and New England in particular, might well exercise some self-criticism, in view of its slave-trading past. Thus President Nott reminded the smug critics of the South of the thought-provoking fact that "if the planter of the South has long appeared in the odious character of *receiver of stolen men*, the trader of the North has as long appeared in the still more *odious character of man-stealer*."[54]

This emphasis on national, rather than sectional, responsibility for the Negro problem showed the theocrats at their best, as spokesmen of the nation's Christian conscience. At the same time it revealed them as ardent "unionists," and they were proud to be known as such. An investigation of their sermons and other writings, however, discloses yet another motive for supporting the colonization scheme: their hope for the ultimate abolition of slavery.

Ultimate Abolition

Samuel Mills already had voiced this hope of the theocrats which Southern clergymen did not, or dared not, share. The founding of a colony in Africa, he wrote to Ebenezer Burgess in 1817, would "ultimately be the means of exterminating slavery in our country." It would "eventually redeem and

[53] Miller, *op.cit.*, p. 6.   [54] Nott, *op.cit.*, p. 10.

emancipate a million and a half wretched men."⁵⁵ Some of the earliest abolitionist ministers, like Asa Cummings of Maine, later editor of the abolitionist *Christian Mirror*, at first endorsed colonization for the sole reason that it would "hasten the abolition of slavery," or at least "do something to mitigate the many injuries we have done them."⁵⁶ Bishop William Meade of Virginia also expressed the conviction that the Society's work would facilitate the process of voluntary emancipation.⁵⁷ Leonidas Lent Hamline, Methodist Bishop of Ohio, estimated that "a fund of a million and a half dollars, annually renewed, to transport and colonize seventy thousand Negroes every year," might end slavery in the United States by their total removal, since "in something less than one hundred years this would launch the last cargo of blacks from our shores."⁵⁸ Most of the theocrats, however, entertained no such fantastic hopes, but looked forward to the day when colonization, by providing an effective check to the dangerous increase of the Negro population and by exerting a moral influence upon the slaveowners, would bring to an end American domestic slavery. Occasionally even clergymen in the South would openly voice this hope. Robert J. Breckinridge, for instance, speaking "as a slaveowner," urged federal and state subsidies for the American Colonization Society, with a view to the final cessation of slavery itself, which he regarded as being "at war with every law of nature, with every lesson of experience, with every conclusion of reason."⁵⁹

Unfortunately, the discretion of the theocrats in dealing with the South and the repeated affirmation of their hope that

⁵⁵ Samuel J. Mills, in *Memoirs of the Rev. Samuel J. Mills*, by Gardiner Spring (New York, 1820), p. 139.
⁵⁶ Asa Cummings, *A Discourse delivered at Brunswick, Maine, April 6, 1820* . . . (Brunswick, 1820), p. 31.
⁵⁷ William Meade, "Address delivered at Winchester, Va. . . ." *African Repository*, vi (1830), 292.
⁵⁸ Leonidas Lent Hamline, "An Address delivered on July 5th, 1830, at Zanesville, Ohio . . ." *African Repository*, vi (1830), 292.
⁵⁹ Robert J. Breckinridge, "An Address delivered before the Colonization Society of Kentucky," *African Repository*, vii (1831), 176.

colonization would not be interpreted as an instrument of abolitionism, did not convince the Lower South, where hostility to the Society was rising rapidly. The auxiliary society in Georgia, which had been so hard to organize, was short-lived. A widely circulated South Carolina pamphlet, entitled, *The Crisis; or, Essays on the Usurpations of the Federal Government*,[60] bluntly accused the Society of a projected alliance with the Philadelphia abolitionists, and cited its reception of federal subsidy as a proof of its being a weapon of the government directed against the South. Ironically, the Society had been pleading for federal aid on the ground that its objective was of nationwide scope and interest, but its pleas had been falling on deaf ears, if we discount the small salary received from the government by the colonial agent.[61]

Southern clerical colonizationists did their best to repair the breach and to maintain the national character of the colonization effort. Charges that the American Colonization Society "espouses the cause of indiscriminate emancipation and is stirring uneasiness and disaffection among your slaves" are wholly unfounded, preached Stephen Foster of Tennessee.[62] And Daniel P. Bestor, of Huntsville, Alabama, reminded his congregation that the legislatures of Virginia and Maryland—both slave states—had endorsed the Society and did not regard it "as carrying on any operations detrimental to their interests."[63]

But the fears of the Lower South could not be allayed, nor did the Society ever officially disavow its hope for the eventual emancipation of the slaves. Far from concealing this hope, Gurley affirmed it with as much defiance as a man of his gentle ways could muster. Mildly rebuking the "morbid sensitiveness" which seemed to prevail in the Lower South, and which,

[60] Charleston, 1828. Reviewed in *African Repository*, IV (1828), 58-60. Opposition in this state was, of course, closely linked with the prevailing hostility to the tariff, which led to the Nullification Controversy of 1832.
[61] Fox, *op.cit.*, pp. 66, 70, 76.
[62] "An Essay for the Fourth of July," *African Repository*, IV (1828), 373.
[63] "Address delivered before the LaGrange Colonization Society, Huntsville, Ala.," *African Repository*, VI (1830), 130.

he felt "approaches the ridiculous, since our Society has received the unqualified approval of nearly every . . . religious denomination in the land,"⁶⁴ Gurley reaffirmed the nationwide scope of the Society, stressed its record of noninterference with the institution of slavery, but noted just as candidly its "persuasive influence in favour of voluntary emancipation."⁶⁵

By the turn of the fourth decade, however, neither tact nor candor availed any longer: the Lower South had renounced colonization. At the fifteenth annual meeting of the Society, held in Washington in January 1832, the southernmost delegation was that of North Carolina, and even of its three delegates two were Quakers with a long record of antislavery work in that state.⁶⁶

Summary

The year 1831 marked a dividing line in the history of the American Negro and consequently in the attitude of the theocrats toward the racial problem he embodied.

The theocrats were unanimous in their conviction that, whether slave or free, the Negro had no place in American society. They endorsed the idea of colonization because of their desire for the evangelization of Africa. They believed that the existence of a successful Negro colony in Liberia would raise the Negro's prestige and improve his lot in this country and elsewhere. They found colonization to be an excellent safety valve against that danger to national security which a quarter million freedmen seemed to represent. They urged their speedy removal, even though they realized that it might further the interests of the "advocates of perpetual slavery." "It matters not that some . . . would prosecute the colonizing of free people of colour from the southern states in order to secure a more effectual power over the slaves," remarked Episcopal theocrat Jonathan Wainwright of New York City. "What alone matters is that the project itself be a good one."⁶⁷

⁶⁴ R. R. Gurley, "South Carolina Opinions of the Colonization Society," *African Repository*, VI (1830), 194.
⁶⁵ *ibid.*, p. 202.   ⁶⁶ *African Repository*, VII (1832), 368-369.
⁶⁷ Quoted in *African Repository*, IV (1828), 202-203.

Above all, the theocrats were "unionists." From 1817 to 1831 the American Colonization Society, supported by the Protestant clergy of the nation with hardly any exceptions, labored powerfully to incarnate and preserve the unionist viewpoint. Led by Gurley, the theocrats endeavored to include Southern clergymen in the effort in order to keep it on a truly national basis. They did not cease to urge moderation and patience toward the South.

This middle-of-the-road character of the theocratic pattern for the American Negro was its chief strength, but it also sealed its fate in the end. Like the Christianity of the Laodiceans, it was "neither hot, nor cold,"[68] and therefore doomed to fail, when the more extreme views came increasingly to the fore after 1831.

1831-1848
The Slaveholder's View

On January 1, 1831, William Lloyd Garrison launched *The Liberator*. Within a year the defense of the Southern slaveowners crystallized in the "positive good theory." First formulated at the time of the controversy over the admission of Missouri into the Union,[69] it came into its own in the early thirties as a reaction to abolitionism. Several slave rebellions further fanned the flames.[70] Under these provocations the slaveowners abandoned their former apologetic attitude and stepped forth as unabashed champions of a social system which the South had found satisfactory and which the North had neither the right nor the power to change.

Jenkins submits a wealth of proof to the effect that the "positive good theory was an outgrowth of the twenties," and that it "antedated the Garrisonian movement, instead of com-

[68] Revelation 3: 16.
[69] See the brilliant antislavery essays of Boston theocrat Jeremiah Evarts, entitled, "The Missouri Question," *Panoplist and Missionary Herald*, XVI (1820), 15-24, 59-72.
[70] The standard monograph on this subject is Herbert Aphteker, *American Negro Slave Revolts* (New York, 1943).

ing ... as the answer to abolition propaganda."[71] This may be true, so far as Garrisonian abolitionism alone is concerned, but it leaves out of account the influence of the American Colonization Society, with the repeated affirmation, mostly by theocratic spokesmen, of its hope for the gradual abolition of slavery. We suggest that this factor played a considerable part in turning Southern sentiment against the North, in spite of all the attempts of the Society at retaining the favor of the South. By 1832, then, the theocratic pattern for the Negro had failed, at least so far as the Lower South was concerned, because its chosen instrument, the American Colonization Society, had fairly reached the end of its usefulness.

Southern criticism of the American Colonization Society was leveled not only at its ideology but at its accomplishments. In that respect it was irrefutable, for the Society had not been able to perform a fraction of what it had proposed. Between 1821 and 1833 less than three thousand emigrants had actually embarked for Liberia under the auspices of the Society.[72] This spectacular failure can be accounted for and excused by pointing to a number of factors: the nature of Liberia, the failure to obtain adequate federal support and the insufficiency of the funds made available by the legislatures of Maryland and Virginia, by churches and private benefactors; the unwillingness of more masters to emancipate their slaves with a view to their colonization and the inability of some masters, willing to emancipate, to provide for their transportation to the ship;

[71] William Sumner Jenkins, *Pro-Slavery Thought in the Old South* (Chapel Hill, University of North Carolina Press, 1935), p. 77.
[72] A "Special Report of the Board of Managers," *African Repository*, x (1834), 8-17, gives the following figures:

1820-1825	390
1826-1829	781
1830	259
1831	441
1832	790
1833	108
Total:	2769

and, last but not least, the attitude of the freedmen themselves, which has never been properly gauged.[73]

The great work by a Southerner expounding the "positive good theory," was *An Essay On Slavery* by Thomas Roderick Dew, President of William and Mary College in Virginia.[74] Slavery, Dew contended, was as old as the human race and had been an accepted social institution even among the Chosen People.[75] Thus it is clearly a "necessary result of the laws of mind and matter," marking "some benevolent design" and "intended by our Creator for some useful purpose."[76] Specifically, it tends to check the frequency of war by attaching primitive men and tribes to a sedentary society; it fits savages, who are naturally indolent, for productive work, and raises them far above any standard of living they could ever have attained had they remained in their savagery; it also gives the women of the slave races a measure of social status and actual physical security far beyond anything they may have enjoyed prior to their enslavement.

Having thus shown the advantages of slavery to the slaves themselves, Dew proceeds to justify the slave trade. He admits the horrors of the capture of slaves and of the middle passage, but ascribes them in large measure to conditions prevailing in Africa and to the ignorance and brutality of the traders. He minimizes America's "share in the original sin by which slavery

[73] An interesting "Memorial of the Free People of Colour" of Baltimore, dated December 11, 1826, *African Repository*, II (1826), 293-298, presents a group of freedmen as giving their grateful and unreserved endorsement to colonization. This, however, was an extreme reaction. The other extreme was represented by David Walker's notorious *Appeal . . . to the Coloured Citizens of the World* (Boston, 1829), which totally rejected the scheme. A self-educated Boston freedman, Walker wrote his pamphlet to call for a world-wide Negro rebellion. Walker claimed that the colonization scheme was devised "by a gang of slaveholders, to select the free people of colour from among the slaves, that our more miserable brethren may be the better secured in ignorance and wretchedness, to work their farms and dig their mines, and thus go on enriching the Christians with their blood and groans." Quoted from Benjamin T. Brawley, *A Social History of the American Negro* (New York, 1921), pp. 155-159.
[74] Richmond, Va. [1832], 1849.
[75] *ibid.*, p. 7.   [76] *ibid.*, p. 24.

was first introduced into this country," blaming it on the British who would not "allow the colonies to check or discourage in any degree a traffic so beneficial to the nation."[77] Then, turning to what constitutes the bulk of his work, Dew exposes the impracticality first of "Emancipation and Deportation," then of "Emancipation without Deportation." The former, which embraces the efforts of the American Colonization Society, he rejects because it barely begins to scratch the surface of the problem and cannot hope to do so even with federal aid (which he staunchly opposes). The latter he rejects because "the slaves, in both an economical and moral point of view, are entirely unfit for a state of freedom among the whites."[78] This last point was, of course, granted by the colonizationists so that the argument really hinged on the practicality or impracticality of colonization.

Insofar, then, as Dew's argument against colonization was based on population facts, it was irrefutable. It gave the continuation of slavery in the United States both a rational basis and a moral justification. The slaves were unfit for emancipation and incapable of colonization; on the other hand, slavery was a beneficial institution not only for the whites but for the slaves; hence slavery should be perpetuated and defended. Thus the "positive good theory," propounded by Dew and embraced by the South, successfully destroyed the alternative proposed by the theocrats, at least so far as the South was concerned.

The Abolitionist's View

If the colonization scheme was not "cold" enough for the slaveholders, neither was it "hot" enough for the abolitionists. Most of the leading abolitionists were renegades from the colonizationist camp. This was true of Gerrit Smith and James G. Birney, and even of Garrison himself whom these two prominent colonizationists joined in the middle thirties.[79]

Garrison's biographers, writing with a partiality both filial and unhistoric, make light of the fact that in 1829 he preached

[77] ibid., p. 38. [78] ibid., p. 77. [79] Fox, op.cit., pp. 175-176.

the Fourth of July sermon in a Boston church, that he asked the congregation "to sustain Congress in any future efforts to colonize the coloured population of the United States,"[80] and that he undoubtedly said a prayer over the special offering designated for the American Colonization Society. Even more significant is the fact that Garrison appealed to "ambassadors of Christ everywhere" and to "the churches of the living God, to lead in this great enterprise," the emancipation of the slaves.[81] Clearly he had not yet given up the clergy and the churches as potential allies.

This, however, was 1829. Only three years later Garrison published his *Thoughts on African Colonization*[82] with which he struck as fatal a blow against colonization in the North as President Dew did in the South.

At least Garrison's attack on colonization should have cleared the Society of Southern charges of abolitionist sympathies. It is quite probable that the attack had some such effect, at least on Southern clergymen who continued to support the Society. On the whole, however, its influence upon the colonization effort in the North was devastating.

Garrison's first charge bore squarely upon the moral aspect of colonization. "The question is not, whether the climate of Africa is salubrious, or any other specific issue but whether the doctrines and principles of the Society accord with the doctrines of and principles of the gospel, whether slave-holders are just proprietors of their slaves, whether it is not the sacred duty of the nation to abolish the system of slavery now, and to recognize the people of color as brethren and countrymen who have been unjustly treated and covered with unmerited shame. This is the question—the only question."[83]

It was true that, depending on the reaction of the slaveholders, colonizationists were willing to forego immediate emancipa-

[80] William Lloyd Garrison, "Dangers to the Nations" (1829), in W. P. Garrison and F. J. Garrison, *William Lloyd Garrison* (4 vols., New York, 1885), I, 137.
[81] *ibid.*, p. 136.
[82] Reprinted, in condensed form, in Garrisons, *op.cit.*, I, 290ff.
[83] Garrisons, *op.cit.*, pp. 290-291.

tion for the sake of ultimate emancipation and the preservation of the Union.[84] But Garrison scorned such caution. Instead he made it clear that he would "oppose this Society, even if its doctrines were harmless," because "it effectively seals up the lips of a vast number of influential and pious men" on the subject of slavery. They may refer to it, to be sure, at least every Fourth of July," but they content themselves with "representing slavery as an evil . . . *and not as an individual crime*. . . ."[85] This was the crux of the abolitionist attack: the definition of slavery as a sin *per se* and the demand for its immediate cessation. Garrison even went so far as to say that "if it were evident that only by a short delay, he [the slave] could be better prepared to receive the book of liberty, still the slave ought to be a free man *now*. . . ."[86]

Garrison attacked the American Colonization Society not only on principle, but also for strategic reasons. He realized that its enormous prestige would have to be destroyed before the "slavocracy" itself could be effectively invaded. The Society appeared to him as a formidable shield behind which the slaveholders were able to carry on "business as usual."[87] An organization of such magnitude and such universal support, engaged in protecting sin, had to be destroyed before the sinners themselves could be effectively dealt with. No longer hoping for anything but hostility from the churches, Garrison admitted: "I have been almost as cruelly opposed by ministers of the Gospel and church members as by any other class of men."[88]

This was only natural, since he had rejected every one of the motives which animated the theocrats in their support of colonization. He would not consider ultimate emancipation at the price of perpetuating sin. He had no regard for the union. "If the slave states haughtily spurn our assistance," he wrote, "then the fault is not ours, if a separation eventually take

[84] Fox, *op.cit.*, p. 127.   [85] Garrisons, *op.cit.*, p. 293.
[86] *The Liberator*, March 7, 1835; quoted in Fox, *op.cit.*, p. 133.
[87] *ibid.*, December 13, 1834; quoted in Fox, *op.cit.*, p. 133.
[88] Garrisons, *op.cit.*, pp. 293-294.

place."[89] He held that only immediate emancipation could safeguard the nation from the danger of a Negro rebellion. Abolition, he affirmed, would be accomplished either by reform or by a revolution "such as will blot out the remembrance of the horrors of Santo Domingo."[90] Above all he scoffed at the missionary vision of the theocrats, claiming that Liberia had received little evangelization, but plenty of "wars, rum, and tobacco," so that there were now "*two* ignorant and depraved nations to be regenerated instead of just *one*."[91] With biting irony he proceeded to point out the inconsistency of the missionary argument. "One of these nations is so incorrigibly stupid or infathomably deep in pollution (for such is the argument), that although surrounded by ten millions of people living under the full blaze of the Gospel light, and having every desirable facility to elevate and save it, it can never rise until it be removed at least three thousand miles from their vicinage!—and yet, it is first to be evangelized in a barbarous land, by a feeble, inadequate process, before it can be qualified to evangelize the other nation!"[92]

This charge was almost unanswerable. Denying the chances of freedmen in the United States did not refute it, because Garrison insisted that the Negroes were to be recognized as "brothers and countrymen." If public opinion would not allow them to rise in the social scale, Garrison proposed to change public opinion. First, however, the American Colonization Society had to be liquidated. Then slavery itself, "a curse, debasing in its effect, cruel in its operation, fatal in its continuance,"[93] had to be abolished; at last, to be sure, the masses of emancipated Negroes would have to be assisted in adjusting to their new condition.

It seems that the general public in the North responded far more rapidly and favorably to Garrisonian abolitionism than did the theocrats. Beginning with the thirties, more and more churches closed their doors to colonizationist lectures and

[89] "Dangers to the Nation," in Garrisons, *op.cit.*, pp. 132-133.
[90] *ibid.*, p. 135.   [91] Garrisons, *op.cit.*, p. 291.
[92] *ibid.*   [93] "Dangers to the Nation," *ibid.*, p. 129.

agents because of the minister's fear that his members would object.⁹⁴ A few clergymen, to be sure, had advocated immediate abolition even before 1831, and had joined either Garrison or the more moderate American Anti-Slavery Society,⁹⁵ but the theocrats—with hardly an exception, opposed abolitionism and continued to favor colonization.

Theocrats versus Abolitionists

As an illustration of the opposition of the theocrats to abolitionism we may cite a famous article by Charles Hodge. In this article the eminent Princeton Seminary professor rejects abolitionism on Biblical grounds by disclaiming that slavery is not condemned as a sin *per se* in the Scriptures. "If the present course of the abolitionists is right, then the course of Christ and the apostles was wrong," he remarks dryly.⁹⁶ Colonization, on the other hand, he hails "as one of the noblest enterprises of modern benevolence.⁹⁷ Hodge was further convinced that the strategy of abolitionism was dangerous, leading to antagonism in the South and to dissension among the friends of the Negro in the North, and threatening "to produce the disunion of the states and the division of all ecclesiastical societies in the country. . . ."⁹⁸ In conclusion, he echoes the doctrine of William Paley, expressing his hope for the termination of slavery through a gentle, gradual elevation of the Negro.⁹⁹

Thus Hodge condemned abolitionism as dangerous to the union, holding out the possibility of emancipation as an ultimate hope, and endorsing colonization as an immediate good both to the Negro and to the United States. No longer did

⁹⁴ Fox, *op.cit.*, p. 64.
⁹⁵ This society was an indirect outcome of the great Western revivals conducted by Charles G. Finney in the twenties. It came into being with the patronage of New York philanthropists Arthur and Lewis Tappan and through the leadership of Finney's greatest convert, Theodore Dwight Weld. See Gilbert H. Barnes, *The Anti-Slavery Impulse, 1830-1844* (New York, 1933), *passim*, but particularly Chapter IV.
⁹⁶ "Review of 'Slavery' by William Ellery Channing," *Biblical Repertory*, VIII (April 1836), 276.
⁹⁷ *ibid.*, p. 305.   ⁹⁸ *ibid.*, pp. 298-299.   ⁹⁹ *ibid.*, p. 300.

even the theocrats believe that colonization alone would solve the entire Negro problem. Horace Bushnell referred, somewhat wistfully, to "the belief, too hastily admitted by some, but now given up," that Colonization is to be a complete remedy for slavery.[100] However, their concern over the mounting tension between North and South was so great that, far from abandoning the colonization scheme, they rallied to the support of the Society even more fervently. "Let the North and the South become arrayed against each other on the subject of our coloured population, and we may indeed tremble for our country," wrote Gurley, adding: "Never, while I live, will I cease to urge every friend of the coloured race, every friend of freedom and the Union, to cultivate peace...."[101] In the same vein Elihu Baldwin, President of Wabash College in Indiana, contemptuously referred to abolitionism as "the thing sometimes misnamed Christianity, that modern Hercules with his lion's skin and his club going to rid the world of political monsters," and asserted that not abolitionism but colonization was in keeping with the "meek, inoffensive, and peace-speaking religion of Christ...."[102] An editorial, entitled, "Some Reasons for not Abandoning Colonization," in the *New York Observer*, warned rather awkwardly that "if the Colonization Society should be allowed to die now, it might be thought guilty of the sins laid to its charge by the Anti-Colonizationists, and thus an indelible stigma be fixed on the American character."[103] In other words, according to this writer in the largest Presbyterian weekly and one of the most influential theocratic journals, resisting abolitionism had become an integral part of the colonizationist platform.

But the theocrats did not stop at such verbal defense, or

[100] Horace Bushnell, *A Discourse on the Slavery Question* (Hartford, 1839), p. 24.
[101] "Remarks on the Principles of the Colonization Society," *African Repository*, x (1834), 72.
[102] Elihu Baldwin, "Address to the Indiana Colonization Society," *African Repository*, XII (1836), 123.
[103] *New York Observer*, September 13, 20, 27; quoted in *African Repository*, x (1834), 293-299.

even attack. They also increased their personal participation in the colonization effort. New faces began to appear at the annual meetings of the national Society in Washington: Philander Chase, pioneer Episcopal bishop of Ohio; Jeremiah Day, President of Yale; William McKendree, Methodist bishop in the West; and Wilbur Fisk, President of Wesleyan College in Connecticut. Other prominent theocrats who were not free or did not think it necessary to journey to Washington, volunteered for responsible posts in their state and local societies. Episcopal bishop William White was active in the Pennsylvania society; Jonathan Going, organizer of Baptist home missions, served as Vice-President of an auxiliary society in Massachusetts; Nathan Bangs, historian of Methodism, held the same position in the New York City Colonization Society, one of the strongest auxiliaries in the thirties, which also enlisted the talents of William Duer, President of Columbia College; George W. Bethune, brilliant minister to the Reformed Dutch Church; Alexander Proudfit, who served as its secretary and collection agent; and Philip Milledoler, President of Rutgers College. The New Jersey Society counted among its most active workers Asa Hillyer and George Cheever, as well as Princeton professors Dod and McLean. The Young Men's Colonization Society of Pennsylvania, a new and powerful group, boasted the services of John Breckinridge, Henry Augustus Boardman, and Episcopalian Stephen Tyng. A strong auxiliary was organized at Pittsburgh in 1836, with Elisha P. Swift, founder of the Presbyterian Western Theological Seminary, as its Vice-President.

All these theocrats held much the same views as Charles Hodge, implacably opposing abolitionism, though hoping for the eventual disappearance of slavery; cherishing the Union above all, and supporting colonization as a missionary venture, a boon to the freedmen, and an inducement to voluntary emancipation by the slaveholder. Lyman Beecher, for once, represented an outstanding exception in that he tried to be a good colonizationist and a good abolitionist at the same time.

As President of Lane Seminary in Cincinnati, Beecher saw the rise of abolitionist sentiment among the students and did not discourage it. In 1833 he wrote to Arthur Tappan: "I am not apprized of the ground of controversy between the Colonizationists and the Abolitionists. I am myself both, without perceiving in myself any inconsistency."[104]

The following year, however, the famous Lane Debate forced the issue. The trustees of the Seminary proceeded against the abolitionist students, particularly against Theodore Dwight Weld, and Beecher could not persuade them to be lenient, nor could he induce the students to submit to their disciplinary measures. A wholesale exodus followed. When the members of the Cincinnati Colonization Society gathered in November for their annual meeting, Beecher addressed them in almost defensive accents: "No hindrance of the Colonization Society to the cause of abolition could well become as great an evil, as the controversy, likely to be introduced, by an effort to put it down."[105] However, before the end of his speech, the defensive mood gave way to firmness, the timid reformer to the staunch theocrat, and he concluded: "But if, after all, the abandonment of Colonization is demanded as the only condition of peace, then we have made our election. If it be possible, as much as in us lieth, we will live peaceably, but we cannot abandon the one hundred million of Africa!"[106] Thus Beecher, in spite of his abolitionist sympathies, remained primarily a theocrat and therefore a colonizationist.

The Southern Clergy after 1831

What about the Southern clergy's attitude after 1831? For one thing, they were convinced that gradual progress had been made in the South toward the disappearance, or at least the mitigation, of slavery, but that it was being destroyed by

[104] *Autobiography . . . of Lyman Beecher*, edited by Charles Beecher (2 vols., New York, 1865), II, 323.
[105] "Address to the Cincinnati Colonization Society," *African Repository*, x (1834), p. 280.
[106] *ibid.*, p. 283.

NEGRO PROBLEM

the effects of the abolitionist agitation. "I am confident that already material injury has been done in the way of impeding the progress of feeling in this country against slavery," wrote John Holt Rice as early as 1827. "There is a march of opinion on the subject, which would, if uninterrupted, at no distant date, annihilate the evil in Virginia. I have no doubt of it. And every step gained by true religion is a step towards the accomplishment of this object."[107]

It is more than doubtful, however, whether Dr. Rice's optimism was justified. We would rather give credence to the estimate of a modern historian of the South who writes: "Although the abolition movement was followed by a decline of antislavery sentiment in the South, it must be remembered that in all the long years before that movement began, no part of the South had made substantial progress toward ending slavery. The free and full discussion in Virginia in 1832 was promising, but the decision was in the negative. The trends are not clear enough to warrant prophecy as to what the South would have done, had it not been disturbed by the abolitionists, but it is at least certain that before the crusade began Southern liberalism had not ended slavery in any state."[108]

Opposition to abolitionist ideas early aroused the Southern clergy to examine slavery in the light of the teachings of the Bible. They concluded, like South Carolina's leading Baptist minister, that slavery was not a sin *perse*, so long as "just and humane masters" ruled their slaves "according to Christian principles."[109]

On Biblical grounds the Southern defenders of slavery undoubtedly carried the day. The literal meaning of Scripture could not be stretched to yield an outright condemnation of

[107] John Holt Rice, "Letter to Archibald Alexander, April 14, 1827," in Maxwell, *op.cit.*, p. 312.
[108] Charles S. Sydnor, *The Development of Southern Sectionalism, 1819-1848* (Baton Rouge, La., 1948), p. 243.
[109] Richard Furman, *Exposition of the Views of the Baptists relative to the Colored Population of the United States* (Charleston, 1823); quoted in A. Y. Lloyd, *The Slavery Controversy, 1831-1860* (Chapel Hill, N.C., 1939), p. 163.

slavery, and appeals to the "spirit of the Bible" were not acceptable to the Biblical literalism of Protestant orthodoxy, South or North. When an occasional theocrat attempted a more liberal interpretation of Scripture, he was at once repudiated. For instance, when Francis Wayland objected to the application of apostolic precepts to the Southern slave system in order to justify it,[110] or when Philadelphia theocrat Albert Barnes exclaimed that "if the Bible could be shown to defend and countenance slavery, it would make thousands of infidels,"[111] they had to face sharp rebuttals not only from Southern pro-slavery clerics like Richard Furman, Thomas Witherspoon, or Richard Fuller, but also from their Northern fellow theocrats, such as Gardiner Spring,[112] Moses Stuart,[113] and countless others. What was worse, they laid themselves open to the devastating charge, leveled at them by the foremost Presbyterian clergyman of the South, James Henley Thornwell, who declared roundly that the "so-called Christian argument against slavery" is based upon "the abstrusest of all speculation upon the vexed question of human rights, and not the obvious teachings of the Bible."[114] The "spirit of rationalism," rather than the spirit of Biblical Christianity, "lies at the foundation of modern speculation in relation to the rights of man." Indeed, "such opposition to slavery has never been the offspring of the Bible," asserted Thornwell.[115]

Thus, by suggesting that abolitionism was not of Christian but of infidel origin, the Southern clergy could rest secure in their pro-slavery views which few of the theocrats could or

[110] *Domestic Slavery Considered as a Scriptural Institution: in Correspondence between the Rev. Richard Fuller and the Rev. Francis Wayland* (New York, 1845), p. 84.
[111] *The Scriptural View of Slavery* (Philadelphia, 1846), p. 381.
[112] "The Influence of the Bible on Slavery," in *Obligations of the World to the Bible* (New York, 1835), quoted in A. Y. Lloyd, *The Slavery Controversy, 1831-1860* (Chapel Hill, 1939), pp. 214-251.
[113] "Letter to Wilbur Fisk" (1836), quoted in Lloyd, *op.cit.*, p. 168.
[114] *Relation of the Church to Slavery* (1847, 1851); in *The Collected Writings of the Rev. James Henley Thornwell* (4 vols., Richmond, 1873), IV, 389.
[115] *ibid.*, p. 393.

dared attack.[116] On the positive side, however, theocrats and their Southern colleagues, continued to work together for African colonization and, to some extent, for the improvement of the lot of the slave. One common venture of the latter type was the education of slaves.

Education of the Slaves

It is a strange fact that the Southern ministers on the whole did more for the Christian instruction of the slaves than the theocrats in the North did for the freedmen. The attempts of the theocrats to train Negro preachers and teachers for Liberia had been signally unsuccessful for want of funds. The African School of the Presbyterian Synod of New York and New Jersey, founded in 1816, did not long survive. The Episcopal African Mission School Society at Hartford was even more short-lived.[117] The *African Repository* noted the founding of an African Education Society in Washington in 1829, proposing "to afford to persons of color destined to Africa, such an education in Letters, Agriculture, and the Mechanic Arts, as may best qualify them"[118] for colonization, but apparently nothing ever came of the venture. To be sure, Negroes were admitted to the public schools in the North, as well as to a few colleges and seminaries, but their attendance was not much enforced on the lower levels, nor was it much encouraged on the higher ones.

In the South, on the other hand, increasing efforts were being made to give the slaves at least a rudimentary Christian instruction during the thirties and forties. This at least is the

---

[116] It is interesting that clerical abolitionists constantly used Biblical arguments, often outdoing in literalism and fanciful interpretation the Southern pro-slavery clergy. See John Rankin, *Letters on American Slavery* (Boston, 1833), chapters xi and xii; LaRoy Sunderland (Methodist, editor of *Zion's Herald*). *The Testimony of God Against Slavery* (Boston, 1835), *passim*. Theodore D. Weld, *The Bible Against Slavery* (New York, 1837), *passim*. For a summary of these arguments, see C. L. Shanks, "The Biblical Anti-Slavery Argument, 1830-1840," *Journal of Negro History*, xvii (1931), 132-157.

[117] *African Repository*, iv (1828), 202-203.

[118] *ibid.*, vi (1830), 46.

impression given by the foremost teacher of the slaves, the Reverend Charles Colcock Jones of Georgia, an active colonizationist, who spent twenty years of his life instructing some six thousand of them in the fundamentals of Christianity.[119] In his book, *The Religious Instruction of the Negroes in the United States*,[120] he has left us an extensive and informative review of accomplishments as well as suggestions for future efforts. He was not a controversialist, but the facts he marshaled came to be used far and wide in countering abolitionist attacks on the Southern churches and their clergy.

Even before the publication of Jones' book, Southern ministers had been casting up their superior efforts on behalf of the slaves to their Northern critics. R. W. Bailey of South Carolina, for instance, pointed out to Asa Cummings, abolitionist editor in Maine, that in South Carolina only one-ninth of the whites over against one-seventh of the slaves were church members. "You have in New England 20,000, and in the free states more than 100,000 blacks. I should be glad to see a comparison of their religious condition with our slaves in this one item. Do you believe that one-twentieth of them are church members? And will you find, in New England, as here, a greater proportion of blacks than whites in the churches?"[121]

In the same vein, James W. Douglass, pastor of the First Presbyterian Church of Fayetteville, North Carolina, suggested a constructive outlet for the "exuberant compassion" of the enemies of slavery. He urged them, if they wanted to do something for the slaves, to send them the Gospel. "Pay their proportion of the pastor's salary, say one hundred dollars per year, and they shall have the pastor's services. This will be a blessing that maketh rich, and, unlike some other plans, addeth no sorrow therewith."[122]

We have no reason to accuse these Southern clergymen of conscious hypocrisy. Their arguments could not convert the

[119] *ibid.*, x (1834), 95.   [120] Savannah, Georgia, 1842.
[121] *African Repository*, XII (1835), 76.   [122] *ibid.*, XIII (1837), 96.

abolitionists any more than abolitionist arguments could convert them, but they made a deep impression on the theocrats in the North and forged a further bond between themselves and their Northern brothers.

Continued Southern Support of Colonization

The chief bond, however, between the Southern clergy and the Northern theocrats continued to be the colonization effort, which the Southern ministers kept supporting even when the rank and file of their people had repudiated it. As a matter of fact, they even increased their activity on behalf of the American Colonization Society after 1832. Henry Bidleman Bascom, later a bishop in the Methodist Church, South, and author of the ablest vindication of the seceding body,[123] worked as a collection agent of the Society in the thirties and remained its lifelong friend. William Winans, prominent Methodist pastor in Mississippi, stated at the Methodist General Conference of 1836 that "he was not born in a slave state—he was a Pennsylvanian by birth. He had been brought up to believe a slaveholder as great a villain as a horse-thief: but he had gone to the South, and long residence there had changed his views; he had become a slaveholder on principle; . . ."[124] yet he was one of the most productive collection agents of the Society, and, at the Society's reorganization in 1839, he became one of its new Vice-Presidents, together with two other outstanding Southern Methodists, Thomas Morris of Ohio and James Osgood Andrew of Georgia.[125]

Among the Presbyterians of the South, Philip Lindsley, President of Transylvania University and one of the foremost

---

[123] *Methodism and Slavery: With other matters controversial between the North and the South* (Frankfort, Kentucky, 1845).

[124] James G. Birney, *The American Churches, the Bulwark of Slavery* (New York, 1836), p. 37.

[125] *African Repository*, xv (1839), 167. Andrew, incidentally, became the reluctant direct cause of the Methodist division of 1844, and was elected bishop in the new Methodist Church, South. The other new bishop was Joshua Soule of New York, a theocrat who deserted the Northern church on conviction and who was also a colonizationist.

educators of his time, served as President of the Tennessee Colonization Society in the thirties. The active participation of Robert Breckinridge and John Clarke Young of Kentucky has been noted already. William S. Plummer of Richmond, Virginia, who became notorious for saying that "if abolitionists will set the country in a blaze, it is but fair that they should receive the first warming at the fire,"[126]—and who was so sensitive on the subject that he publicly denounced an anonymous donor for sending him a few handkerchiefs depicting scenes of slavery[127]—was also an active member of the Virginia Colonization Society. Professing his faith in colonization in the course of a visit to New York, he likened abolitionism to the impulsive Don Quixote, adding that the American Colonization Society, unlike the Don, "runs a tilt at nobody, but proposes a remedy for all the evils of slavery, which has been found on trial to be both peaceful and efficient."[128]

Even Thomas Witherspoon of Alabama, who during his chairmanship of the Presbyterian General Assembly's committee on slavery kept all antislavery petitions off the floor, and who wrote to an abolitionist editor that he considered "Judge Lynch . . . one of the most welcome and salutary remedies for Northern fanaticism,"[129] appeared in Pittsburgh on the same platform with Lyman Beecher and Elisha P. Swift, advocating colonization.[130]

Among the Southern Episcopalians, Bishop L. S. Ives of North Carolina signed an appeal alongside Bishop Onderdonk of New York and Bishop Kemper of Missouri and Indiana, pleading for funds for a ship to be leased or sold to freedmen who would operate it as a regular packet between the United

[126] Birney, *op.cit.*, p. 38.
[127] Beriah Green, *Things for Northern Men to Do* (New York, 1836), p. 16. Green was a Presbyterian minister and a professor at Western Reserve College. He had been converted to abolitionism by Theodore D. Weld. Birney, too, was a convert of Weld. See Barnes, *op.cit.*, pp. 39-40.
[128] *African Repository*, xii (1836), 191.
[129] Birney, *op.cit.*, p. 39.
[130] *African Repository*, xii (1836), 205.

States and Liberia.[131] Participation by Episcopal rectors in the Southern auxiliary societies was also widespread.

The Baptists are the only major denominations in the South whose colonizationist activities we have been unable to trace beyond their contributing to the Society's Fourth of July collection. There is ample evidence, however, of their support of the colonization effort in the North, and in the West their greatest promoter, John Mason Peck, helped raise funds for the American Colonization Society.

At its reorganization, in 1839, the American Colonization Society came under New England dominance almost entirely, but even then it did not lose its Southern support. The Southern theocrats at least remained loyal to it, because their love of the Union and their devotion to the missionary enterprise made the colonization of the freedmen appear to them as highly desirable. The same men who had experienced the utmost forbearance on the part of their Northern colleagues, were undoubtedly ready to forbear in their turn and to keep their places on the common platform of colonization, until the swelling tide of events swept them off on opposite sides. The Methodists and the Baptists divided in 1844 and 1845 respectively; the Old School Presbyterians only at the outbreak of the Civil War. The Congregationalists and the Episcopalians did not divide at all, the former because they were confined to the North, the latter because of their superior diplomacy.

Summary

It may be helpful, by way of summary, to systematize the opinions of the entire Protestant clergy concerning the Negro problem toward the end of our period, in order to bring into relief the significance of colonization as the cornerstone of the theocratic pattern, even after the advent of Northern abolitionism and Southern retrenchment had doomed its noble hopes to failure.

[131] *ibid.*, XIV (1838), 317.

1. The abolitionists asserted that slavery was a sin. The theocrats and the clergy of the South denied this assertion on Biblical grounds. Most of the theocrats regarded slavery as an evil and hoped for its ultimate disappearance through voluntary emancipation and colonization. Many Southern clergymen, to be sure, accepted slavery as a positive good, but far more of them agreed with the theocrats, and all of them, though acting from mixed motives, endorsed the idea of colonizing the freedmen of the South.

2. The abolitionists argued that little had been done for either the freedman or the slave in the way of material and spiritual improvement. They demanded that both freedmen and slaves should at once be admitted to all the privileges of American citizenship. The theocrats were signally unsuccessful in their efforts to elevate the freedmen, but they had their own half-heartedness to blame, for they did not really believe that the Negroes would ever be accepted by the dominant white race. Hence, while making a few efforts for their uplifting, they concentrated their energies on colonization. The Southern clergymen also acknowledged that little had been done for the improvement of the slaves, but they were making slightly more successful efforts at instructing and evangelizing them. However, they also held that the Negroes would be best off by themselves, and therefore favored the colonization of at least the freedmen, but often also of the slaves, if voluntarily manumitted for that purpose. Only a minority of the Southern clergy dared suggest that the slaves should be kept in the United States and in bondage forever, because of the desirability of their situation under Christian masters.

3. The abolitionists had little or no love for the Union and were ready to sacrifice it to their cause. The theocrats, on the other hand, were devoted to the Union and wished to preserve it at all costs. So were, for the most part, the ministers of the South. Colonization, both these groups felt, was not relieving the country of any spectacular numbers of Negroes, but at least it provided a safety valve for sectional tension, while

opening a whole pagan continent to Christian missions. Therefore they continued to hope that at the cost of harder work, larger funds, and better organization, Liberia might yet become the solution of America's Negro problem, draining off first the freedmen and then eventually, the slaves.

CHAPTER VI

THEOCRATIC SOLUTIONS TO OTHER SOCIAL PROBLEMS

Ideological Background

Between 1812 and 1848 American society changed far more radically than it had during the entire colonial era. The greatest single factor in this process of change was, of course, the westward surge. The political, social, and economic influence of the West grew apace with its territorial growth. Another significant factor was the coming to America of the Industrial Revolution, the beginning of the industrialization of the Eastern seaboard and the rise of a self-conscious working class. Immigration from Europe played a large part in both these phenomena. The theocrats, however, dealt with the problem of the immigrant primarily from the religious point of view, that is, in terms of the challenge of Roman Catholicism. On the other hand, the social changes brought about by the influence of the frontier and by the rise of the working class were indigenous challenges. The subjects of these changes were, for the most part, native Americans of Protestant upbringing. Forsaking the simple life of pre-revolutionary America, thousands migrated to the West or into the cities in search of economic betterment. In so doing they cut themselves off from the religious and moral influences under which they had grown up. It was against this background of social upheaval that the theocrats developed their pattern for American society.

A Calvinistic, pessimistic view of human nature lay at the foundation of this pattern. In this view the theocrats were wholly out of tune with their environment, in which, at the opening of the nineteenth century, there seemed to be unlimited possibilities for both individual and social improvement. Deism, propagated among the common people of the nation by

OTHER SOCIAL PROBLEMS

such men as Tom Paine, Ethan Allen, and Elihu Palmer, preached a doctrine based on the dignity and freedom of man rather than on his sinfulness. Man, asserted the Deists, was a product of his circumstances rather than a helpless heir and propagator of original sin, and was able to improve himself and his circumstances indefinitely.[1] The liberty achieved by the American Revolution was only a beginning: America was now standing on the threshold of an era of incalculable progress, if only she would free herself from the remaining traces of aristocratic and priestly overlordship; the people were at last on the march toward the affirmation of their natural rights and the attainment of true liberty.

Such infidel doctrines filled the theocrats with dismay. For a time they were helpless. Then came the Second Awakening in which thousands of people returned to Protestant orthodoxy. By the end of the War of 1812 the progress of infidelity was checked, but its moral effects were apparent to the theocrats on every side. It was high time to bring back the religious and moral restraints which, under the influence of infidelity, had been so dangerously relaxed.

In contemplating the task which lay ahead, Lyman Beecher set the tone by reasserting the doctrine of universal depravity. "Our fathers were not fools; they were as far from it as modern philosophers are from wisdom. Their fundamental maxim was that man is desperately wicked, and cannot be qualified for good membership in society without the influence of moral restraint. With great diligence, therefore, they availed themselves of the laws and institutions of revelation, as embodying the most correct instruction and the most powerful moral restraint. . . ."[2]

The theocrats had only scorn for that shallow, optimistic view of man which refused to take him "as he *is*, a fallen, depraved creature; naturally proud, indolent, evil, and unthank-

[1] Merle Curti, *The Growth of American Thought* (New York, 1943), pp. 158, 171.
[2] Lyman Beecher, *A Reformation of Morals Practical and Indispensable* (1812), *Works* (3 vols., Boston, 1852), II, 92.

ful," and insisted on picturing him "as he *should* be, holy, industrious, humble. . . ."[3] They heartily agreed with Thomas Baldwin's cry, uttered at the execution of a group of pirates: "Every day furnishes new and convincing proof of the universal corruption of human nature!"[4]

In the light of their dim view of human nature, it is not surprising that the democratization of American society which filled the rank and file of the citizenry with glorious visions of America's future, turned the theocrats rather to a wistful contemplation of the past. To be sure, they gloried in the achievement of national independence. Many of the older ones had helped bring it about, while even the younger ones had stirring recollections of the early days of a nation struggling to come to birth. Their social conservatism, however, led them to believe that the conditions which prevailed prior to the Revolution could not and should not be altered. "Our ancestors have not devolved upon us the difficult task of framing, in a degenerate age, all the necessary laws for the punishment of evil doers, the prevention of crimes, the encouragement of sobriety and industry; and whatever else is essential to the well-being of society. Almost everything is prepared to our hands, and has come down to use from our ancestors, the pious fathers of New England."[5]

Thus spoke the future President of Amherst College in 1818. Fifteen years later Lyman Beecher was still of much the same mind. The political and social changes of the intervening years had, if anything, reinforced his conviction that America's golden age lay in the past, and he profoundly deplored and resented the spirit of the age which made light of the Puritan fathers. "The energetic virtue of our Puritan ancestry, while we refuse not the blessing it has sent down to us . . . we are beginning to make the subject of apology and the butt of

[3] Heman Humphrey, *On Doing Good to the Poor* (Pittsfield, Mass., 1818), p. 17.
[4] Thomas Baldwin, *The Danger of Living Without the Fear of God* (Boston, 1819), p. 3.
[5] Humphrey, *op.cit.*, p. 40.

ridicule. From generation to generation, the threadbare story is going down, that they were too strict; while every son, who, in religion and moral rectitude, resembles his Puritan sire, is made the subject of patriotic suspicion that he is plotting against the liberties of his country."⁶

Even a theocrat of a rather independent turn of mind like Horace Bushnell could not say enough of the "glorious and auspicious distinction" of having "an ancestry, who, after every possible deduction, still overtop the originals of every nation of mankind...."⁷

Thus a pessimistic view of man, coupled with such a "backward look," caused the theocrats grave concern regarding America's future. They believed that the young nation, after conquering her freedom from foreign tyranny, now stood to lose it at the hands of a far more subtle foe: internal decay.⁸

This was one of the *Leitmotifs* of the theocrats: that their endeavors were in the interest of freedom, that Christianity alone could guarantee the preservation of freedom, and that the worst enemy of freedom was its abuse by a people morally unfit to enjoy it.⁹ The theocrats argued plausibly that this complete dependence of American freedom on Christian morality was inherent in the nature of the American political experiment, "which recognizes no other sovereignty than the will of the people."¹⁰ In other countries, Heman Humphrey pointed out, the government maintains order with a rod of iron; therefore the people can afford to be heedless of moral standards. However, "our government is not a government of force, but of influence. Its only basis is the virtue and piety of the people...."¹¹

⁶ Lyman Beecher, *The Perils of Atheism to the Nation* (1833); *Works*, I, 107.
⁷ Horace Bushnell, "The True Wealth and Weal of Nations" (1833); *Works*, I, 107.
⁸ Beecher, *op.cit.*, p. 112.
⁹ John Codman, *Home Missions* (Boston, 1826), p. 10.
¹⁰ William B. Sprague, *The Claims of Past and Future Generations on Civil Rulers* (Boston, 1825), p. 24.
¹¹ Heman Humphrey, *The Way to Bless and Save Our County* (Philadelphia, 1831), p. 16.

Refusing to admit that any healthy social morality could exist without religious sanctions, the theocrats attributed the prevailing "moral declension," evidenced, for instance, in the nation's growing intemperance, directly and solely to the neglect of Christian institutions. The gradual extension of the franchise and the rapid accession of new states to the Union further aggravated their misgivings and accentuated their feeling of social responsibility. "The power is passing from the hands of the less numerous to those of the more numerous classes of society; and there is nothing in the nature of our institutions to prevent its thus passing," warned Francis Wayland. "It is our duty to provide that it be wielded by intelligence and virtue."[12]

A few years later Wayland worked out this view systematically by giving the prevalent "compact theory" of society a distinctive theocratic twist. In a republic, he argued, the majority rules; hence the minority and the individual have "no safeguard against oppression, except that which exists in the conditions of the compact on which society is formed, and the feeling of moral obligation to observe that compact inviolably." Thus the form of government does not necessarily determine the degree of civil liberty, since a majority may be as oppressive as a minority. "And to a man of sense it is a matter of small consequence, whether oppression proceed from one or from many; from an hereditary tyrant or from an unprincipled majority. The latter is rather the more galling, and surely at least as difficult to remedy."[13]

By a strange inversion, freedom had come to mean to the theocrats the opposite of what it meant to their fathers during the Revolution and of what it still meant in radical democratic thinking. The revolutionary cry for freedom had been raised in terms of protecting the rights of an oppressed majority from

[12] Francis Wayland, *Encouragements to Religious Effort* (Philadelphia, 1831), p. 14.
[13] Francis Wayland, *The Elements of Moral Science* (Boston, 1835), p. 349. This was the outstanding "sociology" textbook of the theocrats, superseding William Paley's *Moral and Political Philosophy*.

OTHER SOCIAL PROBLEMS

a tyrannical minority, of the people of the colonies from the British Crown and Church. The theocrats of the Jacksonian era now demanded freedom in terms of protecting an oppressed minority from a tyrannical majority, that is, the privileged classes (including themselves) from the rising masses. Hence when they spoke of Christianity as the only safeguard of American freedom, they meant that the sanctions of Christianity alone could act as an adequate check on the surging, turbulent population of the frontier and the radical elements of the Eastern cities.

We need not interpret this concept of "freedom-as-restraint" solely in terms of classbound self-interest. The theocrats were undoubtedly sincere. They had the welfare of the whole nation at heart. As a matter of fact, they were so concerned for the common people that they wanted to save them from the consequences of their own shortcomings. The theocrats had witnessed the bloody transformation of popular sovereignty into dictatorship in France, and they could not forget it. They feared that Americans, if freed from religious and moral restraints, would not only reenact the nightmare of the Reign of Terror, but would also ultimately forfeit their own liberties at the hands of a tyrant raised from their own ranks. Christianity, then, appeared as the only safeguard, not only of the survival of the privileged classes, but of the American republic as well. If Christianity, with its wholesome fear of God and its doctrine of eternal rewards and punishments did not keep abreast of the "emancipation" of the masses, America, in Lyman Beecher's words, "would soon experience the vandal tendency of political atheism. If the iron governments of Europe, justified by age, custom, power, and the sanctions of eternity, perverted to sustain them, could not stand, how shall we of yesterday escape. . . ? To us it would be like the falling of the dam, and the desolation of unobstructed flood—like the extinction of the orb of day,—like the suspension of gravity and the reign of chaos."[14]

[14] Lyman Beecher, *The Perils of Atheism to the Nation*, p. 100.

OTHER SOCIAL PROBLEMS

Evangelizing the West

The first object of concern to the theocrats was the West, with its godlessness and lawlessness. The expanding frontier of the close of the eighteenth century had been effectively subdued by the influence of the Second Awakening. Ohio, Kentucky, and Tennessee were adequately supplied with institutions of Protestant orthodoxy, though the largest share of church members had been reaped by the Methodists and the Baptists, who did not meet with the unqualified approval of the theocrats. Their contribution to the taming of this frontier was readily acknowledged, but while the theocrats were gradually overcoming denominational prejudices within their own ranks, that is, in New England and the Middle Atlantic States, they could not help viewing the West in a spirit of denominational competition.[15] Reporting on his exploratory tour at the end of the War of 1812, Samuel J. Mills observed: "The Baptist and Methodist denominations are exerting themselves to gain a footing in the Territories. . . . Why then, it may be asked, should we not leave it to them? We answer, the field is large enough for us all!"[16]

Then, commenting on the frontier's need for Christian preaching and Christian institutions, he added: "The character of the settlers is such as to render it peculiarly important that missionaries should be sent among them. Indeed, they can hardly be said to have any *character* at all, assembled as they are from every state of the Union and originally from every nation of Europe. The majority, although by no means regardless of religion, have not yet embraced any fixed principles

---

[15] Even among themselves the theocrats had not conclusively conquered the spirit of rivalry. The Presbyterian-Congregational plan of Union of 1801 continued to have many opponents and was an important factor in the Presbyterian division into Old School and New School in 1837.

[16] Samuel J. Mills and Daniel Smith, *Report of a Missionary Tour through that part of the United States, which lies West of the Allegany* [*sic*] *mountains* (Andover, Mass., 1815), p. 19.

OTHER SOCIAL PROBLEMS

concerning it. They are ready to receive any impressions which a public speaker may attempt to make."[17]

This estimate of the West's spiritual pliability, for good or ill, was by no means unrealistic. The Eastern emigrant, when he left his farm or shop to go West, cut himself loose not only from the traditional Christian institutions of Sabbath observance and organized worship, but also from the accustomed community control of morals which bound him to an extent, even if he was not himself a professing Christian. The ratio of church members, for that matter, was extremely low at the beginning of our period, in spite of the gains made in the Second Awakening. Even in New England hardly more than one out of every ten persons was a church member. Yet established sanctions of Christian morality continued to affect, to a considerable extent, all the inhabitants of the settled East, and the theocrats were well aware of their power. "Long established institutions and habits have a mighty influence over the whole population of old settlements. When these institutions and habits are good, they operate as so many checks upon the corrupt propensities of our nature. Every man acts under the public eye, and feels a responsibility which restrains sinful inclinations and serves to regulate his daily deportment."[18]

The relaxing of these institutions and habits on the westward trek prompted the theocrats to unusual evangelistic efforts. Already during the War of 1812 missionary societies in New England and New York were exploring the new settlements and their religious needs. After the two major tours by Samuel J. Mills at least one thing became evident: there was a dire scarcity of Bibles and other religious literature among the frontiersmen. Accordingly the American Bible Society came into being in 1816 and forty thousand dollars' worth of Bibles and Testaments were distributed during the first year

[17] *ibid.*, p. 20.
[18] Heman Humphrey, *An Address to the Emigrants from Connecticut and from New England generally in the new settlements in the United States* (Hartford, 1817), p. 5.

159

of its existence.[19] The New England Tract Society, founded in 1814, also speeded up its output and many new tracts were published with a special slant to the West. In 1825 this society merged with a similar society in New York to form the American Tract Society, which accounted for the distribution of over ten million printed pages during its first year of operation.[20] Printed matter, however, could not be relied upon to do the job alone. The most significant step for the taming of the West through evangelization was taken in 1826 with the founding of the American Home Missionary Society in New York City.

From its organization the American Home Missionary Society was overwhelmingly a Congregational and Presbyterian venture. The first roster of its officers shows only Andover and Princeton graduates and their lay following.[21] The fifth annual report of the Society presents essentially the same picture, with the addition of two clergymen of the Reformed Dutch Church.[22] Yet the Society intended to operate as a national institution, since "its object must not be considered as accomplished until every parish in the nation is supplied with an able and faithful minister. . . ."[23] The Society's *Address to the Christian Public* stated this objective in forthright terms, recalling that "Congregationalists and Presbyterians of different names, who are already represented in the Society, are probably the largest denominations of Christians in the United States," and that "other denominations *may* hereafter make this Society the channel through which to convey their con-

---

[19] American Bible Society, *First Annual Report* (New York, 1817), p. 26. Theocrats of all the major denominations were represented in this society from the start. The only defection from its ranks occurred in 1837 when the Baptists withdrew because of the Society's refusal to translate the word "baptizein" as "to immerse." They then founded the American and Foreign Bible Society of their own denomination.

[20] *American Quarterly Register*, II (1829), 40-41.

[21] American Home Missionary Society, *First Report* (New York, 1827), pp. 4-6.

[22] American Home Missionary Society, *Fifth Report* (New York, 1833), pp. 4-6.

[23] American Home Missionary Society, *Address to the Christian Public* (New York, 1826), p. 3.

OTHER SOCIAL PROBLEMS

tributions to the destitute," so that the founders of the Society "could hardly be charged with presumption in having given it the style of a National Institution."[24] Yet, such criticism was soon forthcoming, particularly since the Baptist and Methodist Churches were missionary churches by definition, which led them to resent the name. Even they, however, found it expedient before too long to establish separate societies for home missions work, thus officially sanctioning denominational rivalry on the frontier.[25]

Regardless of the denominational limitations, however, the motives of the theocrats for evangelizing the West were primarily national and patriotic. George Bush, pastor in the village of Indianapolis, Indiana Territory, and charter member of the American Home Missionary Society, made it clear to his little flock that "many enlightened and cordial friends of the country" when viewing the growth of the West, "are looking with trembling anticipation." "They see the banks of our Western Waters, the Ohio, the Wabash, the Mississippi, the Missouri, peopling with swarming tribes of emigrants, to be multiplied in their prosperity ten thousand fold; but they see not a proportionate growth in virtue, knowledge, and godliness ... and they dread the consequences of such a vast numerical and physical power holding an unsanctified preponderance in the councils of the nation and over the destinies of men. Hence the great movements in the churches of the East in favor of the growing myriads of the West."[26] This sentiment continued to be voiced in the yearly reports of the American Home Missionary Society, and in the sermons and other propaganda writings of the theocrats on behalf of the home missionary cause.[27]

---

[24] ibid.
[25] Robert Baird, *Religion in America* (New York, 1844), pp. 140ff.
[26] George Bush, *Lack of Vision, the Ruin of the People* (Indianapolis, 1826), p. 11.
[27] The most widely read book against "infidelity" during our period was the work of a home missionary, David Nelson, who wrote his *Causes and Cure of Infidelity* while stationed in Illinois. The American Tract Society published it in 1841 and it was reprinted more often than any other of its publications before the Civil War.

The classical elaboration of the argument, however, came from the pen of Horace Bushnell.

Expected to play on the theme of the Roman Catholic menace which was then uppermost in the minds of the theocrats, Bushnell startled them by exclaiming before the annual meeting of the American Home Missionary Society: "Our first danger is *barbarism*; Romanism next!" Then, likening conditions in the West to the conditions prevailing during the times of the Judges, Bushnell went on to say that "if ignorance, wildness, and social confusion" were allowed to create "a race without education, law, manners, or religion, we need not trouble ourselves farther on account of Romanism, for to such a people Romanism, bad as it is, will come as a blessing."[28]

It is quite apparent that sectional feeling played a large part in the theocrat's concern for the West. This appears clearly from the patronizing attitude assumed—unconsciously, no doubt—by Humphrey, Bushnell, Lyman Beecher, and others.[29] It appears even more forcibly in the reaction of the frontier preachers who opposed home missions chiefly because they resented the interference of the Eastern clergy whose political and social thinking they regarded as "aristocratic" and foreign to the West. This motive figured prominently in the antimission movement,[30] and was forcefully endorsed by John Leland. "Nothing can be more false," he wrote, "than the idea that the Valley of the Mississippi is peopled with irreligious characters altogether, who are perishing for want of missionary preaching. The truth is that many religious people remove into the valley, and many of the preachers go with them. Many also are turned to the Lord in the place, and a portion of them commence preaching."[31]

[28] Horace Bushnell, *Barbarism the First Danger: A Discourse for Home Missions* (1847); *Works*, v, 230-231.
[29] See particularly Lyman Beecher's famous *Plea for the West* (Cincinnati, 1835).
[30] See John Taylor, *Thoughts on Missions* and Daniel Parker, *Public Address to the Baptist Society*, the two principal statements of the antimission point of view, both published in 1820.
[31] John Leland, *Free Thoughts on Times and Things* (1836), in *Writings* (New York, 1845), p. 673.

OTHER SOCIAL PROBLEMS

In the same spirit a Baptist evangelist in Missouri published a volume on prophecy in St. Louis, with the pointed prefactory remark: "From the locality of its publication, the truths contained in this volume will be brought to bear on the minds of hundreds and thousands that all the mechanism of Eastern literature could never have reached."[32]

Yet, in spite of the sectional imprint of the theocrats' concern for the West, we still accept the conclusion of Colin B. Goodykoontz: "In general the home missionary movement was an expression of nationalism. . . . Nationalism as applied to religion and morals, that is, a desire that the whole country might be dedicated to sound principles and free, democratic institutions, was a more important motive than sectional pride."[33]

Pointing to the loyalty of the Northwest to the Northeast during the Civil War, Goodykoontz attributes it largely to the influence of home missions. "Moral and spiritual ties had been drawn between the East and the West that were stronger than the forces that tended to drive them apart. . . . And these bonds, which were moral and sacred, and therefore indissoluble, had been drawn by the humble home missionaries."[34]

Thus the political by-product of home missions bears an eloquent witness to the patriotic motivation of the theocrats, absolving them in large measure from the charge of sectional bias. Nevertheless, it is easy to understand why their motives were suspect. They were not content, like the Baptist and Methodist frontier preachers, to convert individuals. They insisted on transplanting to the frontier the institutions and standards of a settled, organized community. In so doing they hoped to preserve some of the organic, communal character of Christianity over against the frontiersmen to whom individual liberty and freedom from restraint had an irresistible appeal.

[32] Isaac T. Hinton, *The Prophecies of Daniel and St. John Illustrated in the Events of History* (St. Louis, 1843), p. 5.
[33] Colin B. Goodykoontz, *Home Missions on the American Frontier* (Caldwell, Idaho, 1939), p. 422.
[34] *ibid.*, pp. 423-424.

The frontier preachers thought of individuals only as isolated entities, as souls to be saved. They had no concept of society and of the individual's relatedness to society. Neither did they give much thought to America as a nation with a national heritage to be safeguarded and a national destiny to fulfil. Their Christianity, just like their whole way of life, was individualistic. They were "on their own" and they labored among people of the same stamp. Such classical frontier documents as the autobiographies of James B. Finley and Peter Cartwright abound in missionary adventure, but give no indication whatever that their authors had any social concept of their task or any patriotic motivation for going about it with such persistent courage.

The theocrats, on the other hand, defined their task in terms of the community pattern which had proved its worth in the East. "To establish a pastor in every neighborhood . . . is the only effectual means of giving the Gospel its proper and necessary influence," wrote Charles Hodge;[35] and Bushnell concluded his classic on home missions with the solemn pledge: "We will not cease, till a Christian nation throws up its temples of worship on every hill and plain."[36] Being both more pessimistic and more realistic about human nature than the frontier preachers and distrusting the durability of individual conversion without Christian institutions to socialize its effects, the theocrats sought to establish the church in the West in the same prominence which she had enjoyed in early New England. The church, affirmed Edward Norris Kirk, is the nation's most powerful safety, because, "as salt is endowed with the property of preserving animal and vegetable esculents from decay, so the *Church is the chief conservative power in the moral world*, preserving man and society from that degeneracy, to which they are ever tending."[37]

[35] Charles Hodge, "Anniversary Address," in *The Home Missionary*, II (1829), 19.
[36] Horace Bushnell, *Barbarism, etc.*, p. 267.
[37] Edward Norris Kirk, *The Church Essential to the Republic* (New York, 1848), p. 3.

OTHER SOCIAL PROBLEMS

Evangelization alone could not do it. To save the West and thereby the United States, Christianity would have to be laid on solid institutional foundations; else the twin monsters of "infidelity" and "immorality" would soon destroy her. To stem the religious and moral decline, however, a third monster had to be identified, attacked, and vanquished. This monster—parent of the deadly twins—was ignorance, and only education could hope to slay it.

Educating the West

Protestantism is by nature a literate religion. The Reformation originated in the rediscovery of the Bible and in its translation into the language of the common people. To be able to read it, however, the people had to be taught how to read: they had to be educated. Hence modern education is far more deeply indebted to Protestantism than it is usually willing to admit.

In the New England colonies, heirs of the British Puritan tradition, religion and education were inseparable. "The child began his reading with that time-honored device, the hornbook—a printed alphabet list of one-syllable words, together with the Lord's Prayer, held in a wooden frame, the whole covered by a sheet of horn. He was advanced next to the spelling book, and thence to a primer and a catechism. 'In Adam's Fall / We sinned all' begins that most famous of American readers, *The New England Primer, or Milk for Babes*, of which it is estimated that seven million copies were printed before 1840."[38]

"Dreading to leave an illiterate Ministry to the Churches, when our present Ministers shall lie in the Dust,"[39] the fathers of New England made the raising of an orthodox and learned ministry the primary object of education. Consequently, the colonial clergy controlled education from hornbook to sheep-

[38] Perry Miller and Thomas H. Johnson, *The Puritans* (New York, 1938), p. 696.
[39] "New England's First Fruits" (1643), reprinted *ibid.*, p. 701. The immediate reference is to the founding of Harvard College.

skin. Clerical control was most conspicuous in New England, but was equally strong in all the colonies, because the same texts were used everywhere.[40]

In spite of the inroads of deism and rationalism, the clergy retained considerable control over education in the young republic. "Not only did the churches maintain considerable supervisory power over elementary education—in Connecticut, for example, the schoolmaster had to be certified by the nearest minister of the established Congregational Church—but the curriculum stressed religious and moral precepts. In Noah Webster's spellers, Jedidiah Morse's geographies and John Pierpont's readers the Christian spirit permeated the pupil's lessons, constantly reminding them of the hand of God in human affairs."[41] Patriotic instruction was added to Christian indoctrination, investing patriotism with the sanction of religion by affirming that all sound government was founded on God's moral order in the world and that American republican institutions were traceable directly to God's will.[42] This satisfying equilibrium, however, was disrupted when, at the end of the War of 1812, the population began to move across the Alleghanies, leaving not only their churches but also their schoolhouses far behind them.

Frontier religion of the Methodist and Baptist type did not inspire confidence in the theocrats. "Many of their preachers," observed Samuel J. Mills with distaste, "are exceedingly illiterate; and this circumstance . . . has been a very great injury to the cause of Christ in many places. . . ."[43] Educational institutions had to be provided for the emigrants in order to insure their continued receptivity to theocratic influences.

The first effort of the theocrats consisted of supplying the frontier with Christian reading matter, notably Bibles and tracts. In its *Address to the People of the United States* the

[40] Alice Felt Tyler, *Freedom's Ferment* (Minneapolis, 1944), p. 277.
[41] Krout and Fox, *The Completion of Independence* (1790-1830). Volume v of *A History of American Life*, p. 183.
[42] *ibid.*, p. 184.
[43] Mills and Smith, *op.cit.*, p. 19.

OTHER SOCIAL PROBLEMS

American Bible Society warned of the "dreadful consequences which ensue from a people's outgrowing the knowledge of eternal life, and reverting to a species of heathenism, which shall have all the address and profligacy of civilized society, without any real religious control."[44]

The *First Annual Report* of the American Tract Society reproduced excerpts of letters from the West, of which this one is typical: "The importance of Religious Tracts in this part of the country . . . is becoming more and more apparent. Great is the ignorance of many of the inhabitants. Errors and delusions are prevailing. The people are 'destroyed for lack of knowledge.' "[45]

The activities of the American Bible Society and the American Tract Society were an early venture in adult education, but because of their wholesale approach to the problem of religious illiteracy, their effectiveness was hard to determine. They served undoubtedly as an important stop-gap between the end of the War of 1812 and the middle twenties, when the frontier situation became even more critical for the theocrats because of the renascence of popular freethought.

Dormant since the death of Elihu Palmer in 1806, organized infidelity was revived by a group of freethinkers representing Robert Owen's social teachings. Within a decade a vigorous, popularly written freethought press grew up around the *New Harmony Gazette*, official organ of Owenism published by Robert Dale Owen, Frances Wright, and others at the model community of New Harmony, Indiana. Most of these papers were short-lived, to be sure, but they enjoyed a wide circulation in the West because they were anti-aristocratic, anti-clerical, and sensational.[46]

The theocrats soon realized that the frontier mind was no longer just a vacuum, but that it was becoming an all-impor-

[44] New York, 1816. Quotation from page 17.
[45] New York, 1826. Quotation from page 20.
[46] Albert Post, *Popular Freethought in America, 1825-1850* (New York, 1943), pp. 28-29, 34-39.

OTHER SOCIAL PROBLEMS

tant area for which they now had to contend with a purposeful opponent. The stakes were too high to entrust the battle to the printed word alone. Only institutions of learning could hope to defeat infidelity in the present generation and prevent the rising generation from being contaminated with its virus. The Sunday School and the denominational college became the twin prongs of the theocratic counter-offensive in the struggle for the Western mind.

The patriotic motivation of these educational movements did not differ materially from other expressions of theocratic concern for the religious and moral conditions of the growing West. As early as 1812 Lyman Beecher had stated the primary reason for concentrating on the children and youth of the nation. "Immoral men," he said, "do not live forever. If good heed is taken that they draw no new recruits from our families, death will achieve for us a speedy victory."[47] The *Annual Reports* of the American Sunday School Union and the *Anniversary Sermons* delivered before that body by outstanding theocrats echoed the same assurance in all the keys of the theocratic scale.[48] A generation later Lyman Beecher, as vigorous as ever, took the initiative in organizing the Society for the Promotion of Collegiate and Theological Education at the West, to bolster the sagging finances and prestige of five home missions colleges founded by the theocrats between 1826 and 1834.[49] The first report of the Society, after noting the melancholy decline of interest in these colleges and in their strategic significance both from a patriotic and from a religious stand-

[47] Lyman Beecher, *A Reformation of Morals* . . . (1812), p. 9.
[48] The Union was founded in 1824. In five years it had established supervision, direct or indirect, over some six thousand Sunday Schools, enlisting over fifty thousand teachers and three hundred and fifty thousand scholars, cf. *American Quarterly Register*, II (1829), 34. At its Annual Conventions held in Philadelphia sermons were heard by Francis Wayland (1830), Heman Humphrey (1831), Charles Hodge (1832), J. P. K. Henshaw (1833), Isaac Ferris (1834), and James B. Taylor (1836), indicating the genuinely interdenominational character of the Union; cf. American Sunday School Union, *Anniversary Sermons* (Philadelphia, 1860), *passim*.
[49] S.P.C.T.E.W., *First Report* (New York, 1844), pp. 1, 7.

OTHER SOCIAL PROBLEMS

point, asked the rhetorical questions: "Has it ceased to be true ... that the destinies of the East and the West are bound up in the same bundles ... that the great battle of American institutions is to be fought in the valley of the Mississippi? ... Has it ceased to be true that the tendency of our national character ... is toward a common level, and that, in order to protect itself from a disastrous reaction, social and religious, as well as political, the East must educate and Christianize the West?"[50]

Then, recalling the newness and the fluid social conditions of the West, the report stressed with passionate earnestness, the need for Christian intellectual influences upon the young men —the future leaders—of the West. "Amid these shifting social elements, we want principles of stability, we want a system of permanent forces, we want deep, strong, constant influences that shall take from the changefulness and excitability of the Western mind, by giving it the tranquility of depth, and shall protect it from delusive and fitful impulses by enduing it with a calm, profound, and pure reason."[51]

Thus, during three short decades, the patriotism of the theocrats enabled them not only to evangelize the West by sending out missionaries, but to flood it with Bibles and tracts, to organize Sunday Schools equipped with libraries which became the forerunners of the modern public library,[52] and to found so many church-related colleges that the historian of the subject has called the period the "denominational era in American higher education."[53] Beecher's oft-quoted cry, "We must edu-

[50] *ibid.*, p. 21.
[51] *ibid.*, p. 26. The moving spirit of this Society was the Reverend Theron Baldwin, its Corresponding Secretary. The first roster of officers included such important theocrats as Nathan S. S. Beman, Absalom Peters (Corresponding Secretary of the American Home Missionary Society), Thomas H. Skinner, Leonard Bacon, Emerson Davis, author of *The Half Century* (a theocratic history, published in New York in 1851), and Horace Bushnell.
[52] Alice Felt Tyler, *op.cit.*, p. 260.
[53] Donald G. Tewksbury, *The Founding of American Colleges and Universities before the Civil War* (New York, 1932), pp. 66-70.

cate or we must perish by our own prosperity!"[54] had not been sounded in vain. In spite of the colossal political and social changes of the times, the West was, by 1848, well supplied with educational institutions and agencies intended to safeguard it from infidelity and anarchy, since, in the minds of the theocrats, the latter was an inevitable adjunct of the former. It is an interesting sidelight on the educational achievement of the theocrats that by the middle thirties the Baptist and Methodist Churches were feverishly founding and building colleges! Whether the spirit of denominational rivalry or the contagion of a good example caused this change of heart, the fact remains that the Methodist and Baptist theocrats of the East were doing their utmost to overcome the frontier preacher's distrust of "book larnin'" and his contempt for an educated ministry. Except for the survival of some antimission elements, they were signally successful. Even such a notorious opponent of ministerial education as Peter Cartwright eventually helped establish two colleges in Illinois. As a member of the Illinois legislature he also introduced the first bill for the establishment of a state university.[55]

The Public School Issue

In contrast with the success of the theocrats in Sunday School and college education, their efforts at retaining control over the nation's growing public school system ended in failure. Strangely enough the secularization of the public school began in the most theocratic of all states: Massachusetts. The long survival of an established church was probably responsible for this fact: the harder the Congregational theocrats fought for their primacy over the schools, the harder the leaders of other denominations battled to achieve equality. By pressuring the legislature, they obtained as early as 1826, the passage of a statute authorizing school boards to select textbooks, provided

[54] Lyman Beecher, *A Plea for the West*, pp. 31-32.
[55] W. W. Sweet, *Religion on the American Frontier, 1783-1840. Vol. IV: The Methodists* (Chicago, 1946), p. 67.

OTHER SOCIAL PROBLEMS

"that said committee shall never direct any school books to be purchased or used, in any of the schools under their superintendence, which are calculated to favor any particular religious sect or tenet."[56]

At this point the Congregational theocrats realized that they could no longer dominate the public school as a denomination. Instantly they changed their strategy, endorsing "nonsectarian" religious instruction. The Reverend Charles Brooks of Quincy went so far as to assert that lack of such instruction was already responsible for "half the crime and more than half the unhappiness of society."[57]

For a time it seemed as if such nonsectarian teaching might preserve a measure of Protestant influence over the public schools. Even Horace Mann believed in the beginning that "in every course of studies, all the practical and perceptive parts of the Gospel should be sacredly included; and all dogmatical theology and sectarianism sacredly excluded. In no school should the Bible be opened to reveal the sword of polemic, but to unloose the dove of peace...."[58]

Even in 1848 Mann affirmed his belief in a nonsectarian use of the Bible in the public school. "Our system," he wrote, "inculcates all Christian morals; it founds its morals on the basis of religion; it welcomes the religion of the Bible; and in receiving the Bible, it allows it to do what it is allowed to do in no other system, to speak for itself."[59]

Some of the theocrats apparently shared Mann's hope that Christian morality could be inculcated in the public schools by letting the Bible "speak for itself." Robert Baird, for instance, was favorable to the idea.[60] Other theocrats, however, realized the inadequacy of uninterpreted Bible reading with its implied divorce from Christian doctrine. In its place they proposed Protestant parochial education as the only means of saving American youth for Christianity. The Presbyterian Synod of

[56] Quoted in Anson Phelps Stokes, *op.cit.*, II, 53.
[57] Charles Brooks, *Elementary Instruction* (Quincy, Mass., 1837), p. 11.
[58] Quoted in Stokes, *op.cit.*, II, 56.   [59] Quoted in Stokes, *op.cit.*, II, 57.
[60] Robert Baird, *op.cit.*, p. 148.

OTHER SOCIAL PROBLEMS

New Jersey warned in 1845 that the "race of irreligious and infidel youth, such as may be expected to issue from public schools," would not be "fit to sustain our free institutions." On the other hand, if the denominations would organize their own system of schools, they might then, "with a fair prospect of success, apply for a Rule of the State, that every taxpayer, every man when he pays his tax for education, may signify to what denomination of Christians it shall be applied. . . . If any should decline exercising their privilege, their money would be entirely at the disposal of the State."[61]

During the next decade over two hundred and fifty Presbyterian parochial schools were organized all over the country, but inadequate financial support and the improvement in public school systems arrested the trend. For better or for worse, the Protestant clergy lost all influence over public education, not only in Massachusetts but in the whole United States. On the other hand, the Catholic church was able to develop an extensive parochial school system.

It seems as if in the twentieth century the Catholic minority might obtain what the Protestant majority a century ago could not secure for themselves: state aid for parochial schools. Catholic demand for such aid dates back as far as 1840 when Archbishop Hughes of New York petitioned the New York Public School Fund to this effect. Failing to win his point, Hughes continued to protest against the use of the "Protestant Bible" in the New York schools and against all attempts to subject Catholic children to Protestant influence. The reaction of the theocrats, grounded in their Biblical literalism, was of the kind which today we would expect from the Catholic church only, as well as from a few small sects. Defending the use of the Protestant version in the New York schools, George B. Cheever argued that "there is such a thing as ultimate and absolute truth, and . . . such truth is in the word of God. No rights, either of majorities or minorities, either of law

[61] Quoted in Conrad H. Moehlman, *School and Church: The American Way* (New York, 1944), p. 67.

or conscience, can be pleaded against that...."[62] Then, turning to the public school system itself, Cheever denounced it as "a bold proclamation against Christianity and religion of every creed."[63] By this time, however, the public school system was here to stay.

The Challenge of the City

The other major area of American society in which the traditional influence and prestige of Christian orthodoxy was being most severely challenged during our period was the city. The rise of cities with a self-conscious working class was an important political and social development in the first half of the nineteenth century. To the theocrats the challenge was not fundamentally different from the one encountered in the West. As in the West, so in the Eastern cities, the theocrats viewed the advance of infidelity as a menace to American political and social institutions. They expressed their concern for the mind of the workingman in patriotic terms all the more readily since the doctrines and movements agitating him were inspired largely by foreigners.

In 1832 Robert Dale Owen, the Englishman, and Frances Wright, the Scottish woman, realized that New Harmony, Indiana, was too far removed from the centers of population. Hence they abandoned the *New Harmony Journal* and launched the *Free Enquirer* in New York City in association with another English freethinker, Robert L. Jennings. The *Free Enquirer* supported the most radical demands of the workers and contributed much to the shaping of a labor ideology.[64]

Another factor which stimulated unrest among the workers was that under Jackson's administration they found, for the first time, a government aware of their existence and sympathetic to their problems. Democratic newspapers often took their part. Democratic politicians defended unions in the

[62] George B. Cheever, *The Right of the Bible in our Public Schools* (New York, 1854), p. 77.
[63] *ibid.*, p. 252. [64] Post, *op.cit.*, p. 39.

courts. Labor's greatest victory of the period was won by Massachusetts Democrat Robert Rantoul, Jr., in *Commonwealth vs. Hunt*.[65]

The close connection between the growing power of the working class on the one hand and infidel social theory on the other, brought forth an early reaction from the natural leader of the theocrats: Lyman Beecher. Between 1832 and 1835 Beecher lectured extensively on the menace of an atheistic social ideology and eventually published his lectures, dedicating them "to the workingmen of our nation."[66] In his preface, he comments on the expression, "political atheism," noting that he has selected it, because, "in France and here, its theories extend to the modification of the religious, civil, and social state of man—contemplating nothing less than the abolition of marriage and the family state, separate property, civil government, and all sense of accountability, and all religious worship;—an effort to turn the world upside down, and empty it of every institution, thought, feeling, and action, which has emanated from Christianity, to unite mankind under the auspices of atheism."[67]

Anyone taking the tirades of the freethinkers and social radicals at face value might find it easy to agree with Beecher. For instance, H. D. Robinson, another Englishman and later editor of the *Free Enquirer*, dedicated one of his books "to priestcraft," specifically, "to you, who inculcate the bliss of ignorance and condemn inquiry into the intention of Scripture writings as blasphemous.... To you whose power is unlimited to shelter the vicious, as the resistance to it is circumscribed to protect the virtuous.... To you whose victims rot in prison, whose vassals crouch in palaces, and to whom the rich of the land bend their knees...."[68]

Beecher and his fellow theocrats did not perceive the absurdity of such fanaticism. Desperately earnest, wholly lack-

[65] Schlesinger, *op.cit.*, p. 339.
[66] *Lecturers on Political Atheism* (1835), in *Works*, I, Preface.
[67] *ibid.*, Lecture I, *The Being of God*, p. 20.
[68] Quoted in Post, *op.cit.*, p. 42.

OTHER SOCIAL PROBLEMS

ing in any sense of humor, and acutely mindful of the social changes taking place in Britain as well as on the continent, Beecher used the whole vast store of his rhetoric on his intended audience—the workers—in the hope that they might heed his warning. "Infidels are republicans in theory and in tongue, but not in deed and in truth. They are not your friends; but *God* is your friend. He has predicted and projected and will accomplish your elevation. . . ."[69]

Beecher's hope of a hearing among the workers was rather naïve. While many of them were undoubtedly influenced by the more extreme and utopian theories of free thought, the majority were too busy organizing unions against great odds, fighting for small local gains, and asserting a series of specific demands, which were much the same everywhere, notably "1. equal universal education, 2. the abolition of imprisonment for debt, 3. the abolition of licensed monopolies, 4. a less expensive legal system, 5. equal property taxes, 6. an effective lien law for laborers on buildings, 7. no legislation on religion and the removal of all religious restrictions."[70]

While these demands were gaining gradual acceptance with the American government and people, the theocrats steadfastly refused to see the need for labor unions and to admit that there might be some good in them. As a specimen of the attitude of the theocrats toward unions, there is the collection of essays by James Waddell Alexander, published originally under a pen name, because "the author doubted whether the name of a clergyman would add any currency to lucubrations on such a subject."[71] Speaking of unions, Alexander affirms: "Nothing can fail to be so disorganizing and ruinous, which tends to set the rich against the poor, or marshals these two classes into con-

[69] Lyman Beecher, *Lectures on Political Atheism*, Lecture III, *The Perils of Political Atheism*, in *Works*, I, 135.
[70] Tyler, *op.cit.*, pp. 214-215. For an extensive treatment of the early history of organized labor in the United States, see John R. Commons and Associates, *History of Labour in the United States* (2 vols., New York, 1934), vol. I, parts I-IV.
[71] James Waddell Alexander, *The American Mechanic and Workingman* (New York and Philadelphia, 1847, 2 vols.), Preface.

flicting hosts; and such is the tendency of that fearful system which is beginning to spread itself among our happy yeomanry."[72]

As for any specific reforms, the theocrats believed that they would come automatically, if they were justified and if the workers, by their good behavior, would earn them. Consequently their approach to social reform consisted in an endeavor to achieve the moral reformation of individuals. This is a strange paradox. The theocrats who thought in terms of society as a whole and specifically in terms of American society from a patriotic standpoint, rejected every suggestion of reforming society as such except by means of regenerating individuals. The antitheocrats, on the other hand, gave little or no thought to society or to the nation as such, except in terms of the individual, yet they set about reforming the institutions of society in order that the individual might have a better life. What, then, was the basic social outlook of the theocrats?

Theocratic Paternalism

The first thing the theocrats rejected was the social reformer's doctrine of human nature, which Andrew Jackson so eloquently voiced in his inaugural address of 1829: "I believe man can be elevated; man can become more and more endowed with divinity; and as he does, he becomes more God-like in his character and capable of governing himself. Let us go on elevating our people, perfecting our institutions, until democracy shall reach such a point of perfection that we can acclaim with truth that the voice of the people is the voice of God."[73]

The same unbounded belief in man characterized the utopian reformers, Owen, Wright, Brisbane, and so forth. They taught that "man becomes a wild, ferocious savage, a cannibal, or a highly civilized and benevolent being, according to the circumstances in which he may be placed from his birth."[74]

[72] *ibid.*, I, 123.
[73] Quoted in Tyler, *op.cit.*, p. 22.
[74] Robert Owen, quoted in Hillquit, *op.cit.*, p. 52.

OTHER SOCIAL PROBLEMS

The theocrats were deeply antagonized and alarmed by the notion that man could be improved merely by improving his circumstances. In an extensive article on Fourierism, Methodist theocrat George Peck summarized their view in a few crisp words. "Here, then, is the antagonism of Fourierism to Christianity; the latter teaches that evil comes from *within*; the former, that man's nature, his instincts, his passions, his tendencies, are essentially holy, and that evil proceeds from causes *extraneous*; from causes which press his natural instincts and impulses, and prevent their full and free and harmonious development. Fourierism proposes to take off these causes . . . and then will be ushered in the reign of universal unity."[75]

Presbyterian theocrat John M. Krebs had only scorn for those "profound illumanati, both of foreign and domestic growth, who meet in World Conventions, and gravely resolve that the whole organization of society is wrong and needs to be recast . . . by devices as notable and ingenious as the famous projects of the philosophers of Laputa, to extract sunbeams from cucumbers."[76]

So fearful were the theocrats of the consequences of the reforming ideologies that they consistently advocated the maintenance of the *status quo* in terms of a social and economic paternalism enhanced with the sanctions of religion. It was no longer possible to bring back the "good old days" of the Massachusetts theocracy: the least they could do for their country was to "hold the line."

The basic tenet of theocratic paternalism was the belief in social and economic inequality as being not only inevitable but desirable, since it gave both rich and poor the proper scope for the practice of the Christian virtues peculiar to their respective stations. Matthew 14:7, "For ye have the poor with you always," was a favorite text of the theocrats. Preaching

[75] George Peck, "Fourierism," *Methodist Quarterly Review* (New York, 1845), p. 592.
[76] John M. Krebs, *Education and Progress* (Easton, Pa., 1847), p. 21.

on this text in 1818, Heman Humphrey ascribed all poverty to individual and moral causes, notably to "want of capacity," "insanity," "prodigality," "pride," "idleness," and, above all, "intemperance."[77] The more the poor were cared for through public charities, he asserted, the more their numbers would increase, until "the call of distress will multiply . . . faster than you can possibly furnish the means to relieve them."[78] The whole problem of poverty, he concluded, should be treated at the root, with the "moral and religious preventives of poverty."[79]

This view of the theocrats was carried over unchanged into the Jacksonian era. Gardiner Spring went so far as to caution the poor—in their absence, to be sure!—"Do not envy the rich!" "The poor cottager with all his poverty and rags, whose daily bread is scarcely earned by the sweat of his brow, but whose piety spreads a charm around his humble dwelling, you may well envy; but not the rich worldling. Will you envy a man that which ensnares his soul?—which presents an obstacle to his eternal salvation? which throws mountains in his way to heaven?"[80]

So typical was this view of poverty that Francis Wayland included the subject in his chapter on "Benevolence to the Unhappy."[81] On the other hand, the theocrats tried to balance it with a patronizing, aggressively encouraging attitude toward the workers, who, while in a sense on probation, pending proof of their moral worth, were yet beneficiaries of American political institutions and American prosperity, which should in itself stimulate their self-respect. "In America," James Waddell Alexander pointed out, "posts of honor are open to all classes of men," so that "no poor mother who looks on her sleeping babe, can predict with certainty that this very child

[77] Heman Humphrey, *On Doing Good to the Poor* (Pittsfield, Mass., 1818), pp. 9-16.
[78] *ibid.*, p. 20.   [79] *ibid.*, p. 23.
[80] Gardiner Spring, "Wealth a Fearful Snare to the Soul," *American Preacher*, IV (1830), 377-378.
[81] *Elements of Moral Science* (Boston, 1835), pp. 376-381.

OTHER SOCIAL PROBLEMS

may not one day be President of the United States."[82] Alexander considers it important that American workers should be informed about their superior advantages, "in order to show them how unreasonable are their murmurs." "Take the case of the common labourer: he is better clothed, better lodged, and better fed in America than in any other country on earth."[83] Furthermore, "the prospect of wealth is spread before him"; and "if he is so happy as to be a member of any Christian church, he finds that there is no privilege, trust, or office from which he is excluded by his having been a labouringman."[84]

The adoption by the theocrats of the social and economic doctrines of the privileged classes has never been put before the public as fully as in a recent work by Joseph Dorfman entitled *The Economic Mind in American Civilization.*[85] Dorfman concentrates on systems of economic theory and does not draw very much on occasional writings, but it is precisely the amount of systematic economic thinking by theocrats during our period which is remarkable. In spite of many minor variations among them, Dorfman's findings fully justify the label of paternalism, with a sacred regard for private property, a consistent advocacy of the interests of the merchant class, and an uneasy attitude toward the working and under-privileged classes.[86]

"The aristocracy of blood and wealth is fast passing away," remarked Philip Milledoler, President of Rutgers College, in a commencement address. "We are persuaded that no other

[82] Alexander, *op.cit.*, I, 164. (Some of the leading Unitarians were equally conservative, cf. W. E. Channing, *On the Elevation of the Laboring Classes* [1840], while others, like Theodore Parker, were among the extreme radicals.)
[83] *ibid.*, II, 141-142.   [84] *ibid.*, II, p. 143.
[85] Three volumes (New York, 1946-1949).
[86] See especially chapter XIX on "The Higher Learning, 1789-1829," and chapter XXV on "The Higher Learning, 1829-1861," in Dorfman, *op.cit.*, vol. II, for the economic views of theocratic college presidents and professors, like Charles Nisbet of Dickinson, Samuel Stanhope of Princeton, James M. Mathews of New York University, Laurens P. Hickok of Union College, and Joseph Haven of Amherst.

will be tolerated among us, but that of talent and virtue. This is the aristocracy, if so it may be called, which God and enlightened men delight to honor, and the only one that will take root in the United States."[87] In other words, since aristocracy can no longer be secured merely by inheritance, it will henceforth be safeguarded for "talent and virtue," that is, for those who can afford to cultivate their talents and who will practice the accepted virtues.

In a similar setting a Baptist theocrat left even less to the imagination. "We want that mixing and mingling of all classes," exclaimed the President of Georgetown College, Kentucky, "which shall break up the odious horizontal line which separates rich and poor. This can be done only by the operation of benevolence, individual and associated. The church, the temperance society, and a hundred other such combinations, give an opportunity for the free intercourse of all classes, which will knit them together in bands stronger than even interest. The mass will then be ruled as scepters and constitutions never ruled. Vast wealth and deep poverty will remain, yet will there be the holiest and happiest community of goods earth ever saw."[88]

Was there not one among the countless social reforms of the period which the theocrats wholeheartedly approved and supported? The answer is a qualified "No." They rejected the "reforming spirit," as well as such major social movements for human betterment as abolitionism, public education, and labor organization. All social experiments were suspicious to them, even those with religious overtones. They might express only mild scorn for the peaceful Shakers, but the spurious "theocracy" of Joseph Smith and the Mormons elicited their most violent condemnation.[89] Even the struggle of women for higher

[87] Philip Milledoler, *Address . . . to the Graduates of Rutgers College* (New York, 1831), p. 9.
[88] Howard Malcom, "Address to the Graduation Class . . . ," *Western Baptist Review*, IV (1848-1849), 38.
[89] See the scathing article on "Mormonism" in the *Methodist Quarterly Review*, XXV (1843), 111-127.

OTHER SOCIAL PROBLEMS

social status found them solidly aligned with the opposition. Gardiner Spring could discourse most eloquently on *The Excellence and Influence of the Female Character*, but eventually disappointed his "fair auditors" by warning them that their character should be cultivated only in "the various spheres of usefulness peculiar to their sex and station."[90] Horace Bushnell could only plead: "Do save us one half of society from the boils and bruises and arts of demagogy. . . . Let a little of the sweetness and purity, if we can have it, of the simple religion, of life remain. God made the woman to be a help to man, not to be a wrestler with him."[91] In the same vein Princeton Seminary's ancient and venerable Samuel Miller devoted a lengthy sermon to the delicate subject of *The Appropriate Duty and Ornament of the Female Sex*.[92] Even such minor reforms as the improvement of prisons and of the penal system did not enlist the theocrats, though some of the outstanding (and otherwise conservative) Unitarians were very active in their promotion.[93]

The only reforms which the theocrats supported were moral reforms, which might have social implications but were directed primarily at the individual. Beginning with Lyman Beecher's call for a "moral reformation" in 1812, the theocrats spent a great deal of time and energy on the extirpation of such "immorality" as they saw abound in the country, whether in the raw West, among the industrial workers, or even in idyllic rural New England.

Some of the practices which the theocrats branded as immoral were of a purely ecclesiastical, institutional nature, and need not concern us. For instance, if the people did not go to church as faithfully as they used to go, clergymen in any age and under any social conditions would endeavor to obtain a

[90] New York, 1825. Quotation from page 30.
[91] *American Politics: A sermon, etc.* (1840), in *Life and Letters*, p. 94.
[92] *American Politics*. Printed in J. T. Duffield, *The Princeton Pulpit* (Philadelphia, 1850).
[93] Gordon A. Riegler, *Socialization of the New England Clergy* (Greenfield, Ohio, 1945), pp. 97-102.

OTHER SOCIAL PROBLEMS

more regular attendance. The theocrats wrestled with these typical problems as much as any clerical group at any time, but their efforts to solve them were not distinctive: ministers of antitheocratic convictions were doing likewise. The outstanding exception to this rule was, of course, the Sabbath controversy, in which the neglect of a Christian institution caused the theocrats to conduct a truly national campaign.

Again, the theocrats branded as immoral certain pastimes or amusements which had been at least frowned upon, and more often forbidden, by their colonial forbears. Such "vices" as card-playing or going to the theater came in for severe but sporadic criticism during our period but were never selected as targets for any reforming crusade. The same was true of the notorious custom of duelling which received nationwide attention because of the fatal encounter of Alexander Hamilton with Aaron Burr in 1805. The theocrats never failed to condemn duelling and everywhere exerted pressure for its moral and legal outlawry.[94]

Yet the exercise of such moral criticism cannot properly be called reform, since it involved little or no organized effort and was of slight social consequence. It merely serves as an index to the direction of theocratic concern. The aim was, as usual, to restrain the individual from giving free rein to his evil passions, lest social morality suffer.

At the opening of our period the theocrats still believed that private morals could be controlled by means of the strict enforcement of existing laws. Such laws still existed, especially in the New England states. They breathed the strangely pathetic moral earnestness of men like Increase Mather, author of *An Arrow against Profane and Promiscuous Dancing, Drawn out of a Quiver of the Scriptures*.[95] Realizing that pri-

[94] Stokes, *op.cit.*, II, 5-12, deals with the anti-duelling efforts of theocrats like John Mitchell Mason, Timothy Dwight, Eliphalet Nott, and others. Once again Lyman Beecher was the pioneer. *His Sermon on Duelling* (1806) was the earliest and the most widely circulated of them all.
[95] Boston, 1684. Reprinted in Miller and Johnson, *op.cit.*, pp. 411-413.

vate morals always had social implications, the Puritans considered their supervision to be incumbent upon the constituted authorities. In 1813 Lyman Beecher still held this opinion. "Civil rulers," he wrote, "are ministers of God, appointed for this very thing, and bound to exercise their best discretion to provide for public safety."[96] Even then, however, the fate of the Establishment was sealed, and it is to Beecher's credit that he read the signs of the times correctly and that, while continuing to fight for the "old firm of Moses and Aaron" till its dying gasp, he managed to shift more and more of his vast energy to organized effort through voluntary societies. From the founding of the Connecticut Moral Society in 1813,[97] moral societies began to spring up all over New England, gradually spreading to the Middle Atlantic states and to the West. Originally they proposed to do what the "civil arm" was no longer able or willing to do: to control private morals for the public good under clerical guidance. Within a very short time, however, their objective narrowed down to the conquest of just one vice, intemperance, which in its prevalence as well as in its social significance far outstripped all the others.

The Temperance Crusade

The beginning of the temperance movement has been authoritatively treated by a contemporary historian who does full justice to the outstanding part played in it by the Protestant forces and by the theocrats in particular.[98] In colonial times the use of alcoholic beverages was not considered a social problem, though the Puritan clergymen were quick to condemn individual excesses. The ravages of drinking became

[96] Beecher, *A sermon, delivered at Hartford, Connecticut . . . subsequent to the formation of the Connecticut Moral Society* (Hartford, 1813), p. 16.
[97] Beecher, *Autobiography*, I, 255-256. Among its founders were Heman Humphrey, Timothy Dwight, and Calvin Chapin, as well as Lyman Beecher and several distinguished laymen.
[98] John Allen Krout, *The Origins of Prohibition* (New York, 1925). The subsequent discussion is heavily indebted to this monograph.

OTHER SOCIAL PROBLEMS

rather more apparent during the Revolutionary era and were first brought before the public from the medical standpoint by Dr. Benjamin Rush, in his pamphlet entitled *An Inquiry into the Effects of Spiritous Liquors on the Human Body and Mind*, published in 1784. In 1808 this pamphlet fell into the hands of Lyman Beecher, then pastor at East Hampton, Long Island. It made an indelible impression on him. At once he resolved upon a crusade.[99]

Beecher's initiative soon began to bear fruit. In Massachusetts Jeremiah Evarts took the lead through the pages of the *Panoplist*, enlisting Jedidiah Morse, Eliphalet Porter, and other theocrats. The Massachusetts Temperance Society resulted.[100] The example was contagious. Local societies sprang up all over New England, coalescing into state societies. At last, in 1826, the American Society for the Promotion of Temperance was organized. In addition to the leaders of the Massachusetts society, this national body included such prominent New England theocrats as Leonard Wood, Francis Wayland, Benjamin B. Wisner, William Jenks, and Warren Fay.[101] Justin Edwards was employed as full-time Secretary, soon joined by Nathaniel Hewit. So successful was the work of this society that before long nearly all the major denominations officially endorsed the Temperance Crusade.[102] Only the Lutherans and the Episcopalians remained lukewarm. The records of the society also show that within the first decade of its existence nearly three thousand ministers of all denominations had individually pledged themselves to the support of its program.[103]

Meanwhile, however, another more truly national body had come into being under the name of United States Temperance Union. It was organized in Philadelphia in 1833 and Stephen Van Rensselaer became its first president. In 1836 the two

[99] Beecher, *Autobiography*, I, 177.
[100] E. C. Tracy, *Memoir of Jeremiah Evarts, Esq.* (Boston, 1845), pp. 75-76.
[101] *First Annual Report of the ... American Society for the Promotion of Temperance* (Andover, 1828), p. 7.
[102] *Sixth Report* (New York, 1833), pp. 14-18.
[103] *Seventh Report* (New York, 1834), p. 94.

OTHER SOCIAL PROBLEMS

bodies merged into the American Temperance Union at a national convention held at Saratoga, New York, which furnished the greatest single demonstration of the power of the crusade up to that date. At the same time, however, dissension appeared within the ranks. Several of the theocrats, including Lyman Beecher and Justin Edwards, wished to ban only strong drinks and to exempt beer and wine from the general condemnation. Episcopal bishop Alonzo Potter shared their views and ridiculed the "teatotallers" by exposing their syllogism, "Alcohol is a poison—wine contains alcohol—therefore wine is poison" by countering with one of his own, notably "Carbonic acid gas is poison—the atmosphere contains carbonic acid gas —therefore the atmosphere is poison."[104] Yet, in spite of the efforts of these more moderate theocrats, the forerunners of Prohibition came to dominate the scene more and more and the emphasis on individual "pledging" gave way to the demand for legislative restrictions.

In this connection, it may be worth while to observe the fluctuations of the strategy of the theocrats. After the War of 1812 they felt that there was no longer any hope for government support of their programs, and that the voluntary societies would have to do the job alone. In the late twenties they reversed themselves by entering wholeheartedly into the Sabbath controversy, petitioning for legal redress for the violation of the Sabbath. At the same time, however, they were engaged in the early phases of the temperance crusade with little or no thought of enlisting the civil authorities, except insofar as they might respond to propaganda. Then, in the early forties the temperance cause was carried into politics by the more radical element among them, until the enactment of the Maine Law in 1851 raised legislative action to the rank of its primary objective, culminating eventually in the Eighteenth Amendment. What accounts for these fluctuations? It seems that in times of comparatively little political and social tension the theocrats were ready to entrust their causes exclusively to the voluntary

[104] Quoted in Calvin Colton, *Protestant Jesuitism* (New York, 1837), p. 263.

societies. This was the case during the so-called "Era of Good Feelings" between the end of the War of 1812 and the election of Jackson in 1828. This again was the case during Jackson's second administration when they realized that Christianity had weathered the onset of militant democracy after all. On the other hand, the turbulent years of the War of 1812, the convulsions during Jackson's first term, and the economic depression after 1837 shook the theocrats' faith in the effectiveness of voluntary societies, unaided by political action. Even when reinforced by the sanctions of religion and by relentless propaganda, the principle of moral restraint seemed adequate for bringing private morals under public supervision only in times of comparative ease. In times of stress and strain the authority of public opinion over the private citizen decreased until the voluntary societies had to admit that they were unable to cope with wholesale moral defection. Then, recalling that their primary motivation was patriotic, that they were guardians of the moral welfare of the American people and that their pattern was the guarantee of the fulfillment of America's divinely appointed destiny, the theocrats reminded the civil authorities of their responsibility to apply legal restraint, in order to help the voluntary societies in the discharge of their task.[105]

For as much as they opposed the social reforms of the day because of the "infidel" philosophy underlying them, as much they bent every effort to the moral reformation of the American citizen, not only to make him receptive to the Gospel but to make him a valuable and loyal citizen of his nation. In this sense intemperance was obviously subversive to patriotism. "When excess has despoiled the man of the natural affections of husband, father, brother, and friend, and thrust him down to the condition of an animal, we are not to expect of him com-

[105] Krout, *op.cit.*, pp. 302-304, attributes the entrance of the temperance crusaders into politics to their disappointment at the slowness of the cause's progress by voluntary methods. He suggests that their "optimistic belief" in man's perfectibility was shaken. So far as the theocrats were concerned, this explanation is not adequate: they did not hold such a belief.

OTHER SOCIAL PROBLEMS

prehensive views, and a disinterested regard for his country."[106]

Every day furnished new illustrations of the ravages of strong drink in terms of pauperism and crime which the theocrats could not fail to note. But the greatest menace to the nation, they thought, lay in the political realm. "For the laboring classes constitute an immense majority, and when these are perverted by intemperance, ambitions need not better implements with which to dig the grave of our liberties, and entomb our glory. . . . These are the troops of the future Caesars, by whose perverted suffrage our future elections may be swayed, and ultimately our liberties destroyed."[107]

The unanimous advocacy of temperance by the theocrats gave rise to certain ironical situations. On the one hand, secular "patriots" who opposed all reform movements because they regarded them as un-American, did not always distinguish between those of foreign and those of native origin. If they had, they would have recognized the temperance crusade as a purely American phenomenon. Lacking such discernment, a Democratic politician from Virginia denounced the Temperance Union because it repudiated the "principles of seventy-six—the right to life, liberty, property, and happiness."[108] On the other hand, the theocrats in the crusade often found themselves allied with individuals whom they would normally consider more dangerous than John C. Young's 480,000 drunkards.[109] For instance, they had to welcome the support of Judge Thomas Hertell, one of the nation's leading infidels,[110] and be

---

[106] Lyman Beecher, *Six Lectures on Intemperance*, Lecture III, in *Works*, I, 383.
[107] *ibid.*, pp. 387-388.
[108] Quoted in Curti, *Growth of American Thought*, p. 392.
[109] In an *Address on Temperance* (Lexington, 1834), John C. Young, President of Centre College, declared that if the country could be rid of her 480,000 drunkards, it would be the greatest safeguard to American liberty, since he would rather see America "menaced by the bayonets of four hundred and eighty thousand foreign foes" than by the same number of drunkards.
[110] Cf. Thomas Hertell, *An Exposé of the Causes of Intemperate Drinking* (New York, 1819). For a theocratic estimate of Hertell, see *Methodist Quarterly Review*, xxv (1843), 5-23.

content to collaborate with Horace Greeley whose low opinion of them was well known.

Basically, however, the temperance crusade was a positive theocratic reform program for the saving of American social morality. William Warren Sweet rightly stresses its significance on the frontier. "The basic moral problem which confronted the average community," he writes, "grew directly or indirectly out of the abundant supply of intoxicating liquor."[111] This, incidentally, accounts for the Protestant clergy's rigid attitude toward drinking even a century later. "On every frontier from the Alleghenies to the Pacific these [the clergy] were the people who fought the battle for decency and order, and to a large degree saved the West from semibarbarism, and the attitudes created by these struggles remain to this day."[112]

What Sweet establishes concerning the West also applies to America's urban "frontier." "There is no question that there was room for reform. Foreign travelers remarked American intemperance, some kindly passing it off as a concomitant of rigorous pioneering in a new country of great climatic extremes. But there was an abundance of hard liquor drunk along the long-settled seaboard where pioneering had passed. . . . By 1819 one could scarcely find a town in Connecticut or Rhode Island without a rum distillery. . . ."[113]

For this reason whatever opposition the theocrats encountered in their reforming efforts was directed not so much at their objective as at their methods. John Leland professed to abhor drunkenness as much as anyone, though he also recalled the apostolic injunction about the propriety of a little wine, "for thy stomach's sake."[114] He even commended the temperance societies for "directing public opinion while leaving individuals at their liberty."[115] He rebelled only against those

[111] W. W. Sweet, "The Churches as Moral Courts of the Frontier." *American Historical Review*, II (1933), 21.
[112] *ibid.*
[113] Dixon Ryan Fox, "The Protestant Counter-Reformation," *New York History*, XVI (1935), p. 31.
[114] John Leland, "Facts and Questions" (1829), *Writings*, p. 56.
[115] Leland, "Transportation of the Mails" (1830), *ibid.*, p. 565.

who "would pronounce the best men drunkards because they will not list themselves nor their names into a mixed society, never instituted by Jesus Christ."[116] Calvin Colton, the colorful and implacable enemy of "Protestant Jesuitism," agreed with Leland. He felt that the object of the temperance crusade was praiseworthy, but that its attainment should be left to the church, "the only and the very society under commission given by Jesus Christ, which he authorized to be employed by his professed disciples for the reformation of morals and manners in the world. . . ."[117] In the light of Colton's checkered career in the ministry it seems strange that he should adopt such a churchly attitude.

Episcopal Bishop John Henry Hopkins, on the other hand, could fittingly hold such views, since he was a High-Churchman and an aristocrat, cast in the same mold as his more famous British namesake and contemporary, John Henry Newman. Naturally averse to anything that might vulgarize Christianity by taking it into the highways and byways of human life, Hopkins rejoiced that the Episcopal Church did not endorse the temperance societies, because "the church of Christ always was, and, with all its faults . . . is to this hour, the only sure school for temperance and for every other virtue."[118]

The theocrats, by and large, were unmoved by such objections. They did not need any instruction in good churchmanship. They had created the voluntary societies not to compete with the churches but to assist them. Above all they were using them as a weapon to ward off the threats of infidelity and immorality to their beloved country. Their pattern for American society was to be achieved by evangelization, education, and the exercise of moral restraint. "It belongs to this plan of taking a nation in the mass for religious purposes, that the mass be Christianized throughout. A general evangelical virtue, congenial to the work of the spirit on individual men, must be dif-

[116] Leland, "Note on Temperance" (1834), *ibid.*, p. 727.
[117] Colton, *Protestant Jesuitism*, p. 131.
[118] John Henry Hopkins, *The Primitive Church* (Burlington, 1835), p. 148.

fused through the nation. As God rears a plant from the soil no less by tempering the hemisphere than by specific appliances to the root, so he conducts his moral discipline of men as much by common allotments and motions of nations, as by direct dealings with particular persons."[119]

Summary

It is hardly possible to conceive of a more concise summary of the theocratic pattern for American society. To be sure, the theocrats were socially conservative, but their conservatism was not merely a sign of self-interest, a rationalization of their desire to maintain the *status quo*. America was undergoing a process of social change so manifold and in many respects so radical, that a conservative influence was to be welcomed, even though some of its champions might wield it for narrow purposes. Furthermore, the theocratic pattern for American society revealed a delicate balance between Christianity and patriotism, which in an age of excessive nationalism on the one hand and of excessive individualism on the other, served as a prophetic leaven in the rising loaf of the nation. "The Christian citizen of an evangelized nation," wrote a Presbyterian theocrat, "may regard his country as an abode of the church, and love his country the more without loving the kingdom of Christ the less; the more he is a patriot, the more he is a Christian."[120]

[119] "Annual Report of the Board of Missions . . . of the Presbyterian Church . . ." (1849), in *The Princeton Review and Biblical Repertory*, XXI (1849), 314.
[120] *ibid.*, p. 315.

CHAPTER VII

THE THEOCRATIC PATTERN FOR TERRITORIAL EXPANSION

Expansion Before 1812

AT the turn of the nineteenth century the United States was still much the same geographically as the thirteen original colonies had been. The westward migration had begun, to be sure, but by far the larger part of New York and Pennsylvania was unsettled frontier territory and the movement into the new "southwestern" states—Kentucky and Tennessee—was barely getting under way. Three European nations, all mightier than the United States, continued to possess vast empires in North America. Britain ruled Canada, whose boundaries extended farther south than they do now. The Indian tribes of the Northwest were also largely under British influence. Spain held the title to what is now Florida. Mexico and the largely unexplored regions to the north which were to become Texas, New Mexico, Arizona, and California, were also under Spanish dominion. The Louisiana Territory, which had belonged to France and been ceded to Spain, passed again under French control in 1800. With the present state of Louisiana at its base, it spread far to the north, virtually splitting the continent in half.

The acquisition of Louisiana by purchase in 1803 was by all tokens the outstanding event in American history between 1800 and 1812. Profiting by one of Napoleon's weakest moments before his ultimate downfall, American diplomacy stumbled into an unbelievable bargain. For one thing, the purchase of Louisiana eliminated France from the North American continent. This is all the more significant if we remember that at the time Napoleon ruled all of continental Europe and that only the British Navy stood between him and world conquest. Again, the purchase of Louisiana added about twice as much territory to the United States as she then possessed.[1] To be sure, it was largely a wilderness which the nation thus acquired, but it was a wilderness adjacent to her own settled lands rather than three thousand miles away.

The reaction to the Louisiana purchase was indicative of the whole trend of American politics. The Federalists, who had been responsible for the first attempts to create a nation out of a loose federation of states and who had been insisting on a broad interpretation of the Constitution, were losing their platform to the Republicans and adopting more and more the former position of their opponents. It was one of the most startling changes of position in all political history. The same Jefferson who had written the Virginia Resolutions of 1798 found himself, in 1803, negotiating the transfer of Louisiana, persuading Congress to ratify the transaction in record-breaking time, and justifying it before the Federalists—and before his own conscience—in terms of America's "natural right" to the area![2] Even the boldest, most "nationalistic" Federalist would not have dared either to stretch the Constitution so far or to interpret the well-known philosophical doctrine in such novel terms.

This change of position influenced decisively not only the course of party politics but also the moral overtones of America's subsequent territorial expansion. The theocrats, being New Englanders or at least men of a New England stamp and with a New England outlook, were largely identified with the Federalist party. They had been vocal in their support of the early "nationalism" of their party, but then, profoundly alarmed by the Republican victory of 1800 and perplexed by the rising nationalism of the government, they followed their party into its ideological retrenchment. Throughout the first half of the nineteenth century, the theocrats were "unionists" in all their pronouncements and aspirations, but always with

---

[1] Edward Channing, *History of the United States* (8 vols., New York, 1938), IV, 298ff.

[2] Albert K. Weinberg, *Manifest Destiny* (Baltimore, 1935), pp. 29-30.

the proviso that the nation would adopt their pattern—which so closely coincided with the political platform first of the Federalist, then of the Whig party—whether for her racial and religious complexion, her social morality, or her territorial expansion. In other words, the theocrats were trying to think as Americans rather than as New Englanders and conservatives, but were unsuccessful most of the time.

Beginning with the Louisiana Purchase, the United States entered upon an era of growth, which, within less than two generations, pushed her borders to the Pacific Ocean. This startling expansion came by stages, to be sure, but it was always championed by the popular party of the day: first by the Republicans, then by the Democrats. The conservative party, Federalist or Whig, consistently opposed the acquisition of new territory. It may sound rather harsh that "the New England Federalists would have been content to keep the nation, however small and feeble, forever under New England domination."[3] Yet it would seem to be no exaggeration.

From the beginning, however, the opponents of American expansion were running counter to popular feeling. The sentiment of the country was "expansionist." Pratt has proved that the real cause of the War of 1812 lay not in anything the British had or had not done, but rather in the aggressive temper of the War Hawks, who, backed by their frontier constituents, coveted new lands from Canada to Florida.[4] Weinberg has traced the story of *Manifest Destiny* from the War of 1812 to our own day, showing the intricate relationships between the desire for aggrandizement and its political and moral justification.[5] The story of the opposition to America's territorial expansion has yet to be written. It would have to be culled from the Congressional Record and from the leading Federalist and Whig papers of the day. It can be found, however, in the writings of the theocrats, since their arsenal contained all the argu-

[3] Krout and Fox, *The Completion of Independence* (1790-1830), p. 203.
[4] Julius W. Pratt, *The Expansionists of 1812* (New York, 1925).
[5] Albert K. Weinberg, *op.cit., passim.*

ments of the more sensitive conservative politicians, plus such theological and ideological ammunition as was distinctly their own.

The Causes of the War of 1812

Officially there were four reasons for going to war with Britain. In the first place, the British "Orders in Council" of 1807, which reduced American merchant shipping in European waters to virtually nothing, had not been revoked, in spite of many promises to that effect. Secondly, British cruisers were hovering in American coastal waters to enforce the Orders. In the third place, the British had not halted their impressments of American seamen in spite of numerous protests by the United States. Fourthly, the aggressiveness of the Indians of the Northwest under Tecumseh's leadership seemed to be traceable to British influence. Yet, by the time President Madison declared war, the Orders of Council had been revoked and there is reason to believe that this news was deliberately withheld from the American people. With the revocation of the Orders, the British cruisers automatically withdrew from American waters. The friction with the Indians continued, but could be ascribed as readily to the aggressiveness of American settlers as to British instigation. Thus, "technically, the impressment grievance must stand as the *Casus belli* in 1812."[6]

It was a flimsy cause. There were serious grievances in regard to France, which would have made a declaration of war upon that nation just as plausible. On July 6, 1812, Madison sent to Congress a list of vessels captured by Europeans since 1803. It disclosed that the French had seized 558 vessels since November 1807, the British 389.[7] To be sure, England was still remembered by the revolutionary and post-revolutionary generations as America's traditional oppressor. Yet, Napoleon's despotism was far more to be feared than blockade-locked

[6] Homer Cary Hockett, *Political and Social Growth of the United States* (New York, 1941), p. 417.
[7] Channing, *op.cit.*, IV, 453.

PATTERN FOR TERRITORIAL EXPANSION

Britain. The explanation of the government's action must be sought in the fact that France had been eliminated from North America in 1803, whereas Britain still had Canada, which the War Hawks coveted for the United States. Of course, there was still Spain, but her hold on Florida was so tenuous that the War Hawks were ready to take her in their stride along with Britain. As a matter of fact, being able to pair off Florida with Canada furnished an excellent political platform on which North and South might unite in the common endeavor of national aggrandizement.[8] Pratt's analysis of the sectional factors behind the War of 1812 is conclusive. "The nation in 1812 was divided by a twofold cleavage. There was, first, the line between East and West, or more accurately, between the frontier crescent from New Hampshire to Georgia and the more settled and stable portions of the country. Here war men and annexationists, all Republicans, were opposed, in the north by New England Federalism, and in the Middle States, from New York to North Carolina, by the factious and antiwar Republicans with a scattering of Federalists. Cutting across this line at right angles was a second line of cleavage between the commercial and the planter states, the free and the slave states. In terms of bitterness and distrust, this line cut far deeper than the first."[9]

The annexation of Florida was anticipated with eager enthusiasm in the South. Weinberg shows that the peninsula was considered by the expansionists as belonging to the United States by a kind of "geographical predestination."[10] The conquest of Canada, on the other hand, did not seem to offer any real compensation to the antiwar elements in the North. It was not any Northern politician but Grundy of Tennessee and

[8] A similar sectional bargain was proposed in the forties when Texas and Oregon were linked together in the platform of the Democratic party in order to allay the feeling of rivalry between North and South.
[9] Pratt, *op.cit.*, pp. 134-135.
[10] Weinberg, *op.cit.*, pp. 47-48, reproduces a letter of Madison to Monroe expressing this view within a year after the Louisiana Purchase. The subsequent pages contain further evidence.

PATTERN FOR TERRITORIAL EXPANSION

Clay of Kentucky who kindled whatever zeal there was for an American invasion of Canada.[11] What is more, the hurried and ill-prepared attempt to invade Canada led to such military disasters that any enthusiasm there might have been, cooled at once. By 1813 the War Hawks had to realize that their prey was not as ready for the kill as they had so confidently hoped. Yet, Northern boycott was not alone accountable for the American defeats on the Canadian frontier. In spite of all the protests of the Federalists, even New England and New York did their share in raising money for the war, though Massachusetts and Connecticut refused to contribute their contingent of militia.[12]

Thus the theocrats opposed "Mr. Madison's war" both as Northerners and as Federalists. They rejected the government's reasons for going to war and exposed the "immorality" of the war with all the religious fervor and all the eloquence at their command.

Antiwar Arguments of the Theocrats

The first argument the theocrats advanced in their opposition to going to war with England had to do with their hatred and fear of France. Their unanimity on this point was complete. Whether Bourbon, Revolutionary, or Napoleonic, France was a hotbed of infidelity as well as a welter of anarchic forces which could be controlled only by despotic power. The saintly old Seth Payson, Congregational pastor in Rindge, New Hampshire, for over half a century, summarized the theocratic view of France as clearly as anyone. "Previous to the revolution, an atheistical philosophy had been silently extending its influence over the French nation, and gradually eradicating every principle of virtue and morality. Still, while the monarch remained,

---

[11] "I feel anxious not only to add the Floridas to the South, but the Canadas to the North of this empire!" asserted Grundy in the Senate; and Clay declared, "The conquest of Canada is in your power!" Quotations from Hockett, *op.cit.*, p. 416.

[12] Channing, *op.cit.*, IV, 470-471.

PATTERN FOR TERRITORIAL EXPANSION

the spirit of licentiousness was restrained by the strong hand of power; but no sooner was this last obstacle to licentiousness removed, than the hateful passions of the heart burst forth with unrestrained fury. . . . Such will republics be, when religion, and the restraints of law, lose their operation. The late Emperor Napoleon reduced these wild passions under an iron yoke of despotism. His usurpations were readily submitted to by the more discerning part of the nation, as preferable to the state of anarchy with which they were convulsed. And cruel as his exactions and conscriptions were, this strong hand of power seemed to be necessary to save them from national ruin."[13]

Following the meteoric career of the Corsican, the theocrats had taken great pains to prove that he was, indeed, the Antichrist of prophecy, and that hostilities with England would be so much grist for the Antichrist's mill. As early as 1808, Elijah Parrish, a theocrat of vehement Federalist convictions, faced his hearers with the startling alternative, *Ruin, or Separation from Anti-Christ.*[14] Two years later Isaac Braman, while also starting with Biblical prophecy, expounded his anti-French views on a more practical level, in the hope of proving the "comparatively greater evil of a close connection with France than of a connection with Great Britain."[15] He pointed out the factor of a common language, expressed his preference for Britain's limited monarchy against France's despotic government, showed how the United States risked becoming an accomplice to France's scheme of world conquest, how France's perfidy in international dealings outweighed that of Britain, and how it was Protestant America's duty to favor Protestant Britain over Catholic France. "It seems to be morally impossible," Braman concluded, "that any man of real piety . . .

[13] Seth Payson, *Two Discourses, preached at Rindge, N.H., at the Annual Fast, April 13, 1815* (New Ipswich, N.H., 1815), p. 8.
[14] Newburyport, Mass., 1808. A sermon based wholly on prophecy.
[15] *Union with France a greater evil than union with Britain* (Haverhill, Mass., 1810), p. 4.

197

should pray for the downfall of England at the present day, or that France might get the ascendancy over her."[16]

The religious condition of France—an infidel nation ruled by the Antichrist—furnished the theocrats with a distinctive viewpoint. When President Madison called for a day of fasting and prayer following the declaration of war, they seized the opportunity avidly. In the chapel of Yale College Timothy Dwight held two services expounding the whole course of Christian history in terms of the prophecy of the seven vials[17] of which the sixth and the seventh, he said, were just about to be poured out upon the world. "To ally America to France," he warned, "is to chain living health and beauty to a corpse dissolving with the plague."[18] The same day in Boston Jedidiah Morse cried out against the folly and calamity of a war destined to "inflame our resentments against a Christian nation" and to "throw us into the fatal embrace of the tyrant of Europe...."[19]

The second argument of the theocrats against going to war with Britain was of a more positive nature. It had to do with their new appreciation of the old foe because of a community of concern born of the missionary movement. The earliest American missionary efforts were all traceable to British examples and the theocrats were not ashamed of their indebtedness. The outbreak of war, coming as it did at a time when the first group of American missionaries had barely begun their work in India and Burma, appeared doubtly disastrous because of its anticipated effects on missions.[20] It was obvious that missionary cooperation between the two countries had to be discontinued until after the war. Then, however, it was resumed

[16] *ibid., passim*; quotation from page 19.
[17] Revelation: 16.
[18] Timothy Dwight, *A Discourse in Two Parts, delivered July 23, 1812* (New Haven, 1812), p. 52.
[19] Jedidiah Morse, *A sermon delivered at Charlestown, July 23, 1812* (Charlestown, Mass., 1812), p. 24.
[20] Nathan S. S. Beman, *A sermon delivered . . . in Portland, Maine, August 12, 1812, on the occasion of the national fast* (Portland, 1812), p. 10.

almost at once, and the theocrats were the first ones to champion it. John Lathrop reflected the reborn missionary optimism when he announced in a sermon of thanksgiving for the return of peace: "Should the peace continue which is now established among the christian nations of the earth, opportunities will offer for the execution of the most benevolent purposes of the human heart."[21]

All the other antiwar arguments of the theocrats were the same as those of the Federalist politicians. They kept pointing out that English monarchy was preferable to Napoleon's dictatorship, that the English-speaking nations should make common cause against him, that the United States would gain nothing from the war and that New England might lose everything. Their only distinctive arguments remained those of a religious nature: the folly of aiding Catholic and/or infidel France; the folly of fighting Protestant and missionary-minded Britain.

Clerical Support of the War of 1812

So far as we have been able to ascertain, there was only one theocrat who wholeheartedly favored the war, and his reasons could be traced to his personal background. Alexander McLeod, pastor of the Reformed Presbyterian Church in New York and author of *A Scriptural View of the Character, Causes, and Ends of the Present War*,[22] had come to America from Scotland in 1792 and had brought with him the fierce anti-British feeling of his "Covenanter" ancestry. As a minister in a denomination consisting largely of Scottish-Americans, he naturally welcomed the opportunity to chasten the British government, which he considered "a despotic usurpation, a superstitious combination of civil and ecclesiastical power, a branch of the grand antichristian apostasy, Erastian in its constitution and administration, and cruel in its policy."[23] Yet

[21] John Lathrop, *A discourse . . . in consequence of the peace* (Boston, 1815), p. 14.
[22] New York, 1815.
[23] Alexander McLeod, *op.cit.*, p. 60.

even he made allowances for the British people over against their hated government, primarily because of "that noble institution, which exceeds any thing that has hitherto been established by christian exertions, *The British and Foreign Bible Society*.[24] Perhaps the most interesting aspect of his work can be found not in what he wrote but in what he omitted, for in the entire volume there is hardly any mention of France. Apparently he did not sympathize with the French, either, but preferred to leave his opinions unsaid, lest he should weaken his case against the British.[25]

Aside from Alexander McLeod who later played a prominent part in the societies of the theocrats, clerical support for the War of 1812 came from the Methodists and the Baptists who represented largely the frontier point of view as well as the lower economic and social strata, and were thus naturally committed to, or sympathetic with, the Republican administration. James Osgood Andrew, who, in 1844, became the immediate cause of the split in the Methodist Church, was riding the circuit on the New York frontier during the war and wrote exultantly of Perry's victory on Lake Erie. "A smile of joy rests on the countenance of every honest Republican," he claimed.[26] An anecdote about the prominent Baptist preacher of western Pennsylvania, David Jones, illustrates the feelings of his denomination. A veteran of the Revolution, Jones was on his way to enlist in the war in spite of his seventy-six years, when he overheard a young man criticize the administration. " 'Yes, indeed,' Jones seemed to agree, 'a miserably weak administration—if President Madison were half the man he ought to be . . . he would have hung, long ago, scores of such confounded Tories as you. . . .' "[27]

[24] *ibid.*, p. 97.
[25] For McLeod's life, see S. B. Wylie, *Memoir of Alexander McLeod* (New York, 1855).
[26] George G. Smith, *Life and Letters of J. O. Andrews* (Nashville, 1883), p. 54.
[27] Biographical notice of *David Jones* by his grandson, Horatio Gates Jones, in Sprague, *Annals of the American Pulpit,* vi, *Baptists* (New York, 1860), 88.

PATTERN FOR TERRITORIAL EXPANSION

In New England where Republicanism was much in the minority, John Leland, another veteran of the Revolution, voiced the convictions of his fellow-Baptists by heaping scorn on the "self-named peace party who are always at war with their own government" and by asserting that "if there were causes of resistance and war in 1775 . . . there is seven times the justification for the present war."[28] It also appears that some of the churches composed of recent immigrants from Europe took the administration's part, both because of their own Republican sentiments and because of their European concept of loyalty to constituted authority. This is true of a sermon by the leader of early American Lutheranism, Henry Augustus Muehlenberg,[29] and of a Fourth of July sermon by a Dutch Reformed minister, himself a recent arrival in the United States.[30]

Thus the lines were rather clearly drawn. On the one hand there were the theocrats, largely Congregationalists and Presbyterians,[31] together with a handful of other New England clergymen. They opposed the war and openly favored England. On the other hand, there were the popular frontier churches and some small Christian groups of relatively new Americans who wholeheartedly backed the government. We may mention one group which did not fit into either category, namely clergymen of normally pro-British leanings who were caught in the midst of the hostilities and whose views were affected by the conduct of the British troops, particularly after

[28] John Leland, *Address to the Association of the Sons of Liberty, Cheshire (Mass.), March 4, 1813.* In *Writings* (New York, 1845), pp. 373-374.

[29] Henry Augustus Muehlenberg, *Busztagspredigt . . . den 20sten August, 1812 . . . in der lutherischen Kirche der Stadt Reading, in Pennsylvanien* (Reading, Pa., 1812). This sermon is completely, even strenuously, American, in all but language.

[30] P. I. Vanpelt, *The goodness of God be praised by men* (New York, 1812). The author is anti-French as well as anti-British and vociferously pro-American.

[31] At this date, with the Plan of Union in full operation, these two denominations were closely identified in their ministries as well as in their political, social, and religious point of view.

the burning of Washington and other needless atrocities. Such a clergyman was John Ewing Latta, lifelong minister of the Presbyterian Church at Newcastle, Delaware. In 1812 Latta greeted the outbreak of the war with all the sorrow of a sincerely irenic nature but also with a definite pro-British, anti-French bias.[32] By 1815, having seen the British troops at close range, he was far more willing to justify the war, though the tenor of his peace sermon—quite properly—was still pacific.[33] Another Presbyterian clergyman, Conrad Speece of Richmond, Virginia, spoke of the war without enthusiasm, dwelt at length on the national sins of the United States, and, probably as a concession to his Southern constituents, expressed his faith in the "sincerity" of the government.[34] At least one Southern Episcopal clergyman preached a bitterly pro-war sermon because of the British plunder of Georgetown and Havre de Grace, but even he did not voice any fundamental criticism of England, while his criticism of France and "liberty" was severe.[35] In short, even among these clergymen, the hatred and fear of France drowned out much of the indignation at British outrages, and whatever resentment they were able to feel they instinctively transferred to their own Republican government, without whose incompetence (so they argued) war with Britain would not have been necessary.

The Theocrats and the Peace of Ghent

It may be interesting to see how the theocrats reacted to the advent of peace, following upon a rather doubtful victory. Britain had simply tired of fighting and did not have sufficient resources to divert from Europe to the American theatre.

[32] John Ewng Latta, *A sermon preached on the 20th day of August, 1812* ... (Wilmington, 1812).
[33] John Ewing Latta, *A sermon preached at New Castle (Del.) on the thirteenth day of April, 1815* ... (Wilmington, 1815).
[34] Conrad Speece, *A sermon ... on account of the war with England* (Richmond, Va., 1813), p. 4.
[35] Philip Mathews, *An oration delivered ... in the Episcopal Church of St. Helena, Charleston, S.C.* (Charleston, 1813), p. 11.

PATTERN FOR TERRITORIAL EXPANSION

Compared to her decisive part in the destruction of Napoleon and his empire, the hostilities with the United States lacked interest. On the American side the war had been so poorly managed and the American forces had suffered so many defeats, at least on land, that the news of peace came as a glorious surprise to the "victors." Ironically, the one great American land victory of the war—Jackson's victory at New Orleans —took place when the two countries were already technically at peace! These facts, known to the theocrats, furnished them with excellent opportunities to rehearse the whole folly of the war from the beginning. Yet, on the whole, they preferred to interpret the fortunate outcome of the war as a token of God's mercy and to look to the future rather than raking over the past.

Some of them, of course, were rankling with bitterness. Nathanael Emmons, for instance, expressed the hope that "the pleasing sound of peace, which brings no positive good, but only mitigates positive evil, will not prove an opiate to lull the people into stupidity and negligence, but serve to animate their exertions for the redress of intolerable burdens."[36] In this spirit, Emmons was able to make his peace sermon into a campaign speech for the 1816 elections, in which, he felt certain, the Federalists would return to power.

"Although we have not yet learned that the objects for which the late war was declared, have been obtained or secured," observed John Lathrop caustically, "we do sincerely rejoice at the return of peace."[37] Others showed themselves more magnanimous and refused to comment on the war, but their views were implied quite clearly. "As to the causes of the war, or how far its objects have been attained, it is as little consistent with my inclination as with my duty, on the present occasion, to offer any opinion," concluded the President of

[36] Nathanael Emmons, *The Choice of their Rulers the Privilege of the People* (1815), in *Works* (Boston, 1840, 6 vols.), II, 286.
[37] John Lathrop, *A discourse . . . in consequence of the peace* (Boston, 1815), p. 14.

Bowdoin College.[38] "Shall I trace back the origin of the war and pronounce concerning its policy and morality; whether it was just or good?" asked a Presbyterian theocrat, answering his own question with a firm "No; I will not."[39]

Most of the theocrats, however, ascribed the victory—or at least, the return of peace—to God alone, without giving any credit to his human agents.[40] Nor can it be said that such an estimate of what had happened was wholly unfounded, no matter how the Republican papers labored to interpret the advent of peace as victory. Nevertheless, the people as a whole welcomed the interpretation which flattered nationalistic feeling and transmuted a defeat, or at best a stalemate, into an American (and Republican) triumph. The theocrats, on the other hand, by ascribing the "victory" to God alone, were also trying to save face. They had been decried as unpatriotic for boycotting the war; they could not risk becoming even more unpopular by wholly resisting the emotional current. For this reason Charles Coffin, President of Greenville College in Tennessee, tried to reconcile his New England view of the war with the opposite views of his students and church members by claiming that there had been a change of heart in the American people during the war which ultimately earned for them God's gift of peace.[41]

For this reason also a Hartford theocrat went so far as to plead with his hearers that "party names be now laid aside." "An odium infallibly attends them; and they are totally inconsistent with that spirit of accommodation which we now ought to cultivate, . . . Let us adopt no names ourselves, nor give

[38] Jesse Appleton, *A sermon . . . on account of the peace recently established* (Hallowell, Maine, 1815), p. 15.
[39] Samuel Blatchford, *A sermon, delivered . . . April 13, 1815* (Albany, 1815), p. 17.
[40] Samuel F. Jarvis, *The Duty of Offering unto God Thanksgiving* (New York, 1815), p. 12.
[41] Charles Coffin, *A sermon, delivered in Rogersville, April 13, 1815 . . . for the restoration of peace* (Rogersville, Tenn., 1815).

any to our fellow citizens, but that of *Americans,* . . . 'Let there be no strife between us, for we are brethren.' "[42]

It is rather ironical that the same theocrats who only three years earlier warned against going to war with the British by quoting the Scriptures, "Let there be no strife between us, for we are brethren," were now applying the same text to their fellow Americans of the opposing political camp.

The Theocrats and American Expansion, 1815-1844

In all these arguments of the theocrats, opposition to American territorial expansion appeared only by implication. To oppose the administration whose avowed purpose was to wrest Canada from Britain and—incidentally—Florida from Spain was tantamount to opposing the growth of the United States. It must have seemed injudicious, to say the least, to admit such a sentiment openly. From time to time, however, some of the more vehement Federalists among the theocrats left no doubt about their real feelings. Jedidiah Morse had stated bluntly that the war would bring nothing to New England except "the ruin of our commerce, the sacrifice of an immense property of our citizens, which is now in foreign countries, beyond our control, or on the ocean," and general economic distress.[43] Elijah Parrish had urged New England to stay out of the war in such uncontrolled language that we wonder how he escaped indictment for treason even in so free a country as the United States. "Let there be no war in your territories!" he thundered. "Proclaim an honorable neutrality! Let the southern heroes fight their own battles, . . . Rise in the majesty of your inconquerable strength, and once more breathe that free, commercial air of New England, which your fathers always enjoyed!"[44]

With an unusual twist of reasoning he argued that the gov-

[42] Abel Flint, *A discourse occasioned by the news of peace . . . February 14, 1815* (Hartford, 1815), p. 10.
[43] Jedidiah Morse, *op.cit.*, p. 24.
[44] Elijah Parrish, *A Protest Against the War* (Newburyport, Mass., 1812), p. 16.

ernment knew it could not carry on extensive warfare against Britain, that the declaration of war would lead Britain to blockade the American coast, and that New England would be the only real victim of the war; hence, "this nefarious declaration of war is nothing more, nor less than a license given by a Virginia vassal of the French Emperor to the English nation, authorizing them in legal form to destroy the prosperity of New England!"[45] More than a year after the declaration of war, Nathanael Emmons still urged that hostilities should be stopped, since the government had dragged the nation, and New England in particular, into a fruitless, suicidal conflict.[46]

Contrary to Emmons' expectations, however, the Federalist party did not return to power, but quietly went out of existence. The further the memories of the War of 1812 receded, the more willing the American people were to consider it as a great victory on which to feast their national pride. Sectional conflict was temporarily submerged in that wave of "good feeling" which gave its name to the years between 1817 and 1828. Yet sectional tensions continued, because the interests of North, South, and West, or, to put it in economic terms, the interests of the manufacturing, planting, and farming sections, were basically different.

Among the factors making for nationalism the sentiment of the West ranked first. Goodykoontz, like Turner before him, notes that the frontier was the breeding-ground of three great American traits: individualism, democracy, and nationalism. "The frontier was nationalistic. The wrench of leaving the old home had torn loose the roots of state and local pride; sufficient time had not elapsed to allow them to dig far down into the soil of the new abode. The foreign-born, many of whom had made their way to the West, had come to 'America' rather than to a particular 'sovereign state' in the Union."[47]

[45] *ibid.*, p. 23.
[46] Nathanael Emmons, *Rights of the People* (1813), in *Works*, II, 271-272.
[47] Colin B. Goodykoontz, *Home Missions on the American Frontier* (Caldwell, Idaho, 1939), p. 170.

PATTERN FOR TERRITORIAL EXPANSION

For six years immediately following the War of 1812 a new state was admitted to the Union every year: Indiana in 1816, Mississippi in 1817, Illinois in 1818, Alabama in 1819, Maine in 1820, and Missouri in 1821. However the theocrats might regret it and apprehend its consequences, the country was growing by leaps and bounds and the center of gravity was shifting away from New England. In addition to these new states, Florida was eventually acquired from Spain without bloodshed by the Treaty of 1819 and another area, twice as large as the New England states (Maine excepted) passed into American possession. In 1825 Florida joined the Union.[48]

Eastern fear of the West was one of the mainsprings of the home missionary movement, which the theocrats originated and continued to sponsor indefatigably throughout our period. So strong was the sectional tinge of their patriotism that they could envision a greater America only insofar as the newer areas reproduced or promised to reproduce the New England pattern. This sentiment occasionally gave rise to almost lyrical expressions of New England pride. For instance, Samuel Worcester wrote: "Go to the villages and cities of the West, and you can tell a New Englander's premises as soon as your eye rests upon them. You see his enterprise, his thrift, his taste, wherever he has been located long enough to frame his house, plant his maize or his wheat, and train the honey-suckle at his door."[49]

And Hollis Read, the theocratic historian, observed with profound satisfaction how the "Puritan element" was placing their stamp upon the whole West, "softening, melting and fusing" all its heterogeneous elements and "running them into the New England mould."[50]

[48] For the diplomatic background of the Florida treaty, see Edward H. Tatum, Jr., *The United States and Europe, 1815-1823* (Berkeley, California, 1936), pp. 157-163, 186-198.
[49] Samuel M. Worcester, *Our country and our work; a discourse* . . . (Salem, Mass., 1843), pp. 22-23.
[50] Hollis Read, *The Hand of God in American History* (Hartford, 1850), p. 365.

PATTERN FOR TERRITORIAL EXPANSION

With the accession of Andrew Jackson to the Presidency, the democratic spirit of the West became a dominant influence in the life of the United States. Yet, we have seen that the theocrats weathered the onset of Jacksonian democracy better than they themselves had dared to hope, and that the taming of the West through home missions, both evangelistic and educational, continued unabated. At the same time, however, the sectional rift between North and South kept widening dangerously year by year.

So far as the Negro problem lay at the bottom of the rift, the theocrats had a clear-cut, well-defined program to overcome it. However, the problem of the Negro was not only a racial problem: it was also a problem of different cultures and divergent economic interests. Superficially united in the emotional brand of nationalism which swept the country after 1815, North and South soon drifted back into their respective sectional positions. After 1829 the history of the South is a story of growing sectionalism. The classical illustration of the trend was furnished by John C. Calhoun, one of the War Hawks of 1812, who before too long emerged as the champion of Southern states' rights—a complete reversal of position.

The tension between North and South was highlighted by the Webster-Hayne debate of 1828. The states' rights platform of the Kentucky and Virginia resolutions, or that of the Hartford Convention, had been less dangerous than that which Hayne presented on Capitol Hill. Oddly enough, Hayne's opponent represented New England as truly as any other national figure, yet his argument was thoroughly nationalistic and remains a classic of American nationalism to this day. The peculiar position of Webster was paralleled by that of the theocrats. Intensely nationalistic and "unionistic" in all their pronouncements and all their conscious objectives, they were yet Northerners and New Englanders to a far greater extent than they themselves realized.

PATTERN FOR TERRITORIAL EXPANSION

Between the annexation of Florida and the annexation of Texas the United States did not grow a great deal. Outlying territories were being populated and consolidated. The infiltration of Texas by Americans led to the Texan war of independence in 1836. The infiltration of the Oregon territory foreshadowed the tensions between Britain and the United States which nearly resulted in war in the early forties. A trickle of American emigrants reached California, but that faraway Mexican possession did not offer any real inducement prior to the discovery of gold in 1849. Only two states were admitted to the Union during this period: Arkansas in 1836 and Michigan in 1837. The usual political pattern required that every new free state should be matched by a slave state. In this way the precarious balance of power between North and South in the Senate continued to be maintained.

There is not much in the writings of the theocrats to indicate any particular awareness of, or alarm at, the sectional tensions of these relatively peaceful years. They believed that harmony between East and West could be insured by means of their efforts at the conversion and moral elevation of the West. They hoped that peace between North and South could be secured through the adoption and furtherance of the colonization movement. If they were conscious of the underlying economic causes of sectional tensions and if they felt any acute misgivings about the long-range fate of the Union, they did not express them. To do so would have been a denial of the efficacy of their pattern for solving the nation's problems. From time to time, however, expressions of pessimism cropped up in unguarded moments.

For instance, when John Holt Rice of Virginia was invited to become a professor at Princeton Theological Seminary, he declined the honor and accounted for his decision in a letter to Archibald Alexander in a revealing manner: "On acceptance, it would at once be said, 'Ah! this is what his love of Virginia has come to. Northern gold has bought him and it can buy any of them.' And thus my influence in the South would be greatly lessened, if not destroyed...."[51]

Rice's great project in life was to cement the ties between South and North by molding theological education in the South after the Northern pattern. To that end he finally succeeded in founding Union Theological Seminary at Richmond. He was also an ardent colonizationist and a close personal friend of many Northern Presbyterian theocrats. His refusal to go to Princeton at a time when sectional feeling was not even very pronounced shows that he was unusually sensitive to the deeper current of distrust and animosity which flowed between North and South and that he chose to remain in a lesser position in order to devote himself more effectively to his unionist activities. As a true theocrat he was also a true patriot.

James D. Knowles, a Baptist theocrat at Boston, showed a similar sensitivity to the menace of sectional divisiveness at an early date. In a Fourth of July sermon in 1828 he openly deplored "the great extent of our country" which was giving rise to sectional feeling "sometimes more powerful than that of patriotism."[52] With ill-concealed apprehension he asked: "Could local jealousies and jarring worldly interests ever lead the disciples of Christ to think of each other as enemies? Can you imagine that Christians in Missouri and Alabama could ever willingly consent to a dissolution of the national compact, which binds them to their brethren in New England? And much less, that they could ever meet each other with hostile bayonets in the field?"[53]

To the outsider, the high degree of cohesion achieved by the United States seemed admirable considering how young the nation was. To be sure, the two-member Baptist deputation from Britain found it hard to answer the persistent question,

[51] John Holt Rice, "Letter to Archibald Alexander, March 5, 1823," in *Memoir* by William Maxwell (Richmond, 1835), pp. 232-233.
[52] James D. Knowles, *Perils and Safeguards of American Liberty* (Boston, 1828), p. 19.
[53] *ibid.*, p. 24.

PATTERN FOR TERRITORIAL EXPANSION

"What do you think of America?" because of local and sectional divergences, yet their over-all impression was favorable. "There is a far greater identity among the confederated republics of America than among the separate kingdoms of Europe," they reported. "Time must be allowed for them to be molded into a general homogeneous uniformity."[54]

Meanwhile, the two major forces which the American environment brought into being—individualism and democracy—militated against the attainment of genuine nationality. Looking at the nation candidly and from the inside, the prospect was disquieting. At least one observer, writing from the New England point of view but largely transcending it, has left us a penetrating analysis.

William Watson Andrews, Congregational theocrat of Connecticut whose restless spirit ultimately led him to England and into sectarianism, noted in 1841 that the trend everywhere was toward centralization, toward concentrating more power in the national government—everywhere, that is, except in the United States, where states' rights provided a wholesome check on this dangerous trend. Up to this point he was not saying anything new, but affirming his belief in the American political system. Then, however, he developed his argument in a novel way. "It is an evil in this land," he wrote, "that the nation is merely the sum resulting from the addition of the parts, which are the states, instead of being a controlling power into which they enter as harmonious, integral forces."[55] He proceeded to warn that the union "is mechanical, not vital; an external band, not an inward law. The band may bear for a time the pressure of growth . . . but in the end it must be broken asunder."[56] Among the things which made the Union so unstable, Andrews observed the influence of immigrants from other than the Anglo-Saxon strain, the poverty of national symbols, in-

---
[54] F. A. Cox and J. Hobey, *The Baptists in America* (New York, 1836), p. 11.
[55] William Watson Andrews, *The Hebrew Commonwealth* (New Haven, 1841), p. 13.
[56] *ibid.*, p. 14.

cluding the utilitarian and uninspiring character of the nation's capital, but above all the lack of a central, integrating principle. "Is Christendom loosening its hold upon us? Are all organized bodies between the state and the isolated individual, losing their permanence and energy? Is society in all its parts growing restless and disjointed more and more? And is it ceasing to express, through symbolic national ordinances and popular customs, those great super-sensual truths, the possession of which is the glory of humanity and the highest source of strength to a land?"[57]

Andrews was not theocrat enough to find in Protestant Orthodoxy and a return to Puritan social morality the integrating principle which he knew was lacking in the United States. His later career proves as much. On the other hand, he did realize that "Christianity," however defined, had been such an integrating principle in times past, and that the individualism of Americans, which was both the parent and the child of American political democracy, was sapping the nation's strength by disrupting whatever collectivity or cohesion had been achieved since 1787.

For this process of disintegration, dramatically illustrated by the tensions between North and South and between East and West, nationalists like Henry Clay offered the abstract ideal of the Union as a remedy. Far more than Jackson who embodied so much of the individualism of the frontier, Clay represented secular nationalism at its best. He appealed constantly to "the spirit which made America a nation," to the "sense of national existence, of power, of bigness, of duty, in a word, of reality. "Without this sense, without this feeling in the hearts of Americans, the Union could not have resisted the corroding influence of slavery and could not have made itself, by a mighty effort, the huge, self-conscious, personal being that it is today."[58]

[57] *ibid.*, p. 23.
[58] Article, "Henry Clay," in *Cambridge History of American Literature*, edited by W. P. Trent et al. (3 vols., New York, 1917-1921), II, 88.

PATTERN FOR TERRITORIAL EXPANSION

Satisfactory as this might sound to the secularized thinking of our century, the theocrats refused to be satisfied with it. Within their own human limitations, of which sectional bias was one, they sought "a nation whose God is the Lord" and they endeavored to make the United States into a likeness of the ideal which they cherished—the Hebrew theocracy. Lacking in historic sense, they thought it possible to transplant the world of the Old Testament into the nineteenth century with only minor modifications. This was the mainspring of their opposition to American territorial expansion: they were afraid that the nation would become too big to be manageable by the means at their disposal, that Western "mobocracy" and Southern "slavocracy" would outstrip their efforts at making the United States the new Israel of God. Yet, during the comparatively peaceful interval between 1815 and 1844 only a few of them stopped to analyze the situation as a whole.

The Theocrats and American Expansion, 1844-1850

Expansionist sentiment reached a new, unprecedented peak in 1844. The Democrats, waging one of the most blatant as well as one of the most successful campaigns in all American history, subtly avoided the slavery question in their platform but included instead the demand for the "re-occupation of Oregon and the re-annexation of Texas." Nor was it altogether a conscious, cynical rationalization. Weinberg has shown that there was in the thinking of the expansionists of the forties a missionary element: they desired to extend the benefits of American freedom to territories and populations as yet unacquainted with it.[59]

The Presidential election of 1844 brought into power a "dark horse" who turned out to be far more spirited than even his supporters had anticipated. James Knox Polk, governor of Tennessee, "was not the nonentity that history often pictures him. Lacking in personal magnetism and dramatic qualities, he was

[59] Weinberg, *op.cit.*, chapter IV, *passim*.

a serious, methodical man of inflexible purpose and great executive capacity. His term was crowded with important events, and judged by his record, he was the greatest expansionist who ever occupied his high office."[60]

The annexation of Texas had been in the air ever since Texas had won her independence from Mexico in 1836. Northern opposition had been the principal factor in delaying its consummation for eight years.[61] The theocrats, though sharing the prevailing Northern apprehension of Southern aggrandizement, were not very vocal in their opposition. Most of them agreed with Francis Wayland that it was not desirable, since the United States did not need any more territory; that there were constitutional objections to it; but that it was a local issue, i.e., something for the Texans to decide, and that the South had no right to urge it any more than the North had a right to prevent it with a national measure.[62] Even in the heat of the campaign of 1844 the theocrats made no attempt to match the vehement pronouncements of the antislavery men who urged the repeal of the Union, should Texas be annexed.[63]

While the theocrats disapproved of the expansionist feelings of Southern ministers, they themselves contributed to the kindling of similar sentiments in the Northwest. As a matter of fact, the annexation of Oregon was considerably facilitated by the home missionary work of Northern Methodists and Presbyterians. The biographer of Jason Lee, pioneer Methodist missionary to Oregon, traces Lee's annexationist activity as far back as 1837 and assigns him a part in that memorial in which the settlers first petitioned Congress for annexation.[64] Lee's

[60] Hockett, *op.cit.*, p. 630.
[61] The standard monograph on the subject is Justin R. Smith, *The Annexation of Texas* (New York, 1919, 1941).
[62] Francis Wayland, *The limitations of Human Responsibility* (New York, 1838), pp. 11-12.
[63] See James Freeman Clarke, *A discourse on the annexation of Texas* (Boston, 1844), p. 15. Clarke was a Unitarian minister, editor and author.
[64] C. J. Brosnan, *Jason Lee, Prophet of Oregon* (New York, 1932), p. 219.

spirit appears clearly in the Oregon Memorial of 1838, composed in all likelihood by himself. It is a skillful blend of missionary propaganda and American nationalism.[65] During the following years, Lee worked ceaselessly to bring the territory into the possession of the United States. At last, the crucial year of 1844 he journeyed to Washington for a personal conference with President Tyler who assured him that Oregon would be annexed and that missionary claims would be respected.[66]

The part played by Marcus Whitman, pioneer Presbyterian missionary doctor in Oregon, was similar to that of Lee, but his relative significance is hard to determine because his colorful life and tragic death at the hands of Indian killers were spun into a legend by a missionary-minded author, until he came to be regarded as the one-man savior of Oregon.[67] It seems certain, however, that he rendered the United States a real strategic service by encouraging Protestant settlers to come to Oregon and by bearing witness to Oregon's potential value to the United States during his famous ride to Washington in the winter of 1842-1843.[68]

Whatever the missionary activities of the theocrats did or did not contribute toward the annexation of Oregon, it was evident that they did not favor it at the expense of war with Britain. We do not know how real the threat of war was, but it rated some attention among them and their view can be summed up in the argument of David B. Coe, pastor of a Presbyterian church in New York: "A narrow strip of bleak, inhospitable wilderness, 3,000 miles off. What a bargain!"[69] Daniel Sharp, a Baptist theocrat at Boston, went even further. He suggested that the United States and Britain might *both*

[65] *ibid.*, p. 221.
[66] *ibid.*, pp. 242-243.
[67] Myron Eells, *History of Indian Missions on the Pacific Coast* (Philadelphia, 1882), pp. 145-202 contains the "Whitman legend."
[68] This more balanced view of Whitman's role is given by C. M. Drury, *Marcus Whitman, M.D.* (Caldwell, Idaho, 1937), chapter xv.
[69] David B. Coe, *War as a means of settling national disputes* (New York, 1845), p. 7.

be better off without Oregon and favored letting it become an independent nation.[70]

In spite of such sentiments, however, it seemed to be the "manifest destiny" of the United States to possess at least part of the Oregon territory as well as all of Texas. The Democratic slogan of 1844 did not go the way of most campaign promises but was partially fulfilled. Texas joined the United States in 1845 and part of "Oregon" was annexed as a territory a year later. The same year of 1846 witnessed the march of the Mormons to Utah, the occupation of California, and the outbreak of the Mexican War. It was one of the most fateful years in American history: the vision of an American continental empire appeared on the horizon and, to make it come true, America plunged into her first imperialistic war.[71]

The Mexican War

There were many similarities between the War of 1812 and the Mexican War. In both wars the shift of the nation's center of gravity from the East to the West was a major factor. In both wars the opposing ideologies—Eastern "aristocracy" and Western "democracy," Northern freedom and Southern slavery —were reinforced and to a considerable extent motivated by the divergent economic interests of the manufacturing, planting, and agricultural sections. In both wars the most vocal opposition by any religious body came from the Congregationalists whose strength lay in New England and the Northwest.

Beyond these similarities, however, there were considerable differences. For one thing, the area of the United States had increased vastly between the two wars. Consequently the relative importance of New England and the North in general was much smaller in 1846 than it had been in 1812. New England and the Middle Atlantic States still furnished a dispro-

---

[70] Daniel Sharp, *A Plea for Peace* (Boston, 1846), pp. 17-18.
[71] The standard monograph on the war is Justin H. Smith, *The War with Mexico* (New York, 1919, 2 vols.).

portionate percentage of the religious and intellectual leadership of the country, but in politics they were far outweighed by the West, South, and Southwest. Again, in the War of 1812 the primary motive may have been expansion, but the justification of the war in terms of American self-defense had a far greater plausibility than it did in the Mexican War. In 1812 the United States might logically feel that the gains of the Revolution had to be consolidated by eliminating British influence from the Northwest and Spanish influence from the South. The nation was small and weak, and the presence of such European outposts might justifiably cause apprehension. By 1846, however, the United States had increased so greatly in population, material resources, and power that neither the British toehold in Oregon nor yet the presence of populous but woefully disorganized Mexico could hold any real threat to her security. Thus, to the extent to which the moral argument for war was weaker, the opponents of war had a better case.

The moral argument against the Mexican War was fully exploited by the Congregational theocrats. They rejected the official version of a "foreign invasion," which the administration used as the immediate justification for war.[72] They exposed the moral fallacy of the concept of "national honor." "What is called national honor," wrote Burdett Hart of Connecticut, "may not perhaps now allow this nation to recede from its present position. But before any decisive measures were taken by force, there was higher honor in treating so weak a neighbor with long suffering and great forbearance...."[73] It is not likely that by this exhibition of brute force "all nations will be taught to respect the American name and not to trifle with our rights," warned Samuel Harris. It is far more likely that history "will point the slow, unmoving finger of scorn" at an American victory over Mexico.[74]

Nor did these Congregational theocrats have any patience

[72] Samuel Harris, *The Mexican War* (Greenfield, Mass., 1877), p. 6.
[73] Burdett Hart, *The Mexican War* (New Haven, 1847), p. 7.
[74] Harris, *op.cit.*, p. 7.

with the "manifest destiny" argument. "The expansionists who talk about the destiny of the United States, observed Milton Braman, "claim that it is a part of the great plan of Heaven that the United States shall push its possessions from one limit to another, till it acknowledges no boundaries but the ocean. The doctrine of predestination seems to be a part of their political creed. I wonder if it is one of the articles of their religious faith also. But how do they know what the divine decree is with respect to the ultimate extent of the Union? The most rigid predestinarians do not pretend to be acquainted only with as much of the divine counsel as has been revealed. Does political predestinarianism assume to know more?"[75]

Behind "manifest destiny" there was the economic interest of the South in extending slavery. Why else would Calhoun have threatened secession, should the Wilmot Proviso become law? It was quite simple, the theocrats maintained. "The South has been indulged until she has become as willful and perverse as a pampered and petted child. For her the Florida and Louisiana purchases were made. For her a long and bloody war was maintained among the swamps of Florida. And when the North has hesitated to yield to her imperious demands, she has threatened a dissolution of the Union."[76]

Instead of seeing any honor or glory accruing to the nation from the war, the Congregational theocrats saw only the obvious evils attendant upon any war and the sure judgment of God for national wrong which the United States could not hope to avoid. Young Henry Ward Beecher proved to be a true son of his aged father when he exclaimed: "Why are men so sensitive, when, with the backing of Christ's whole Gospel, we deplore an unjust and foreign war, in which, by God's decree, every laurel will be made of a branch plucked from our own prosperity, and every honor will be paid for at the price of sure demoralization?"[77]

[75] Milton Braman, *The Mexican War* (Danvers, Mass., 1847), p. 10.
[76] Hart, *op.cit.*, p. 21.
[77] Henry Ward Beecher, *A discourse delivered at the Plymouth*

But the most clear-cut statement of the theocrats' viewpoint came from Milton Braman. The war, he warned, was going to increase the number and the power of new states where "intelligence, virtue, and strength of religious sentiment" were yet only feebly sustained by the necessary institutions. If these institutions cannot be created and/or expanded rapidly enough, the new areas will experience an upheaval which "will shake New England and the Atlantic States like an earthquake . . . if it does not overwhelm them in the same catastrophe. . . ."[78]

Such statements represent the attitude of the Congregational theocrats. Surprisingly enough, however, the theocrats in the other major denominations either remained silent or upheld the war effort.

Clayton S. Ellsworth has made a study of the attitude of the churches toward the Mexican War. According to his findings, the Congregationalists and Unitarians were wholly opposed because of their New England constituency, and so were the Quakers, because of their pacifist creed; the Episcopalians, Lutherans, Dutch and German Reformed were neutral; the Southern Methodists and Baptists wholly favorable; the Presbyterians (both Old School and New School), Northern Baptists and Northern Methodists ranged from lukewarm to favorable, with only individual exceptions siding with the opposition.[79]

Our own findings are much the same. We found only one Old School Presbyterian theocrat condemning the war, and his view was grounded in strong antislavery convictions which were exceptional among members of his denomination.[80] In the New School group Ellsworth found only one, Albert Hale of

---

Church, Brooklyn, New York, upon Thanksgiving Day . . . November 25th, 1847 (New York, 1848), p. 25.

[78] Braman, *op.cit.*, p. 17.

[79] Clayton S. Ellsworth, "American Churches and the Mexican War," *American Historical Review*, xlv, No. 2 (Jan., 1940), 301-326.

[80] Thomas E. Thomas, *Covenant Breaking and its Consequences* (Rossville, Ohio, 1847), *passim*.

PATTERN FOR TERRITORIAL EXPANSION

Springfield, Illinois, whose antiwar sermon brought down upon him the wrath of the Illinois legislature.[81] We may add another, Samuel G. Spees of Indianapolis who indicted the war as "a needless war . . . a war of aggression . . . a war for territory. . . ."[82] Among the Lutherans, Samuel S. Schmucker constituted a one-man exception. At odds with his denomination because of his conviction that Lutheranism should become American in language and thought as fast as possible, Schmucker did not share the unconcern of his brethren for the moral implications of the war, but condemned it as an undertaking which "at the tribunal of true Christianity . . . cannot be vindicated."[83]

We found no opposition to the war among Methodist theocrats, but at least three prominent Baptists went on record as opponents of the war, largely because of their strong antislavery views. These views, just as in the case of the Old School Presbyterians, were exceptional rather than common in their denomination. Morgan J. Rhees, pastor of the Second Baptist Church of Wilmington, Delaware, added to his antislavery convictions a lively interest in pacifism and in the temperance movement. With pitiless logic he expounded the absurdity of Christians in opposite camps praying before battle and then "rushing upon each other with the fury of tigers," while sacrificing all the hard-won gains of public morality in the general demoralization which follows in the wake of any war.[84] William R. Williams, one of the most accomplished writers in his denomination, based his objections to the war on the broad moral ground of justice. Applying the same standards to nations as to individuals, which was a basic principle of the

[81] Ellsworth, *op.cit.*, p. 313.
[82] Samuel G. Spees, *A discourse on the great American idea—universal liberty* (Indianapolis, 1848), p. 24.
[83] Samuel S. Schmucker, *The Christian Pulpit the Rightful Guardian of Morals in Political no less than in Private Life* (Gettysburg, 1848), p. 30.
[84] Morgan J. Rhees, *Our Privileges, the Measure of our Responsibility* (Wilmington, 1846), pp. 8-10.

theocrats, Williams contended that the fate of a "rapacious and unscrupulous nation" was sealed.[85]

Standing on the same broad moral ground, Francis Wayland came close to suggesting a boycott of the war effort. His meticulously logical argument was reminiscent of the restrained passion of Nathanael Emmons. Dissecting the individual's responsibility in a nation embarked upon a wrong course, Wayland concluded that "the fact that our country has commenced a course of wrongdoing in no manner whatever alters the moral character of the action," and that in the end the innocent would suffer along with the guilty for the nation's sin.[86]

Even Wayland's suggestion that it might still be possible to stop the war reads like an echo of the utterances of his spiritual forbears who believed that the War of 1812 could be brought to a speedy halt at any time, if only sufficient public opinion were marshaled against its prosecution. "Let the moral principle of this country only find an utterance," warned Wayland hopefully, "and party organizations would quail before its rebuke."[87]

Why were the Congregational theocrats virtually alone to oppose the War with Mexico, when the moral argument against the war was so much more powerful than it had been in 1812? The answer seems to lie in the nature of the foe. In 1812 the United States faced Protestant Britain; in 1846 the enemy was Catholic Mexico. War with Britain meant the sundering of friendly ties whose strength had just begun to be tested in the nascent foreign missionary movement. War with Mexico, while regrettable, promised an opportunity for missionary expansion into Catholic territory—a most welcome challenge.

This argument was used, of course, by the Southern Baptists and Methodists unashamedly and vociferously. We can trace it from the scathing criticism it received by one who opposed the

---

[85] William R. Williams, "The Prayer of the Church against those who Delight in War" (1847), *Miscellanies* (New York, 1850), p. 386.
[86] Francis Wayland, *The duty of obedience to the civil magistrate* (Boston, 1847), pp. 37-38.
[87] *ibid.*, p. 42.

war. "I care not for the good that may come of it to that miserable, unhappy Republic," wrote Samuel G. Spees. "This will afford us no justification. Napoleon conquered to *republicanize*. For trampling on justice and the rights of nations, God hurled him from his throne. Shall we adopt his policy and conquer to protestantize?"[88]

Yet, the missionary motive applied to a Catholic nation—and perhaps to an entire Catholic continent—fascinated the theocrats of all the major denominations (except the Congregationalists) to the point where their conscientious scruples about the justice of the war were either stilled, or at least considerably quieted. In many sermons preached by theocrats at the return of peace the secular expansionist argument about the "extension of freedom" appears linked with the missionary argument about bringing the Gospel to the Mexicans. Nicholas Murray's statement furnishes a typical and comprehensive example. The Presbyterian theocrat whose literary clashes with Archbishop Hughes had won him nationwide repute as an anti-Catholic of the "sweetness and light" approach, commented on the peace: "We sincerely hope that our recent war, much as all good men deplored it, may be overruled for the good of the benighted and semi-civilized Mexico. . . . However we may object to the manner of obtaining these vast territories, or to the incorporation of their people with ours, there can be no question as to the good resulting to the people themselves. And seeing that the territory is ours, and that its people are our fellow-citizens, the best way to repair the evil of war among them is speedily to send to them the institutions, and the Gospel, of peace. And already are the ministers and missionaries of our own church preaching the Gospel in districts of ancient Mexico, where until recently the voice of a Protestant Minister could not be raised save at the risk of his life."[89]

We have to conclude, then, that denominational rivalry ac-

[88] Spees, *op.cit.*, p. 25.
[89] Nicholas Murray, *Special causes of gratitude* (Elizabethtown, New Jersey, 1848), pp. 7-8.

counts for the apparently inconsistent attitude of the theocrats toward the Mexican War. The Congregationalists opposed it because they had no stake in its gains: their constituents were largely in New England and their missionary outreach, even through the Plan of Union of 1801, had not led to any significant gains for them. The Presbyterians had kept pace with the expanding frontier and were eager to share in the spiritual spoils of the war, though they did not necessarily approve of the war itself. The Northern Methodists and Baptists, having separated from their Southern brethren only a year before the outbreak of the war, had not yet learned to think of themselves as Northerners rather than as just Baptists and Methodists. Hence they could not condemn the war which promised their denominations such obvious rewards, even though by the end of the war they were to awaken to the fact that the booty had passed not into their hands, but into the hands of the Southern bodies.

California and Beyond

Toward the end of the Mexican War, the expansionist fever reached a new height. In spite of Polk's determination not to prolong the fighting unnecessarily, the loudest proponents of "manifest destiny" insisted on the annexation of all Mexico. But Polk was adamant. The treaty of Guadalupe Hidalgo did not make any additional demands on the defeated nation and was ratified by the Senate in February 1848. America had achieved the dimensions of a continental empire, though the immediate result of this colossal territorial expansion was an intensification of the sectional tensions which presaged civil war.

Meanwhile the theocrats, who had been unable to resist the lure of new missionary fields, found that reality outstripped their wildest dreams. To their opportunities in Texas and New Mexico was added California. The discovery of gold in that territory led to a mass migration of men and to an onset of prosperity unprecedented in history. Within a year California was admitted to statehood. The disorders of the Gold Rush have been so thoroughly described that the solid, unspectacular work of missionaries, trying to create communities out of the surging, inchoate masses, has been largely forgotten. Yet, they were there and they persisted against unusual odds. As for the discovery of gold, it only confirmed their belief in America's destiny under God, who had kept "the immense treasures of California . . . even from the keen-scented Spaniard," in order to bestow them upon a Protestant nation.[90]

"The occurrence of the war—the acquisition of this country by it—the establishment of a line of steamships to open communication with it—all this apparently to prepare the way for the great discovery soon to follow and the consequences resulting!" exclaimed Samuel H. Willey, the first emissary of the American Home Missionary Society to reach California.[91]

To be sure, Willey was writing ten years later. Yet, this image of California's destiny and potential glory did not exist only in the retrospect. J. A. Benton, founder and minister of the first church in Sacramento, had such a vision even in the midst of the sordid confusion of the Gold Rush. While realizing all the "ills and vices of progress" due to the lack of the "restraints of love, beauty, and home," he professed his faith that "the wisdom which is guiding the complications of the vast machinery of God's moral government . . . will secure the triumphs of grace and truth on these western shores.[92] Then, triumphantly, he added: "With all the genius of Americans, with all the tact and shrewdness of New Englanders, with all the energy of Saxons, California shall become the richest, mightiest, noblest, and most renowned of all the States that

---

[90] E. L. Cleaveland, "The Home Missionary Argument," *The Home Missionary*, XXVI (July, 1853), 64.

[91] Samuel H. Willey, *Decade Sermons, preached at the Howard Street Presbyterian Church, San Francisco, March, 1859* (San Francisco, 1859) p. 17.

[92] J. A. Benton, *California, as she was, as she is, as she is to be* (Sacramento, 1850), pp. 12-13. Preached on Thanksgiving, 1849.

glitter and blaze in the grand constellation of the north, whose radiance already beams on all the earth."[93]

The same year the two corresponding secretaries of the American Home Missionary Society submitted a report which matched the "imperialistic" enthusiasm of Southern Democratic politicians. After noting that God had saved Oregon and California "for a people of Pilgrim blood . . . for a new empire about to arise in the Pacific world," these two theocrats demanded that the institutions of the Gospel should be speedily established and consolidated on these shores, so that the "cities and villages" springing up there might become "the abodes of regenerate men, and sources of light and salvation to the thousand Isles of the Sea that lie beyond."[94] The acquisition of New Mexico, the report continued, has brought into the United States "a Spanish race under a government which does not shield it from the free access of Protestant Christianity." American influence is bound to extend itself into Central and South America and Protestantism will accompany it. "A Yankee saw-mill now performs its offices, fifteen hundred miles from the mouth of the Amazon; and a 'Down Easter,' who once wielded his axe on the banks of the Kennebec, fulfills the same mission on the shore of the Rio Negro. . . . This ascendance of the vigorous over the feeble nations is not necessarily wrong, it is the natural superiority and irresistible progress of freedom, knowledge, and enterprise, when brought in contact with ignorance and inactivity."[95]

This statement is the more remarkable since it came from Congregational theocrats reporting to a society which by this time had become overwhelmingly Congregational. It took only a year even for the Congregationalists to forget the moral aspects of the war by which these missionary opportunities were secured, and to embody Manifest Destiny in their belief concerning America's world role.

[93] ibid., p. 14.
[94] Milton Badger and Charles Hall, "Correspondence from the Home Missions Field," *The Home Missionary*, XXII (June, 1849) 43, 45.
[95] ibid., pp. 46-47.

Before considering the theocratic concept of America's world role, however, we must pause long enough to determine the attitude of the theocrats toward the problem of war in general. How could the theocrats crusade against the religious and moral effects of war and yet not be wholly opposed to war itself? There was, among the reform movements of the day, a small but growing peace movement. Why did the theocrats not embrace it as an integral part of their pattern for an American theocracy?

The Theocrats and War

The primary reason for the inability of the theocrats to endorse the peace movement was that the letter of the Bible did not forbid war. It was much the same thing as when they were facing the problem of slavery. The Old Testament expressly allowed both. The New Testament did not expressly forbid either. Only the "spirit of Jesus," that nebulous though intensely real and convicting power, condemned both slavery and war. This, however, the theocrats dared not accept as the supreme moral criterion, since it lent itself to speculation which soon left the firm ground of Revealed Truth for the realm of reforming zeal and unbridled fancy.

The outstanding textbook of ethics which continued to be used almost exclusively in the colleges and seminaries of the theocrats until the middle thirties was William Paley's *Moral and Political Philosophy*, which first appeared in London in 1788. Though he could have marshaled the whole Old Testament in support of the rightfulness of war under certain circumstances, Paley's article, "Of War, and of Military Establishments," confines itself to the New Testament, showing that the military profession is not inherently unchristian and that war itself is not intrinsically evil. "The justifying causes of war, are, deliberate invasions of right, and the necessity of maintaining such a balance of power amongst neighboring nations, as that no single state, or confederacy of states, be strong enough to overwhelm the rest. The objects of war are precaution, defence, reparation. In a larger sense, every just war is a defensive war, inasmuch as every war supposes an injury perpetrated, attempted, or feared."[96] Making all moral judgment upon the causes of war a matter of casuistry, Paley proceeds to consider the proper conduct of war in the same spirit, concluding that "if the cause and end of war be justifiable, all the means that appear necessary to that end are justifiable also."[97]

Of course, Paley was not alone responsible for the entire thinking of the theocrats on the problem of war, yet his work was an influential summary of the "just war" theory which the Churches of "classical Protestantism" had embraced and which only the later and lesser Protestant bodies rejected with any degree of consistency.[98]

The oldest consistent pacifism was that of the heirs of the Anabaptists, who in the United States were represented by the Mennonites,[99] the Brethren,[100] and other small sects, largely outside the main stream of American life. What is more, the wars of 1812 and of 1848 were fought by volunteers, so that there was no occasion to test the faith of the nonresistant churches.[101] Younger in years but far stronger in the United States was the pacifist witness of the Quakers.[102] The Disciples of Christ, a growth of the American soil, began as a pacifist sect. All their early leaders, with the exception of Walter Scott, were avowed pacifists.[103] Alexander Campbell, one of the most

[96] William Paley, *op.cit.*, in *Works* (Philadelphia, n.d.), p. 162.
[97] *ibid.*, p. 163.
[98] In this generalization Methodism, though arising two centuries after the Reformation, must be classified with the Anglican tradition. For a summary of the Lutheran, Calvinistic, and Anglican theory, see Roland H. Bainton, "The Churches and War: Historic Attitudes Toward Christian Participation," *Social Action*, January 15, 1945, pp. 22-26.
[99] See Guy F. Hershberger, *War, Peace, and Non-Resistance* (Scottdale, Pa., 1944), the standard monograph on Mennonite pacifism.
[100] See Rufus D. Bowman, *The Church of the Brethren and War, 1708-1941* (Elgin, Illinois, 1944).
[101] Henry C. Smith, *The Story of the Mennonites* (Berne, Indiana, 1941), p. 790.
[102] Margaret Hirst, *Quakers in War and Peace* (New York, 1923), chapter XVI.
[103] Garrison and DeGroot, *The Disciples of Christ* (St. Louis, 1948), p. 335.

original figures on the religious scene in the first half of the nineteenth century, was also the author of one of the strongest and most widely distributed pacifist treatises.[104] Over against the Old Testament emphasis of the theocrats, the pacifists stressed the dichotomy between the "two covenants" and the supremacy of the New Testament. No less literalistic than the theocrats, Alexander Campbell nevertheless worked out an approach whereby he could justify pacifism from the New Testament. Under the "old covenant," he asserted, "wars waged by God's people . . . were waged under and in pursuance of a special divine commission. They were, therefore, right." There is however, no similar warrant under the "new covenant." "What the God of Abraham, did by Abraham, by Jacob, or by any of his sons, as the moral governor of the world, before he gave up the sceptre and the crown to his Son Jesus Christ, is of no binding authority now."[105]

Yet, like William Paley, the theocrats did not need to fall back on the Old Testament for support of the "just war" theory. The fact that the New Testament did not expressly forbid war was enough. This view was shared not only by the overwhelming majority of the theocrats, but also by nontheocrats in the Anabaptist tradition who, rather than resist Caesar, took Christ's words about rendering him his due at face value. John Leland has left us a comprehensive exposition of this point of view.[106]

It appears, then, that the theocrats opposed the War of 1812 and the Mexican War for patriotic (and largely sectional) reasons rather than because of any real opposition to

[104] Alexander Campbell, *Address on War* (1848); in *Popular Addresses and Lectures* (St. Louis, 1861), pp. 342-366.
[105] Campbell, *op.cit.*, p. 350.
[106] Leland, *Free Thoughts on War* (1816); in *Writings* (New York, 1845), pp. 454-468. Constitutionally averse to religious and moral societies, Leland directed these thoughts against the newly-founded Massachusetts Peace Society. For an expression of the same views at the end of our period, see the "Essay on War and Christianity," in *The Gospel Proclamation*, vols. I & II (1847-1848), published at St. Clairsville, Ohio, by Alexander Hall.

war in general. To be sure, the agents of the Massachusetts Peace Society and later of the American Peace Society found ready admittance into their pulpits, and prayers for peace were offered on special days. Yet, although a large proportion of the life members of the Society were ministers, only a relatively small number of them were open advocates of peace.[107] It was easier to endorse peace as a desirable objective than to fight for it at the cost of being called disloyal and unpatriotic. The leaders of the peace movement, including clergymen like Noah Worcester and Samuel J. May, were primarily reformers. They believed in absolute moral principles and fought for their adoption regardless of the cost. Just like the abolitionists, they had scant regard for their country when they felt that their country was morally in the wrong, or for the Union when the Union was being preserved at the price of moral compromise. It was by no means a mere coincidence that the leadership of the abolitionist societies and of the peace societies overlapped to a considerable extent: the fiercest abolitionists—William Lloyd Garrison, Wendell Phillips, Charles Whipple, Amasa Walker, and many others—were also the champions of the most uncompromising antiwar platform.[108]

The only denomination which furnished a number of active participants to the peace societies from among its theocrats was the Baptist denomination. This was probably due to their remembrance of the Anabaptist heritage, though the denomination as a whole remained insensitive to its claims. Francis Wayland, though a noted theocrat and author of the textbook on ethics which virtually superseded Paley's work[109] did not set the tone for the rank and file of his fellow-Baptists, nor yet for the theocrats at large. Noah Worcester was a Baptist, but

[107] Merle Curti, *The American Peace Crusade, 1815-1860* (Durham, N.C. 1929), p. 48.
[108] *ibid.*, p. 81.
[109] *The Elements of Moral Science* (First Edition, Boston, 1835). The section on war, pp. 392-397, goes a long way toward the platform of the peace societies, even to the extent of suggesting that a nation might safely remain defenseless, since its very defenselessness and high moral principle would make it safe from outside aggression, cf. *ibid.*, p. 395.

after 1815 he devoted himself so completely to the cause of peace that his denominational background became irrelevant. Nor did he seem interested in any other reform movement beside his own. Howard Malcom, President of a Baptist college in Kentucky, was fairly prominent in the movement and contributed two articles to an anthology published by the American Peace Society.[110]

The American Peace Society tried to muster antiwar sentiment during the Mexican War and there was, of course, considerable responsiveness among the Congregational theocrats, yet even their resolutions on peace did not condemn war in general. The same attitude was manifest in Northern Methodism. As for the Presbyterians, both Old School and New School adopted the Society's suggestion for a day of confession and prayers for peace, but refused to voice any wholesale condemnation of war.[111]

It is significant that one of the most comprehensive expositions of the problem of Christianity and war which was written during our period came from the pen of a Southern Presbyterian theocrat, Thomas Smyth of Columbia, South Carolina. To hear Smyth—a pro-slavery man defending the Mexican War—condemn the "wild enthusiastic philanthropy" of the reformers "which attempts to be wiser and more merciful than God," one might think he was listening to a Northern theocrat.[112] Christianity's plan to abolish war, Smyth concludes in approved theocratic fashion, "is not by national but by individual reformation. . . ."[113]

Yet even Smyth would not go as far in his acceptance of war as did Hollis Read, a Northerner and a Congregationalist, as soon as the War with Mexico was over. Noticing the "in-

[110] "War Inconsistent with Christianity," and "Criminality of War," in *Book of Peace* (Boston, American Peace Society, 1845), pp. 129-136 and 433-448.
[111] *The Peace Advocate*, VII (1847), 135-136.
[112] Thomas Smyth, *The Relation of Christianity to War* (1847); in *Works* (10 vols., Columbia, S.C., 1908-1912), VIII, 353.
[113] *ibid.*, p. 70.

PATTERN FOR TERRITORIAL EXPANSION

strumentality of war in preparing the world to receive the gospel," Read waxes almost lyrical over its wonderful use by God's Providence. "War is the sledge-hammer of Providence to break in pieces the great things which he will destroy. The wrath of man is made to praise him. . . . When he would demolish the time-honored and seemingly insurmountable obstacles which India presented to ever becoming a Christian nation, he commissioned a people fierce in countenance and skillfull in carnage, . . . first to punish them for their abominable idolatries, and next to remove the difficulties to their evangelization, . . . When he would cut the bars of iron, and break the gates of brass which shut out China from the family of nations and the benign influences of Christianity, he again commissioned the scourge of war and British cannon."[114]

Summary

Thus the Biblical literalism of the theocrats prevented them from condemning war in general, while their intense missionary spirit, combined with their patriotism, induced them to justify—if not the causes, at least the effects—of particular wars. When such wars involved what the American people regarded as the working out of their Manifest Destiny, the theocrats could not long sustain their opposition. This was true in the Mexican War and, half a century later, in the Spanish American War. During World War I the patriotic temper of the country rose to such a feverish pitch that few clergymen cared to or dared to defy it.[115] Ironically, that war was fought in order to establish world peace, as if the cynical words, "Si vis pacem, para bellum" had never been spoken.

In World War II there were fewer illusions and therefore greater self-criticism, in which the clergy shared. Yet, the bit-

[114] Hollis Read, *The Hand of God in American History* (Hartford, 1848-1850), p. 226.
[115] The monograph, *Preachers Present Arms*! by Ray H. Abrams (New York, 1933), shows conclusively the American clergy's uncritical attitude toward the patriotism of World War I.

ing sarcasm of an "Aged Clergyman," writing after the War with Mexico on "When and how certain people would have ministers preach peace," is still as relevant as ever. "Never preach on peace at a time of religious indifference for then more important matters demand attention. Never at a time of religious activity, for then the great work of conversion needs all our efforts. Never in such a manner as to bring our militia system into disrepute. Never in times of peace for it is then unnecessary. Never in time of war, for it might be considered a 'political sermon.' Never carry the principles of Christ so far as to be suspected of any ultra or Quaker notions."[116] If we substitute "armed forces" for "militia system" and "pacifist" for "ultra or Quaker," this satirical tidbit might have been written a hundred years later.

The theocrats were not pacifists but they were able to seek ends beyond the narrow boundaries of sectional or even national selfishness. Their missionary spirit, which helped them to accept the fruits of unwelcome wars, was more than a rationalization of any "Christian expansionism." It was rather a logical extension of the pattern, which, beginning with the United States as God's new Israel, was destined to embrace the whole world of nations. In this sense, they had a fixed and striking idea of America's world role.

[116] *The Peace Advocate*, VIII (1849), 43.

CHAPTER VIII

THE THEOCRATIC PATTERN FOR AMERICA'S WORLD ROLE

IF the theocrats adapted themselves easily to American territorial expansion, in spite of their opposition to the means by which this expansion might be carried out at times, it was because they were filled with a vision of America's world role. This vision represented the final working out of their belief in the United States as God's New Israel. It originated with the Puritan founders of New England, merged with the exuberant optimism of the Enlightenment, and reached its peak in their reaction to the European revolutions of 1848.[1]

The two great facts which helped articulate the theocratic pattern for America's world role were America's growing independence from Europe and the foreign missionary movement. The achievement of America's political independence from England antedated her achievement of emotional independence by at least half a century. The theocrats as a group did much to further this subtle process of "nationalization." Furthermore, the foreign missionary movement which they themselves launched, spearheaded American orientation toward Asia and the Islands of the Pacific, which, in turn, helped speed the attainment of emotional independence from Europe even further. Throughout our period we notice the theocrats' growing conviction concerning the political and religious mission of the United States. This conviction foreshadows American twentieth-century "imperialism," which has, in fact, retained many of the ideological features of the theocratic pattern.

America and Europe

The United States is the child of Europe. The peculiar relationship which always exists between parent and child was

[1] There was a similar ideological outburst in 1917-1918, cf. Ray Abrams, *Preachers Present Arms!* (New York, 1933), *passim.*

very much present in the early days of this nation. "There was a fundamental ambivalence in the relations of the new American nationalism to Europe. Each national idea gains its emphasis by contrasting itself with and differentiating itself from another concept; in the case of America, this concept was Europe."[2]

This dual attitude of admiration and repudiation was most pronounced toward England, the mother country. The theocrats, on the whole, were far more favorable to England than most of their fellow Americans. This was due partly to their New England background, actual or educational, and partly to their indebtedness to the example of British Protestant enterprise. Nearly all their societies had British models. Even the foreign missionary movement originated, at least in its modern sense, in England.

Throughout our era British criticism of the United States was, with some exceptions, violently adverse. "Americans were ridiculed for their execrable taste, their vulgar manners, their unlimited bigotry, their colossal ignorance and vanity. Or they were denounced as a slave-flogging, materialistic, gross, undisciplined people, devoid of true religious feeling. In the United States, it was charged, democracy ran riot, political corruption fouled public life, demagoguery reigned supreme, and property was unsafe from the mob."[3] The *Edinburgh Review* apparently outdid all other British sources in its hostile attitude. British travelers in the United States, only too ready to judge in typical tourist fashion, wrote a number of witty but extremely biased accounts of the young nation. It required a great deal of patience on the part of the theocrats to endure the tone of such criticism, no matter how just some of its contents might be. As early as 1819, John Holt Rice expressed the theocrats' wish for a more temperate attitude on the part of the British press while noting that "the general effect of the

[2] Hans Kohn, *The Idea of Nationalism* (New York, 1944), p. 292.
[3] Merle Curti, *The Growth of American Thought* (New York, 1943), p. 245.

scant praise and abundant censure bestowed on us convinces me that the people of this country, in general, esteem the British more than they do any but themselves, and would rather have their praise and enjoy their friendship, than that of all the world beside."[4] The majority of distinguished British visitors did not come until the thirties and the forties. Their fault-finding attitude was duly excoriated by the theocrats as well as by other patriotic Americans, but the theocrats were always sensitive to the deep-seated spirit of kinship which underlay, or should underlie, British-American relations.[5]

Exchanges of visits between the Protestant forces of England and the United States further helped to cement that friendship which uncharitable criticism rendered so precarious. The visits of Baptist and Congregational "deputations" from England during the middle thirties were received with interest and good will[6] and the semi-official tours of Robert Baird did much to give at least British Protestants a more truthful and more favorable impression of America and of their American brethren.[7]

If British criticism was tolerated, there was no such feeling toward continental Europe. As a matter of fact, the theocrats not only shared but actively fostered that distrust of, and contempt for, Europe, which was so characteristic a symptom of the growing pains of the United States. In the first place, the theocrats shared the contempt of their fellow Americans for the "despotic" governments of Europe. They identified Na-

[4] John Holt Rice, "Letter to Thomas Chalmers, August 14, 1819," in *Memoir* by William Maxwell (Richmond, 1835), p. 169.
[5] This is evident even in such a spirited polemical article as that on "British Tourists in the United States" in the *Methodist Quarterly Review*, xxviii (1846), 508-534, which tears apart the criticisms of Trollope, Martineau, Dickens, and others, yet manages to show a sincere concern for Anglo-American friendship.
[6] See *The Biblical Repertory and Theological Review*, vii 598-626.
[7] Baird's work, *Religion in America*, which was originally published in London in 1835 for British consumption, went through several editions and incidentally helped American Protestants to see themselves in terms of their common characteristics instead of in terms of their denominational differences.

poleon with the Antichrist and rejoiced over his downfall. Yet the members of the Holy Alliance who brought the Little Corporal to his knees were not any more attractive to them than he had been. Metternich's police state became the target of particularly violent criticism because of its alleged Catholic missionary designs upon the United States. The constant wars of Europe furnished more fuel for criticism. As early as 1800 Nathanael Emmons found in the ongoing self-destruction of Europe the proof of his belief that the United States would inherit Europe's imperial power and thus fulfill her divinely appointed destiny.[8]

To the extent that the theocrats scorned despotism, they were naturally in sympathy with European movements for national independence and political and religious freedom. They followed with genuine concern the Greek war of independence and helped organize aid for Greece. Expressions of their sympathetic interest can be found in a number of contemporary sermons and several of the lesser theocrats devoted full-length offerings to the subject.[9] This desire for the success of the Greeks was all the more logical, since the enemy was Mohammedan Turkey. Hollis Read, writing in the retrospect of a quarter-century, made it plain that anything contributing to the downfall of that pagan power "must be considered as a providential instrumentality employed by the great Head of the Church, to prepare for the coming of His kingdom."[10]

Yet this sympathy for nations struggling for liberty was severely restricted by the extreme conservatism of the theocrats. They praised liberty as the highest goal to be fought for,

[8] Nathanael Emmons, "God Never Forsakes His People" (1800), in *Works* (six vols., Boston, 1842), II, 177, 178.
[9] cf. John Wilson, *A Sermon delivered at Leicester (Mass.)* . . . *December 5, 1822* (Leicester, 1823), Gregory J. Bedell; *The cause of the Greeks* (Philadelphia, 1824); Sereno Edwards Dwight, *The Greek Revolution* (Boston, 1824). Nelson and Dwight were Congregationalists, Bedell Episcopalian.
[10] Hollis Read, *The Hand of God in American History* (Hartford, 1850), p. 277.

but they were harshly critical of revolutionary methods. Philip Lindsley contrasted the failure of European revolutions with the success of the American Revolution with considerable smugness by saying that European revolutions could not hope to succeed until the people achieved a higher degree of "political training."[11] He failed to realize that their governments would not give them the opportunity to do so peaceably which made violence inevitable, so that the only hope was for each revolution to bring a somewhat larger measure of freedom.

Horace Bushnell took a more dynamic view of the progress of liberty in Europe, but, in common with all the theocrats, he claimed an exorbitant share of credit for the influence of the United States. "Whatever motion there has been in European affairs for the last half century," he wrote, "all the mitigations of law, the dynasties subverted, the constitutions conceded, the enlarged liberty of conscience and the press, popular education, everything that goes to make society beneficent, has been instigated more or less directly by the great idea that is embodied and represented in the institutions of the United States."[12] The same belief was expressed by Elisha Ballantine, Pastor of the First Presbyterian Church of Washington, D.C. All well-informed observers of Europe, Ballantine noted, have been increasingly aware of the fact that "there is a disturbing power somewhere.... They are not mistaken. In the popular movements, both political and religious, of the last twenty years in Europe, 'America' has been the watchword."[13]

Thus the theocrats were able to reject revolution as a means toward the attainment of freedom and yet give their nation credit for inspiring the revolutions of Europe, from the French

[11] Philip Lindsley, "An address on the occasion of the centennial birthday of George Washington" (1832), in *Works* (3 vols., Philadelphia, 1866), III, 238-243.
[12] Horace Bushnell, "Moral Uses of the Sea" (1845), in *Moral Uses of Dark Things, Works* (8 vols., New York, 1881), VI, 349-350.
[13] Elisha Ballantine, *America, the teacher of nations* (Washington, 1850), p. 8. For a detailed analysis of the Revolutions of 1848 from this point of view, see "The Revolutions of 1848," *Methodist Quarterly Review*, XXX (1848), 535-552.

Revolution to the Revolutions of 1848. At the same time they were gradually getting over their fear of European plots such as the alleged conspiracy of the Leopold Foundation. Toward the end of our period they began to assert boldly that the United States was impervious to such dangers, not so much because of her military power as because of the inherent worthwhileness and stability of her institutions. "As to these revolutions [of 1848]," wrote Nicholas Murray, "we have nothing to fear.... We have no privileged classes, no hereditary nobility, no rulers by divine right, no state and stall-fed ecclesiastics putting forth their preposterous pretensions to the possession of the keys of heaven. We have all that the people of Europe are seeking to gain by their revolutionary efforts."[14]

John Williamson Nevin, noted leader of the German Reformed Church, called the year 1848 the beginning of the "American Epoch." He contrasted the political convulsions of Europe with the peaceful progress of American republicanism and gloried in America's nonviolent expansion into Texas, Oregon, and California.[15] In the same vein the President of a Baptist College in Kentucky complacently noted: "As Americans, we can derive but little help from the study of history, or the observation of the present struggles in Europe. History furnishes us no precedent; and the present races of Europe are neither in character nor condition like our people. With them, reformers must attack and alter the whole structure of society. The correction of a few abuses, and disposition of a few errors, and the elevation of private morals is all we need."[16]

The most blatantly smug reflection on the Revolutions of 1848, however, came from the pen of William A. Scott, Presbyterian pastor at New Orleans. Permanent prosperity for

[14] Nicholas Murray, *Special Causes of Gratitude* (Elizabethtown, 1848), p. 10. Alonzo Potter, Episcopal Bishop of the Diocese of Pennsylvania, reached the same conclusion; cf. "Our Country Admonished" (1848), in *Discourses of Bishop Potter* (Philadelphia, 1858), p. 216.
[15] John W. Nevin, *The Year, 1848; or, The American Epoch* (n.p., 1848), *passim.*
[16] Howard Malcom, "The Genuine Reformer," in *Western Baptist Review,* IV (1848-1849), 421.

America, Scott asserted, was not impossible, no matter what might be happening to Europe. "If a whole nation, or a kingdom, or a continent, should be sunk into the ocean, it would not destroy the rest of the world. So, if one part of the civilized world should go back to barbarism, it would not endanger the existence and diffusive power of the best forms of modern civilization. From the pole to the equator and from ocean to ocean, *God has raised up a people in modern times to be witnesses for political freedom and religious faith*, so that if it were possible for the bosom of destruction to sweep out of existence the Europe of today, in ages to come it would exist in another hemisphere—if not in Australia, yet certainly in America."[17]

World Mission by Example

Thus the theocrats had a Monroe Doctrine of their own. The original Monroe Doctrine, promulgated by President James Monroe in his message to Congress in 1823, contained three major principles: the principle of isolation, which originated in Washington's warning against "entangling alliances"; the principle of paramount interest, which Jefferson formulated with regard to Louisiana and (later) Cuba and Spanish America in general; and the principle of self-determination, which arose largely from American sympathy for the struggle for independence of the Spanish-American colonies.[18]

The theocrats shared the Monroe Doctrine's general distrust of other nations. They were not readily convinced of the application of the doctrine of paramount interest to American territorial aggrandizement, insofar as this benefited the slaveholding South, but they acquiesced in the inevitable for the sake of their own "paramount interest" in the evangelization

[17] William A. Scott, "The Hope of Republics, or, the elements of permanence in modern civilization," *American National Preacher*, xxiii (1849), 67.
[18] The authoritative monograph on the subject is Dexter Perkins, *Hands Off; a history of the Monroe Doctrine* (Boston, 1941).

of Roman Catholic populations. They also shared in the general concern for the success of the struggle for independence of the Spanish colonies, but their well-wishing was never very aggressive not only because they disliked revolutions, but also because they distrusted the nominally Catholic peoples who were fighting them.[19]

Beyond these feelings, however, the theocrats supplemented the Monroe Doctrine with an unshakable belief in the power of the example of the United States upon the world. In this belief their faith in American political institutions and their faith in Protestant orthodoxy blended harmoniously. The peculiar mission of God's American Israel was to keep her political and religious institutions so pure that their excellence would be self-evident and that the rest of the world would be induced to adopt them by sheer force of example.

"Our country has given to the world the first ocular demonstration, not only of the practicability, but also of the unrivaled superiority of a popular form of government," affirmed Francis Wayland.[20] The human race will not experience the "moral renovation" which it needs, claimed Lyman Beecher, unless there are first considerable changes in "the civil and religious conditions of nations"; notably, "the monopoly of the soil must be abolished," "the monopoly of power must be superseded by the suffrages of freeman," and "the rights of conscience must be restored to men." However, "to accomplish these changes, a great example is needed . . . some nation, itself free, must blow the trumpet and hold up the light."[21] "It cannot be," exclaimed Robert Baird, "that God has taken such pains to

[19] Expressions of sympathy with the Spanish-American colonies were always tempered by such misgivings; e.g. Joshua Bates, *The Influence of Christian Truth* (Boston, 1825), p. 19., saw no hope for them, "unless the papal yoke also be broken from their necks," and Lyman Beecher, *The Memory of Our Fathers* (Boston, 1828), p. 22, came to the same conclusion.

[20] Francis Wayland, "The Duties of an American Citizen" (1825), in *Occasional Discourses* (Boston, 1833), p. 61.

[21] Lyman Beecher, *The Memory of Our Fathers* (New Haven, 1826), pp. 6-9.

plant this nation; to watch over it with such care and raise it up to its present greatness, in order only that it might be a *Depository* of his blessed Gospel. Oh, no; he would not have us merely Depositories, but Depositaries—stewards, or *Almoners* rather—to whom he has entrusted this great boon, to impart it to others who have need."[22]

"Our Heavenly Father has made us a national epistle to other lands," affirmed William R. Williams. "See that you read a full and impressive comment to all lands, of the power of Christian principle, and of the expansive and self-sustaining energies of the gospel, when left unfettered by national endowments, and secular alliances. The evangelical character of our land is to tell upon the plans and destinies of other nations."[23]

"We have furnished an example and a model," noted Philip Lindsley with satisfaction, "which has already contributed much to enlighten the world in the theory and practice of government, and which promises incalculable good to mankind throughout all succeeding generations."[24]

In the light of this confident hope it was all the more important that America should be thoroughly Christianized. How else could the example be perpetuated? The theocrats did not believe in the automatic survival of American institutions. Only Protestant Christianity guaranteed their vigor and permanence.[25] In America, Charles Hodge observed, the tragic mistake of Europe's disunity was being speedily corrected. The United States is becoming one people, "having one language, one literature, essentially one religion, and one common soul." Such a nation is bound to exert "a greater influence on the human family than any other nation that has ever existed." Therefore, "our national character being of such unutterable

[22] Robert Baird, *National Prosperity; A Thanksgiving Sermon* (New York, 1847), pp. 11-12.
[23] William R. Williams, "Christ, a Home Missionary" (1836) in *The Missionary Enterprise* (Boston, 1846), p. 93.
[24] Lindsley, *op.cit.*, p. 255.
[25] John Codman, *Home Missions; A sermon* ... (Boston, 1826), p. 11.

importance to the world, it may be questioned whether a generation ever lived on whose fidelity so much depended."[26]

The entire program for the evangelization of America was presented increasingly in terms of America's responsibility to give the world an example of civil liberty and pure religion. It was in this vein that Richard B. Storrs of Massachusetts challenged the American Sunday School Union to double its efforts against "Sectarianism," "Romanism," "Infidelity," and "Atheism": the "prospective influence going forth from us to affect the destinies of the world" demanded as much.[27] In the same vein Gilbert McMaster of Indiana admonished the students of Hanover College that America had to be educated, because "to America is committed the cause of both God and Man, under circumstances very peculiar; circumstances to which other nations have hitherto been strangers."[28]

To forfeit this opportunity seemed to involve a very grave risk. The analogy of ancient Israel could be applied with the utmost consistency. Intended by God to be an example to the world by which all the nations might find their way to Him, Israel betrayed her trust and was punished accordingly. "Greece and Rome with all their foul idolatries were not quickly destroyed; but Jerusalem was suddenly and fearfully overwhelmed. So will it be with us. . . . No wrath is so consuming as that which falls on a people whom God has blessed in vain. The Jews are an example. Like them we are blessed —in mercy may we never share their withering curse!"[29]

Such, the theocrats believed, would be the result of faithlessness. But the fruits of faithfulness would be glorious beyond words. Even now, Philip Lindsley asserted, "I am an American citizen," ranks as high as the ancient "Civis Romanus sum."

[26] Charles Hodge, "Anniversary Address," in *The Home Missionary*, II (1829), 18.
[27] Richard S. Storrs, *The Importance of Religiously Instructing the Young* (Philadelphia, 1845), p. 33.
[28] Gilbert McMaster, *The Obligations of the American Scholar to his Country and to the World* (Madison, Indiana, 1841), p. 12.
[29] Leonidas Lent Hamline, "Christian Patriotism; A discourse . . ." (1841), in *Works* (3 vols., Cincinnati, 1871), I, 413. Hamline was a Methodist bishop.

Only "Christian" ranks higher than "American," and why should the two not be linked forever? "Why should not *American Christian* become the characteristic, distinct appellation of our people? so that we might justly be esteemed as the noblest, holiest, happiest, freest, most disinterested and charitable portion of the human family? Then would the philanthropist, the patriot, the republican, the Christian, be all combined and blended in the one great name, *American*. And he would be joyfully hailed as the missionary of liberty and light, of religion and peace, of mercy and salvation, to an oppressed, benighted, and perishing world."[30]

Thus America's mission to be the political and religious example for the whole human race was defined by the theocrats in terms of both responsibilities and opportunities. However, in a society which was essentially optimistic and activistic, such a sense of mission could not long be contained within the narrow definition of an example. To be sure, the nations had seen and heard; they had responded by unprecedented movements toward civil and religious freedom; their citizens were coming in increasing numbers to the country where these high ideals were being realized. Yet, it was temperamentally impossible for the theocrats to leave it at that. Their pattern for America was not only for America: it was for the whole world, and they were not willing to impart it to the world by example alone any more than they were willing to let the American West develop its potentialities by merely copying the East. It was by no accident that "national missions" and "foreign missions" began at the same time. The theocrats had conceived them not as two separate tasks but rather as two facets of the same task.

The Missionary Outreach

The beginnings of American foreign missions were closely linked with British missions. The London Missionary Society

[30] Philip Lindsley, "Name of Our Republic" (1849), in *Works* (3 vols., Philadelphia, 1866), I, 589.

which came into being in 1795 through the agitation of William Carey, antedated the American Board by fifteen years. As a matter of fact, Judson and Mills were going to be sent out under the auspices of the London Missionary Society, but, owing to the political tension between England and the United States, the Prudential Committee of the newly-founded American Board found it advisable that their journey to Burma should be underwritten by the "Christian public of the United States." "Would it not be a reproach to our character as a Christian nation, as well as an ungrateful distrust of Providence, should we resign our missionaries to the London Society...?"[31]

On February the 6th, 1812, a historic service took place in the First Congregational Chuich of Salem, Massachusetts. Five young men were commissioned by the American Board as "missionaries to the heathen in Asia...." It appears from Leonard Woods' sermon that the significance of their missions was conceived solely in evangelistic terms. The implications of their journey in terms of American influence upon the world had not yet dawned on the theocrats.[32]

The early missionaries were unconscious of any mission beyond converting the heathen. The Foreign Missions School at Cornwall, Connecticut, boasted a number of students from the Sandwich Islands (i.c. Hawaii), but there was no indication of any concern with imposing the "American way of life" upon the converts, though the prime mover of the school, Samuel J. Mills, took it for granted that these young men would not only "Christianize" but "civilize" their islands, once

[31] American Board of Commissioners for Foreign Missions, *First Annual Report* (1811), in *The First Ten Annual Reports of the A.B.C.F.M.* (Boston, 1834), p. 23. The Prudential Committee consisted of Jedidiah Morse, Samuel Worcester, and Jeremiah Evarts.

[32] Leonard Woods, *Sermon, delivered in Salem* (Boston, 1812), *passim*. For the history of the American Board, see William E. Strong, *The Story of the American Board; an account of the first hundred years of the A.B.C.F.M.* (Boston, 1910).

they returned.³³ A recently discovered journal of one of the earliest missionaries to Hawaii discloses the same innocence.³⁴ So far as we could ascertain, no missionary in our period ever expressed the hope that their work abroad might prepare the way for American colonization or even pave the way for American influence. Yet, such was the inevitable by-product of the missionary enterprise. In the case of Hawaii, for instance, the pioneering of the missionaries opened the islands to American commerce which in the course of one generation brought her within the sphere of the Monroe Doctrine's "paramount interest" principle and eventually under American tutelage. John Quincy Adams' Report of the Senate's Committee on Foreign Affairs in 1842 contains an explicit reference to the "mild and gentle influence of Christian charity" which first brought Hawaii within the sphere of interest of the United States until the people of the United States were now bound, "by a virtual right of conquest," to watch over her lest she should fall into the hands of the French.³⁵ Yet, if the missionaries themselves did not conceive of their task in even faintly "imperialistic" terms, the theocrats at home soon connected their evangelistic obligation with the fulfillment of America's mission to the world. They commenced to see this connection as soon as the work of the missionaries began to affect the economic and social structure of non-Christian societies.

To be sure, some of the most prominent theocrats professed indifference to the civilizing effects of missions. Archibald Alex-

³³ *A narrative of five youths from the Sandwich Islands, now receiving an education in this country* (New York, 1816), pp. 43-44.

³⁴ Samuel and Nancy Ruggles, "Missionary Journal, 1819-1820," published in *The Atlantic*, cxxxiv (1924), 648-657. The authors were one of seven couples who, after graduation from Cornwall, went to Hawaii under the auspices of the American Board and succeeded in beginning work by the favor of a prince who built them a "cocoanut grove church."

³⁵ Hiram Bingham, *A Residence of Twenty-one Years in the Sandwich Islands* (Hartford and New York, 1848), Appendix, pp. 588-589. Bingham was one of the original missionaries, along with Ruggles and five others. On the subject of French designs on Hawaii, cf. E. L. Cleveland, "The Home Missionary Argument," *Home Missionary*, xxvi (1853), 63.

ander urged that even "if we could communicate the arts and refinements of civilized life to savages, it is not evident that this would at all prepare and dispose them for the reception of the Gospel."³⁶ Even toward the end of our period no less an authority than Rufus Anderson, Secretary of the American Board, deplored the tendency of the missionary movement to exceed its evangelistic commission by interfering with the social and economic environment of its converts. "The creation among heathen tribes and nations of a highly improved state of society, such as we ourselves enjoy," seemed wholly undesirable to him.³⁷

Yet, the views of Alexander and Anderson represented a minority viewpoint. The majority of the theocrats freely admitted that Protestant Christianity was bound up with the political destiny of the Anglo-Saxon nations. Whether this was a lofty evangelical point of view or one inspired by a rather uncritical nationalism, the fact remains that it was realistic and that it proved right not only for the first half but for the whole of the nineteenth century. For Protestantism's fate continued to be linked, to a large extent, with England and America.

One of the chief aids to their missionary endeavors which the theocrats perceived was the English language. Noting the eminent adaptability of evangelical Christianity which made it, potentially at least, the universal religion, Samuel Miller remarked with satisfaction that "if the time should ever again recur, when the 'whole earth shall be of one language and one speech,' the English, is more likely to be that language than any other."³⁸

The fondness of the theocrats for "Protestant England" became the more pronounced, the more the memory of the Amer-

[36] Archibald Alexander, *Objections Obviated and God Glorified by the Success of the Gospel among the Heathen* (Boston, 1830), p. 12.

[37] Rufus Anderson, *The theory of missions to the heathen* (Boston, 1845), pp. 4-5.

[38] Samuel Miller, "The Earth Filled with the Glory of the Lord" (1836), in *The Missionary Enterprise* (Boston, 1846), p. 154.

ican Revolution faded into the background. As brothers-in-arms in the missionary enterprise, this natural predilection could not fail to grow. Bishop George Washington Doane's affirmation that "Great Britain and America are set for the two hemispheres, to be the buglemen of freedom and the standard-bearers of the Cross,"[39] would have been endorsed by most of the theocrats. The nucleus of America's national character, asserted Bela Bates Edwards, Secretary of the American Educational Society, "is British or English Puritan." This, he thought, was something to be thankful for, because of the prevalence of the English language which is "basically a religious language"; because of the moral integrity which distinguishes England from all the other nations of Europe"; and because of the "desire of this element to diffuse itself widely, that is, its missionary spirit."[40]

The theocrats received some unexpected assistance from Alexander Campbell, who, after starting out as one of the strongest opponents of foreign missions, reversed himself completely and came out as a champion of America's mission to the world. Lecturing in Cincinnati in 1849, Campbell called English "the language of Protestantism" and made a case for the noblest language serving the noblest religion. "Now it is not as strong a proof of the superiority of our ancient Saxon progenitors, as it is of the superiority of Christianity to any form of paganism, that those ancient invaders of England and Ireland, after giving them laws, condescended to receive from them both language and religion? But it may be alleged that they received the language of the conquered because that language had in it a religion more evidently true and rational than theirs. Grant it, and what follows? That our religion will be a passport yet to our language into all the nations of the earth!"[41]

[39] George Washington Doane, "America and Great Britain" (1848), in *Educational Writings and Orations* (New York, 1848), p. 227.
[40] Bela Bates Edwards, "The Influence of the United States on other Nations" (1848), in *Writings* (2 vols., Boston, 1853), II, 848-891.
[41] Alexander Campbell, "Address on the Anglo-Saxon Language" (1849), in *Popular Lectures and Addresses* (St. Louis, 1861), p. 34.

The second great aid which the theocrats found useful in their missionary endeavors was the expanding commerce of England and America. Some of them did not fail to see the damages inflicted upon their work by the commercial spirit with its disregard for human beings, its ruthless competition, its indulgence of demoralizing habits. The same tension between commercial and missionary expansion had become more than evident in dealing with the American Indians. "As soon as the faithful missionary of the cross has begun to succeed in turning the miserable heathen from his idols, and in cleansing them from their pollutions, modern commerce, with its four great maces, war, slavery, intemperance, and disease, beats to the earth the work of heavenly benevolence, and knocks in the head the new-born hopes of regenerated tribes!"[42]

This outcry of an Episcopal theocrat from Brooklyn pictures realistically the ambiguous relationship between the "christianization" and the "civilization" of primitive peoples. Yet, further in his discourse, the same man assumes a very optimistic attitude by proposing to "convert modern commerce," by finding firm ground for hope in the fact that lately Britain and the United States had become the leading commercial nations in the world. "Why has modern commerce fallen mainly into the hands of two of the most Christian nations in earth; of two nations most active in support of Christian mission; of two nations, which, in the irrepressibly enterprising and colonizing genius of their kindred races, command the world;— Great Britain and the United States? Why, but that God is beginning his work of converting this commerce to himself, and thus bringing over the earth the brightest day of glory that ever shone. . . . Commerce, in the hands of Christian nations, can never go back and become what she has been!"[43]

Horace Bushnell, on the other hand, seemed to lack Stone's critical insight but exceeded him in his praise for the help

[42] John S. Stone, "The bearings of modern commerce on the progress of modern missions" (1839), in *The Missionary Enterprise* (Boston, 1846), p. 257.
[43] *ibid.*, pp. 264, 266.

which commerce seemed to be extending to the cause of religion. Commerce, Bushnell believed, had drawn the nations together and had lifted them, from a "footing of barbarism" to a "footing of friendship and civilization." Commerce also advances religion by making it "more catholic." "In this manner we anticipate the day when commerce itself shall become religious, and religion commercial; when the holy and the useful shall be blended in a common life of brotherhood and duty, comprising all the human kindred of the globe."[44]

Thus, both the spread of the English language and the expansion of British and American commercial enterprises which carried it, inspired the theocrats with glorious visions of missionary success. In this sense their pattern for the world seemed to be indissolubly linked with the growth of British and American supremacy. "Whatever may be said of English ambition, or of her pride, avarice, or oppression," wrote Hollis Read, the historian of the theocrats, "whatever opinion the political moralist may form of the justness of her negotiations (which are little else than terms dictated by a stronger to a weaker power), one thing is undeniable; wherever English power is felt, there the arm of protection and assistance is extended to the missionary.... Sheltered under the wings of the Almighty, which are spread over him in the shape of British dominion, he commences his work, confidently expecting to be able to finish it."[45] And if this was judgment of a leading theocrat on the usefulness of British imperialism to the missionary enterprise, how much more might the rank and file of the theocrats welcome the extension of American influence over the world. Yet, just as their patriotism hardly ever degenerated into the "my country right or wrong" variety, so their sanction of American "imperialism" was conditioned upon making American influence worthy of the ideals which the United States professed

[44] Horace Bushnell, *Moral Uses of the Sea*, p. 357.
[45] Hollis Read, *The Hand of God in American History* (Hartford, 1850), p. 160.

and embodied. Specifically, they were careful lest America should make a less-than-Christian impact upon the world.

This abstract principle can best be illustrated by referring to the concern of the theocrats with the evangelization of American seamen. Shortly after the War of 1812 missionary societies were organized to minister to sailors in American ports. Later chapels were erected for their use in various ports all over the world. On the surface this may seem to be just another sign of the thoroughness with which the theocrats set about their evangelistic task. Yet, one of the earliest sermons of this missionary project by a representative theocrat puts the matter squarely in terms of America's world role as a Christian nation. American seamen, noted Edward Dorr Griffin before the New York Marine Missionary Society, "present a bar to the spread of the Gospel, by raising prejudices against the Christian name in every heathen port they visit. . . . But let them be brought under the sanctifying influence of Christianity, and they will become, though not formal, yet efficient missionaries to every part of the world. . . . They will become reconnoitering parties, everywhere dispersed, to make out and present to the eye of the Church a graduated scale of human misery, to show where aid ought first to be applied."[46]

Thus the theocrats fitted this particular project into the global application of their pattern in which a Christian America was destined to bring Christianity to all the world, together with the choicest by-products of Christianity, notably republican political institutions and a lofty personal morality. Truly, exclaimed John Mason Peck, when reviewing the success of the missionary enterprise (though still in its infancy), "Jesus Christ is about to possess the whole earth!"[47] With this

[46] Edward Dorr Griffin, *The claims of seamen* (New York, 1819), p. 15. For a similar viewpoint, see John B. Remeyn, *A sermon . . . for the benefit of the New York Marine Missionary Society* (New York, 1819); Stephen Chapin, *The conversion of mariners will enlarge the praises of Zion* (Portland, 1821); *Sailors Magazine,* published by the American Seamen's Aid Society (New York, 1821).

[47] John Mason Peck, *Fifty Year's* [sic] *Retrospect* (St. Louis, 1825), p. 5.

exclamation the Methodist theocrat struck the keynote of the theocratic pattern for America's world role, which was, of course, the expectancy of the coming of the millennium.

The Millennial Perspective

Much has been written on the strange sects and cults which arose in the tumultuous thirties and forties. The Millerite "end-of-the-world" craze which swept the upper part of New York State received its share of attention. Usually, however, this preoccupation with the imminent return of Christ is treated as a purely sectarian phenomenon, without any awareness of its prevalence among the orthodox clergy. It seems plausible, however, that the practical millenarianism of the theocrats represented the religious counterpart of the buoyant secular optimism which they could not help absorbing from their American environment.[48]

It was a *practical* millenarianism. William Miller and his followers went out on a hilltop to wait for the Lord; the theocrats preferred to hasten his coming by helping him work out his purpose in the world. As early as 1813 Timothy Dwight depicted to the American Board the glory of that day when there would be "one fold and one Shepherd" (John 10:16), reminding his hearers, however, that Christ was going to conquer the world "not by miracles but by means," and specifying that the preparations for that day would be accomplished "by Protestant nations, and, extensively by Us."[49] Francis Wayland minced no words about the grand objective of the theocrats in preparing for the day of the Lord. "Point us to the loveliest village that smiles upon a Scottish or New England landscape, and compare it with the filthiness and brutality of a Caffrarian Kraal, and we tell you that our object is

[48] A. A. Ekrich, *The Idea of Progress, 1815-1860* (New York, 1938), *passim*.
[49] Timothy Dwight, *A Sermon . . . before the A.B.C.F.M.* (Boston, 1813), pp. 21-22.

to render that Caffrarian Kraal as happy and gladsome as that Scottish or New England village."[50]

Samuel S. Schmucker, the Lutheran theocrat, found the Sabbath School system "admirably adapted to train up a generation of Christians for millennial plans and millennial action," since "in that halcyon day of millennial triumph the minor peculiarities of sect will be thrown into the background, and Christians meet on the broad platform of the Bible. . . ."[51]

Struggling with the antimission elements in Alabama, Hosea Holcombe admonished the Baptists that the missionary enterprise was indispensable for the coming of the millennium.[52] In thorough agreement with his humble Baptist colleague, Mark Hopkins, the illustrious President of Williams College, concluded that three things were clearly indicative of the coming of the millennium: "the subjugation of the powers of nature to the use of man"; "the attempt to realize . . . the liberty and rights of the individual man"; and the "benevolent and reformatory movements" of the age. These phenomena, he believed were "a natural, and almost necessary, preparation for the final triumph."[53] There was no doubt in the minds of the theocrats that the working out of their pattern for America, and through America for the world, was laying the groundwork for the Second Advent.

[50] Francis Wayland, *The Moral Dignity of the Missionary Enterprise* (Boston, 1823), p. 9.

[51] Samuel S. Schmucker, *The happy adaptation of the Sabbath-school system to the peculiar wants of our age and country* (Philadelphia, 1839), p. 17. See also Leonard Bacon, "The Day Approaching," *American National Preacher*, xvi (1842), 123-129.

[52] Hosea Holcombe, *A History of the Rise and Progress of the Baptists in Alabama* (Philadelphia, 1840), p. 362.

[53] Emerson Davis, *The Half Century; a History* . . . (Boston, 1851). Introduction by Mark Hopkins, D.D. Quotation from p. xxi.

CHAPTER IX

THE THEOCRATIC PATTERN IN THE RETROSPECT

IN his authoritative study of modern nationalism, Hans Kohn makes much of the "image which a nation forms of itself and in which it mirrors itself...."[1] This image, he observes, is compounded of reality, tradition, imagination, and aspiration, but it transcends its constituent parts in much the same way as personality transcends the sum total of the person's traits.[2] Insofar as such an image becomes articulate enough to furnish a program for action for a party or a group of men, it develops into a *pattern*.

The patriotism of the theocrats exemplified this process. They were Americans wrestling with the realities of a nation in the making. They injected into the struggles of their day the note of a distinct tradition, notably that of political Calvinism, mediated through the New England Puritans. To the extent to which they constantly overestimated the significance of their doings, they were victims of the kind of imagination which lies behind all human endeavors in which emotion plays a large part. Above all, their patriotism embodied an ideal toward which their nation was supposed to be moving by divine decree. This created a tension between America-as-she-was and America-as-she-ought-to-be, and a fervent, sometimes visionary aspiration toward that goal.

The tendency of this patriotism, however, was not so much progress as conservation. The theocrats would have preferred to retain the pre-revolutionary social order, in spite of their hearty endorsement of the American Revolution as a struggle for independence from Britain. They would have been happier, had there been no mass migration of Irish and German Catholics to the United States. They believed that the solution of

[1] Hans Kohn, *The Idea of Nationalism* (New York, 1944), p. 289.
[2] *ibid.*, p. 290.

America's two major racial problems lay beyond the frontiers of the nation and that colonization of the Indians in the Far West and of the Negroes in Liberia would ultimately result in a satisfactory adjustment not only for the United States but for these races as well. They viewed the industrialization of the East and the growth of the West as threats to the social *status quo*, before discovering the challenge and the opportunities inherent in these changes. Consequently their standards of individual and social morality were more in the nature of a reaffirmation of the "Puritan virtues" than of a constructive adaptation of such standards to a new day. Their resistance to American territorial expansion, though based on sound moral arguments, was also influenced by their desire to preserve the dominance of the East over the South and the West. Only their dream of America's world role, couched in missionary terms, seemed relatively free from conscious or unconscious rationalizations. In our estimation, the foreign missionary movement was the most idealistic and most far-reaching part of the theocratic pattern.

This conservative character of the theocratic pattern has been apparent to its twentieth-century critics and they have pointed it out sometimes with more malice than understanding. Parrington applies his anti-Puritan bias to these heirs of the Puritans with damaging results.[3] James Truslow Adams disposes of them with more wit than fairness. "The Puritan had possessed some sterling traits. His descendant became mainly Puritanical. His belief in himself as the chosen of God lingered long after the relationship had probably become repugnant to the Deity: it certainly had to the New Englander's fellow-citizens in other sections."[4]

H. Richard Niebuhr points out that they embodied Puritanism at its institutional stage, at a time when the original

---

[3] Vernon L. Parrington, *Main Currents in American Thought* (3 vols., New York, 1927), II, 321-328, "Liberalism and Calvinism."

[4] James Truslow Adams, *The Epic of America* (Boston, 1933), pp. 158-159.

PATTERN IN RETROSPECT

momentum of the Puritan movement had all but spent itself, and that they adulterated the basic concepts of classical Puritanism by institutionalizing them. "The sovereign God of Lyman Beecher and his colleagues is an absentee monarch who declared his will in a remote past and caused it to be recorded in irrefragable laws . . . conceived to have been once and for all established in nature and published in the Bible, so that the latter comes to be a book of statutes rather than an aid to the understanding of God's living will."[5] This process of institutionalization was accompanied by a corresponding process of nationalization. "The old idea of American Christians as a chosen people who had been called to a special task, was turned into the notion of a chosen nation, especially favored. . . . As the nineteenth century went on, the note of divine favoritism was increasingly sounded."[6]

Thus there is one group of critics who see little or no creative strength in the theocrats and who appraise the theocratic pattern in terms of sterile reaction only. There is, however, another group whose criticism seems to be more suggestive as well as more charitable. Oddly enough, these critics all borrow from the most merciless contemporary critic of the theocrats: Calvin Colton. It was Colton who first compared the strategy of the theocrats, revealed in their associations, to the Roman Catholic Counter Reformation. Colton did little more, however, than indict the "jesuitical" character of these attempts at minority control over society. He granted that the theocrats were marshaling and exercising considerable power, but failed to see any good in their objectives. Evarts B. Greene, reviewing Colton's estimate nearly a century later, arrives at a more mellow conclusion. He traces the resemblance between the Counter Reformation and the theocratic pattern under four headings, notably (1) restatement of orthodoxy, (2) centralization of authority, (3) clerical education, and (4) organized

[5] H. Richard Niebuhr, *The Kingdom of God in America* (New York, 1927), pp. 173-174.
[6] *ibid.*, p. 179.

missionary effort.⁷ To the extent, then, to which the theocrats could be compared to the champions of the Counter Reformation, their pattern could not be dealt with in terms of mere reaction. It was rather a revival and an adaptation of something which had proved its worthwhileness under different circumstances.

Greene's estimate of the theocrats was adopted by another eminent twentieth-century historian, Dixon Ryan Fox. Fox accepts Niebuhr's theory of movement and institution, but does not condemn the theocrats for attempting to preserve, in institutional form, the gains of the Second Awakening. Furthermore, he points out the connection between this "counter-reformation" and American nationalism evidenced in the "nationalization" of the societies of the theocrats.⁸ This aspect of the theocratic pattern is more fully developed by Arthur M. Schlesinger, in his "Biography of a Nation of Joiners," in which he points out that throughout American history "self-constituted bodies . . . reaching out with inter-locking membership to all parts of the country . . . have served as a great cementing force for national integration."⁹

For our part, we have pointed out the extreme political, social, and religious conservatism of the theocrats. We may add that they did not produce many outstanding personalities, though some of them, like Timothy Dwight, Charles Hodge, or Lyman Beecher, were forceful thinkers and capable ecclesiastical statesmen. We may now recall some of the enduring contributions of the theocrats together with the contemporary relevance of their pattern.

Perhaps the greatest achievement of the theocrats was that in an age of intense individualism they bore witness to God's concern for the affairs of human society. To be sure, their application of this principle was narrow and naïve. They took

---

⁷ Evarts B. Greene, "A Puritan Counter-Reformation," American Antiquarian Society, *Proceedings*, n.s., XVIII (1931), 17-46.

⁸ Dixon Ryan Fox, "The Protestant Counter-Reformation," *New York History*, XXXIII (1935), 28.

⁹ *American Historical Review*, L (1944), 25.

over the seventeenth-century "American Israel" motif uncritically and used it with considerable self-righteousness, implying that *they* were America and that others should either conform or remove themselves. Yet, they were at least concerned with God's claims upon the life of the United States, and to the extent to which their patriotism included a measure of self-criticism, it contributed a necessary corrective to the exuberance of early American nationalism. This element of self-criticism, rooted in their conviction of America's destiny in God's plan, could become, with considerable adaptation, a constructive factor in twentieth-century American thinking. "The habit of seeing one's nation under God, under what we may regard as God's criticism, would take most of the poison out of international relations. It would help to break the vicious circle of self-righteous denunciation between Russia and the Anglo-Saxon nations."[10]

Another significant achievement of the theocrats was that in an age of isolationism they pioneered for world-mindedness. Of course, it is anachronistic to use the term isolationism at this stage, but the United States was, in point of fact, isolated from the rest of the world both geographically and by the design of the Monroe Doctrine. Here, too, the theocrats applied a worthwhile principle narrowly and naïvely. Their interest in the world was primarily evangelistic, with little concern for the mundane welfare of other nations and races. Yet, by conceiving a plan for the "evangelization of the world in this generation"[11] by American missionaries, and by enlisting the American Christian public in support of this enterprise, they did much to awaken in the United States a sense of moral responsibility toward the rest of the world. Of course, during the last hundred years such lofty and desirable sentiments have

[10] John C. Bennett, *Christian Ethics and Social Policy* (New York, 1946), p. 67.
[11] A phrase borrowed (anachronistically) from the Student Volunteer Movement and quoted in this context by Robert E. Speer in "Christianity and International Relations," *Christianity and Modern Thought*, edited by Ralph H. Gabriel (New York, 1924), p. 195.

often been used to cloak imperialistic designs, but even the most unsympathetic critics of the United States have not been able to deny the existence of some genuine idealism and altruism in this "messianic complex."[12] It is a great tribute to the theocrats that the foreign missionary movement which they initiated in the United States has been largely responsible for the growth of that world community which today stands more united than ever in a world which is more divided than ever: the ecumenical church. There is now, in spite of two world wars, an unprecedented degree of fellowship and mutual concern among the Christian communities of the nations, seeking "to heal the wounds of war, to reestablish the sense of human solidarity across all boundary lines . . . and to rally men of all cultures and nationalities to a supranational loyalty."[13] The theocrats, of course, could not anticipate the momentous consequences of the movement which they launched, but that should not detract from their merit in launching it.

A third real achievement of the theocrats is closely related to the second. Having foreshadowed the universal rule of Christ, they also were aware of the need for unity among themselves. Their societies, insofar as they were interdenominational or undenominational, were *ipso facto* a unitive force. It mattered little that the early period of harmonious and growing cooperation was followed by an era of intensified denominational rivalry in much the same way as the reasonably harmonious nationalism of the twenties was followed by the increasingly bitter sectionalism of the forties and fifties. The spirit of the earliest ecumenical efforts in America was never wholly lost. That most remarkable document, known as "Schmucker's Appeal," should be cherished by champions of the reunion of Christendom as one of the most far-sighted

[12] See M. J. Bonn, *The American Experiment* (London, 1930), especially chapter IV, "Missionary Fanaticism," for such a grudging admission.

[13] Paul Hutchinson, "Christian Missions and Imperialism," *The Christian World Mission*, edited by William K. Anderson (Nashville, 1946), p. 240.

documents of its kind.[14] To be sure, Schmucker was a prophet "born out of time." His unionist activities made him an outcast among his fellow-Lutherans as well as one of the most widely controverted figures of nineteenth-century American Protestantism. Yet, his "Appeal" did not contain the vision of just one man. It had, at least when it was first submitted to the public (1838) the written endorsement of some of the brightest stars on the theocratic firmament: Justin Edwards, Stephen Tyng, Eliphalet Nott, Thomas H. Skinner, Moses Stuart, Nathan S. S. Beman, Jeremiah Day, and William Cogswell.[15] Regardless of its practical merits or demerits, the "Appeal" constitutes a landmark in the American phase of the history of the Ecumenical Movement. It also reveals the awareness of the theocrats of the need for a common witness and concerted action, which harmonized with their desire for a firmly united nation and their apprehension of national disunity. In both church and nation this striving for unity was going to be thwarted by the course of events, but that does not alter the fact that it did represent an extraordinarily progressive viewpoint for the time.

To sum up: the theocrats stood midway between the church-controlled state of the Middle Ages and the state-controlled church of modern times. They were able to conceive of a nineteenth century "theocracy" because American nationalism was still in its infancy.[16] They struggled to retain a measure of ideological control over the United States, for fear that she might become an ungodly nation. Had they known that the vacuum which Protestant orthodoxy was leaving behind would be filled by the idols of secularism, they would have fought

[14] Samuel S. Schmucker, *The True Unity of Christ's Church*. Gettysburg, 1838. (Reprinted at New York, 1870.)

[15] *ibid.*, 1870 edition, pp. 15-17. These theocrats were all among the original officers of the Evangelical Alliance. Others like Leonard Bacon, Gardiner Spring, Joel Hawes, Robert Baird, were to join them within a decade; see *ibid.*, pp. 29-32.

[16] Ralph H. Gabriel, *The Course of American Democratic Thought* (New York, 1940), p. 38.

even more tenaciously. They would also have exercised even more self-criticism and restraint in their patriotic utterances for fear that anything less than a prophetic voice might help pave the way for the sterile, secularized "Americanism" of the nineteen-fifties.

BIBLIOGRAPHY

OCCASIONAL SERMONS AND DISCOURSES: CONGREGATIONAL

Abbott, Abiel, *Traits of Resemblance of the People of the U.S.A. to Ancient Israel.* Haverhill, Mass., 1799.
Alden, Timothy, *The Glory of America.* Portsmouth, N.H., 1801.
Alger, William R., *Inferences from the Pestilence and the Fast.* Boston, 1848.
Anderson, Rufus, *The Theory of Missions to the Heathen.* Boston, 1845.
Andrews, William Watson, *The Hebrew Commonwealth.* New Haven, 1841.
Appleton, Jesse, *A Sermon . . . on account of the Peace Recently Established between this Country and Great Britain.* Hallowell, Maine, 1815.
Austin, Samuel, *The Apology of Patriots.* Worcester, Mass., 1812.
Bacon, Leonard, *Christian Unity.* New Haven, 1845.
———, *The Day Approaching.* New Haven, 1842.
———, *A Plea for Africa.* New Haven, 1825.
———, *Slavery Discussed in Occasional Essays from 1833 to 1846.* New York, 1846.
Bancroft, Aaron, *A Discourse . . . before the Worcester Auxiliary Society for Meliorating the Condition of the Jews.* Worcester, 1824.
Bates, Joshua, *Influence of Christian Truth.* Boston, 1825.
———, *A Sermon . . . before the Society for Propagating the Gospel among the Indians.* Boston, 1813.
Beecher, Henry Ward, *A Discourse upon Thanksgiving Day.* New York, 1848.
Boudinot, Elias, *An Address to the Whites.* Philadelphia, 1826.
Braman, Isaac, *Union with France, a Greater Evil than Union with Britain.* Haverhill, Mass., 1810.
Braman, Milton, *The Mexican War.* Danvers, Mass., 1847.
Brooks, Charles, *Elementary Instruction.* Quincy, Mass., 1837.
Bushnell, Horace, "American Politics; A sermon" (1840), *Life and Letters*, edited by Mary C. Bushness (New York, 1880), pp. 93-95.

261

BIBLIOGRAPHY

Bushnell, Horace, *Barbarism, the First Danger* (1847), *Works* (New York, 1881, 6 volumes), v, 230-261.

———, *A Discourse on the Slavery Question.* Hartford, 1839.

———, *Moral Uses of the Sea* (1845), *Works*, vi, 344-360.

———, *The True Wealth and Weal of Nations* (1837), *Works*, v, 43-77.

Chapin, Calvin, *A Sermon . . . before the Connecticut Society for the Promotion of Good Morals.* Hartford, 1814.

Chester, John, *A Sermon, in Commemoration of the Landing of the New England Pilgrims.* Albany, 1820.

Codman, John, *The Faith of the Pilgrims.* Boston, 1832.

———, *The Duty of Americans to Send the Gospel to the Heathen.* Boston, 1836.

———, *Home Missions.* Boston, 1826.

Cummings, Asa, *A Discourse . . . for the Annual Fast.* Brunswick, Me., 1820.

Dana, Daniel, *A Discourse . . . to the New Hampshire Colonization Society.* Concord, N.H., 1825.

Dwight, Sereno Edwards, *The Greek Revolution.* Boston, 1824.

Dwight, Timothy, *A Discourse in Two Parts.* New Haven, 1812.

———, *Sermon . . . before the A.B.C.F.M.* Boston, 1813.

Edwards, Bela Bates, "The Influence of the United States on Other Nations" (1848), in *Writings* (Boston, 1848), pp. 477-491.

Edwards, Jonathan, *The Injustice and Impolicy of the Slave Trade and of the Slavery of Africans.* n.p., 1791.

Emmons, Nathanael, "God Never Forsakes His People" (1800), in *Works* (Boston, 6 volumes, 1842), ii, 169-183.

———, "New England's Second Century" (1820), *ibid.*, ii, 323-337.

———, "Rights of the People" (1813), *ibid.*, ii, 263-276.

———, "The Choice of their Rulers, the Privilege of the People" (1840), *ibid.*, ii, 277-287.

Evarts, Jeremiah, *Essays on the Present Crisis in the Condition of the American Indians.* Boston, 1829. (First published under the pseudonym of William Penn.)

Fisk, Pliny, *The Holy Land, an Interesting Field of Missionary Enterprise.* Boston, 1819.

Flint, Abel, *A Discourse Occasioned by the News of Peace.* Hartford, 1815.

Hadduck, Charles B., *The Patriot Citizen.* Hanover, N.H., 1842.

BIBLIOGRAPHY

Harris, Samuel, *The Mexican War*. Greenfield, Mass., 1847.
Hart, Burdett, *The Mexican War*. New Haven, 1847.
Hopkins, Samuel, *A Discourse Upon the Slave Trade*. Providence, 1793.
―――, *The Evils of Gambling*. Montpelier, Vt., 1835.
Humphrey, Heman, *An Address to the Emigrants from Connecticut* . . . . Hartford, 1817.
―――, *Indian Rights and our Duties*. Amherst, 1830.
―――, *On Doing Good to the Poor*. Pittsfield, Mass., 1818.
―――, *The Promised Land*. Boston, 1819.
―――, *The Way to Bless and Save our Country*. Philadelphia, 1831.
Lathrop, John, *A Discourse . . . in Consequence of the Peace*. Boston, 1815.
Lord, Nathan, *A Eulogy on the Honourable John Quincy Adams*. Hanover, Mass., 1848.
Morse, Jedidiah, *A Discourse . . . in Grateful Celebration of the Abolition of the African Slave Trade*. Boston, 1808.
―――, *A Sermon Delivered at Charlestown*. Charlestown, Mass., 1812.
[A.B.C.F.M.], *A Narrative of Five Youths from the Sandwich Islands, now Receiving an Education in this Country*. New York, 1816.
Nelson, John, *A Sermon . . . on the Anniversary Thanksgiving*. Leicester, Mass., 1822.
Niles, M. A. H., *The Sin of Duelling*. Newburyport, Mass., 1838.
Parrish, Elijah, *A Protest Against the War*. Newburyport, Mass., 1812.
―――, *Ruin, or Separation from Antichrist*. Newburyport, 1808.
Park, Edwards A., *The Indebtedness of the State to the Clergy*. Boston, 1851.
Parsons, Levi, *The Dereliction and Restoration of the Jews*. Boston, 1819.
Patton, W. W., *The Duty of Christians to Suppress Duelling*. Boston, 1844.
Payson, Seth, *Two Discourses . . . at the Annual Fast*. Ipswich, N.H., 1815.
Pierce, John, *The Right of Private Judgment Vindicated against the Claims of the Romish Church*. Cambridge, Mass., 1821.

BIBLIOGRAPHY

Proudfit, Alexander, *The Universal Extension of Messiah's Kingdom*. Boston, 1822.
Ruggles, Samuel and Nancy, "From a Missionary Journal," *Atlantic*, CXXXIV (1924), 648-657.
Storrs, Richard, *The Importance of Religiously Instructing the Young*, Philadelphia, 1845.
Stuart, Moses, *Essay on the Prize Question, Whether the Use of Distilled Liquors or Traffic in them, is Compatible at the Present Time, with Making a Profession of Christianity*. New York, 1830.
Woods, Leonard, *Sermon . . . on the Occasion of the Ordination of the Rev. Messrs. Samuel Newell, Adoniram Judson, Samuel Nott, Gordon Hall, and Luther Rice, as Missionaries to the Heathen in Asia*. Boston, 1812.
Worcester, Samuel M., *Our Country and our Work*. Salem, Mass., 1843.

OCCASIONAL SERMONS AND DISCOURSES:
PRESBYTERIAN

Adams, William, *Christianity the End and Unity of all Sciences and Pursuits*. New York, 1847.
Alexander, Archibald, *A Discourse Occasioned by the Burning of the Theatre in the City of Richmond, Virginia*. Philadelphia, 1812.
―――, *Objections Obviated and God Glorified by the Success of the Gospel among the Heathen*. Boston, 1830.
Anderson, W. C., *The Republic and the Duties of Citizens*. Dayton, 1847.
Armstrong, George Dod, *The Study of Natural Science Considered as a Means of Intellectual Cultivation*. Lynchburg, 1841.
Baird, Robert, *The Noblest Freedom; or the Influence of Christianity Upon Civil Liberty*. New York, 1848.
Ballantine, Elisha, *America, the Teacher of Nations*. Washington, 1850.
Barnes, Albert, *Plea in Behalf of Western Colleges*. Philadelphia, 1846.
Beecher, Lyman, *Works*. Boston, 1852, 3 volumes.

Beecher embodied the aspirations of the theocrats more fully than any other man. His active life covered almost exactly our period. If the writings of all the theocrats were

BIBLIOGRAPHY

lost, the theocratic pattern could be reconstructed, at least in its essential structure, from his collected works.

Beman, Nathan S. S., *A sermon . . . on the occasion of the national fast.* Portland, 1812.

———, *The Gospel Adapted to the Wants of the World.* Troy, N.Y., 1840.

———, *Collegiate and Theological Education at the West.* New York, 1847.

Benton, J. A., *California, as she was, as she is, as she is to be.* Sacramento City, 1850.

Blatchford, Samuel, *A sermon on the . . . National Thanksgiving.* Albany, 1815.

Blythe, James, *A Portrait of the Times.* Lexington, 1814.

Boardman, Henry Augustus, *A sermon, occasioned by the death of William Henry Harrison.* Philadelphia, 1841.

Boynton, Charles B., *Oration . . . before the Native Americans of Cincinnati.* Cincinnati, 1847.

Bush, George, *Lack of Vision, the Ruin of the People.* Indianapolis, 1826.

Cheever, George B., *The Elements of National Greatness.* New York, 1843.

Coffin, Charles, *A Sermon Delivered in Rogersville . . . for the Restoration of Peace.* Rogersville, Tenn., 1815.

Duffield, George, *Sermons on American Slavery.* Detroit, 1840.

Green, Beriah, *Things for Northern Men to Do.* New York, 1836.

Griffin, Edward Dorr, "Arguments for Missions" (1826), *The Missionary Enterprise* (Boston, 1846), pp. 22-37.

———, *The Claims of Seamen.* New York, 1819.

———, *Foreign Missions.* New York, 1819.

———, *A Plea for Africa.* New York, 1817.

Hall, Gordon, *The Duty of the American Churches in Respect to Foreign Missions.* Philadelphia, 1812.

Henry, T. Charleton, *A Plea for the West.* Charleston, 1824.

Hodge, Charles, *The Place of the Bible in a System of Education.* Philadelphia, 1833.

Holt, Edwin, *Union of Christians Essential to the World's Conversion.* Charleston, 1836.

———, *Equality of Rich and Poor.* Portsmouth, N.H., 1841.

Jennings, Obadiah, *A Missionary Sermon Preached . . . in Pittsburgh.* Steubenville, Ohio, 1818.

BIBLIOGRAPHY

Junkin, George, *The Integrity of our National Union vs. Abolitionism.* Cincinnati, 1843.

Kirk, Edward Norris, *The Church Essential to the Republic.* New York, 1848.

———, *A Valedictory Sermon.* Albany, 1837.

Latta, John Ewing, *A Sermon, Preached on the 20th Day of August.* Wilmington, 1812.

———, *A Sermon, Preached at New Castle (Del.).* Wilmington, 1815.

Lindsley, Philip, "An Address on the Occasion of the Centennial Birthday of George Washington" (1832), *Works* (Philadelphia, 1866, 3 volumes), III, 229-264.

———, "Name of our Republic" (1849), *Works*, I, 575-590.

McMaster, Gilbert, *The Obligations of the American Scholar to his Country and to the World.* Madison, Ind., 1841.

Magie, David, *Debts.* Elizabethtown, N.J., 1830.

Miller, Samuel, *The appropriate Duty and Ornament of the Female Sex.* New York, Library of the American Tract Society, no date.

———, "The Earth Filled with the Glory of the Lord" (1835), *The Missionary Enterprise* (Boston, 1846), pp. 36-48.

———, *A Sermon Preached at Newark . . . for the Benefit of the African School.* Trenton, 1823.

Murray, Nicholas, *A Sermon Preached November 30th, 1837.* Elizabethtown, N.J., 1838.

———, *Special Causes of Gratitude.* Elizabethtown, N.J., 1848.

Musgrave, G. W., *A Vindication of Religious Liberty.* Baltimore, 1834.

Nott, Eliphalet, "Address to the Candidates for the Baccalaureate in Union College" (1811), *Addresses* (Albany, 1840), pp. 103-131.

———, *Addresses to the New York State Colonization Society.* Albany, 1829.

———, "The Providence of God towards His American Israel" (1801), *Miscellaneous Works* (Schenectady, 1810), pp. 11-35.

———, *Ten Lectures on the Use of Intoxicating Liquors.* Schenectady, 1840.

Paxton, John D., *Letters on Slavery.* Lexington, 1833.

Rankin, John, *Letters on American Slavery.* Boston, 1833.

Rice, Nathan L., *A Discourse on Dancing.* Cincinnati, 1847.

BIBLIOGRAPHY

Skinner, Thomas H., *Thoughts on Evangelizing the World.* New York, 1836.

Smyth, Thomas, "The Relation of Christianity to War" (1847), *Complete Works* (Columbia, S.C., 1908-1912, 10 volumes), v, 353-377.

Speece, Conrad, *A Sermon . . . on account of the War with England.* Richmond, 1812.

Spees, S. G., *A Discourse on the Great American Idea—Universal Liberty.* Indianapolis, 1848.

Sprague, William Buell, *The Voice of the Rod.* Albany, 1841.

Spring, Gardiner, *The Danger and Hope of the American Republic.* New York, 1843.

———, *The Excellence and Influence of the Female Character.* New York, 1825.

———, *The Obligations of the World to the Bible; a Series of Lectures.* New York, 1839.

———, *A Sermon . . . on account of the Malignant Cholera.* New York, 1832.

———, *A Tribute to New England.* New York, 1821.

Thomas, Thomas E., *Covenant Breaking and its Consequences.* Rossville, Ohio, 1847.

Thornwell, James Henley, "Relation of the Church to Slavery" (1847, 1851), in *Collected Writings* (Richmond, 1873, 4 volumes), IV, 381-397.

Willey, Samuel H., *Decade Sermons.* San Francisco, 1859.

Winchester, Samuel G., *The Religion of the Bible, the Only Preservative of our Civil Institutions.* Natchez, 1838.

Young, John Clarke, *Address to the Kentucky Colonization Society.* Frankfort, Ky., 1833.

———, *An Address on Temperance.* Lexington, 1834.

———, "The Destiny of our Country Demands a Numerous, Holy, and Efficient Ministry of the Gospel," *Annual of the Board of Christian Education* (Philadelphia, 1835), pp. 167-193.

———, *Rectitude in National Policy Essential to National Prosperity.* Oxford, Ohio, 1838.

BIBLIOGRAPHY

OCCASIONAL SERMONS AND DISCOURSES:
MISCELLANEOUS

BAPTIST

Baldwin, Thomas, *The Danger of Living without the Fear of God*. Boston, 1819.
———, *Missionary Exertions Encouraged*. Boston, 1817.
Chapin, Stephen, *The Conversion of Mariners will Enlarge the Praises of Zion*. Portland, Maine, 1821.
———, *The Duty of Living for the Good of Posterity*. Portland, Maine, 1821.
Curtis, Thomas, *The Danger of our Public Gratitude Being Polluted by the Leaven of Boasting*. Bangor, Maine, 1835.
Fuller, Richard, *The Cross*. Philadelphia, 1841.
———, *Domestic Slavery, Considered as a Scriptural Institution; a Correspondence with the Rev. Francis Wayland*. Charleston, S.C., 1845.
Hinton, Isaac T., *The Prophecies of Daniel and St. John Illustrated in the Events of History*. St. Louis, Mo., 1843.
Knowles, James D., *Perils and Safeguards of American Liberty*. Boston, 1828.
Leland, John, *The Writings of Elder John Leland . . . written by himself, with additional sketches . . . by Miss L. F. Greene*. New York, 1845.

Leland represents the antithesis of the theocratic pattern as completely as Lyman Beecher represents its essential features. He was opposed to nearly everything the theocrats favored. He also left us a critical "running commentary" on their endeavors, from the point of view of an untamed, old-school Baptist.

Parker, Daniel, *A Public Address to the Baptist Society. . . .* Vincennes, Ill., 1820.
Rhees, Morgan J., *Our Privileges, the Measure of our Responsibility*. Wilmington, Del., 1846.
Sharp, Daniel, *A Plea for Peace*. Boston, 1846.
———, *The Wisdom and Goodness of God in our Calamities*. Boston, 1843.
Staughton, William, *Address at the Opening of the Columbian College in the District of Columbia*. Washington City, D.C., 1822.
Taylor, James B., *The Exigencies and Responsibilities of the Present Age*. Philadelphia, 1836.

BIBLIOGRAPHY

Wayland, Francis, "The Duties of an American Citizen" (1825), *Occasional Discourses* (Boston, 1833), pp. 40-79.
——, *The Duty of Obedience to the Civil Magistrate*. Boston, 1847.
——, *Encouragements to Religious Efforts*. Philadelphia, 1830.
——, *The Moral Dignity of the Missionary Enterprise*. Boston, 1833.
Williams, William R., "Christ, A Home Missionary" (1836), *The Missionary Enterprise* (Boston, 1846), pp. 78-98.
——, "The Prayer of the Church Against Those Delighting in War" (1847), *Miscellanies* (New York, 1850), pp. 367-387.

DISCIPLES OF CHRIST

Campbell, Alexander, "Address on the Anglo-Saxon Language" (1849), *Popular Addresses and Lectures* (St. Louis, 1861), pp. 17-46.
——, "Address on War" (1848), *ibid.*, pp. 342-366.
——, "Sermon on the Law" (1816), in *Historical Documents Advocating Christian Union*, ed. by Charles A. Young (Chicago, 1904), pp. 217-282.

DUTCH REFORMED

Bethune, George W., "A Discourse on the Duty of a Patriot" (1845), *Orations and Occasional Discourses* (New York, 1850), pp. 319-342.
——, *The Relations of the Sunday School System to our Christian Patriotism*. Philadelphia, 1847.
Brownlee, William Craig, *Popery an Enemy to Civil and Religious Liberty*. New York, 1836.
Milledoler, Philip, *Address before the Alumni of Columbia College*. New Brunswick, 1828.
——, *Address . . . to the Graduates of Rutgers College at Commencement*. New York, 1831.
Romeyn, John B., *The Crisis and its Claims upon the Church of God*. New York, 1842.
——, *A Sermon . . . for the Benefit of the New York Marine Missionary Society*. New York, 1819.
VanPelt, P. I., *The Goodness of God to be Praised by Man*. New York, 1812.

BIBLIOGRAPHY

EPISCOPALIAN

Adams, Jasper, *Characteristics of the Present Century*. Charleston, S.C., 1836.

———, *The Moral Causes of the Welfare of Nations*. Charleston, S.C., 1834.

Bedell, Gregory T., *The Cause of the Greeks*. Philadelphia, 1824.

Cary, Samuel, *A Sermon Preached before the Ancient and Honorable Artillery Company*. Boston, 1814.

Darneille, J., *A Discourse . . . on the Subject of Civilizing the Indians*. Washington, 1826.

Doane, George Washington, "America and Great Britain" (1848), *Educational Writings and Orations* (New York, 1848), pp. 224-234.

Gardiner, John S. J., *A Sermon . . . on Fast Day*. Boston, 1808.

Henshaw, J. P. K., *The Usefulness of Sunday Schools*. Philadelphia, 1833.

Hobart, John Henry, *The Security of a Nation*. New York, 1815.

———, *The U.S.A. Compared with some European Countries, particularly England*. New York, 1825.

Jarvis, Samuel F., *The Duty of Offering Thanksgiving unto God*. New York, 1815.

Mathews, Philip, *An Oration . . . in the Episcopal Church of St. Helena*. Charleston, S.C., 1813.

Milnor, James, *A Plea for the American Colonization Society*. New York, 1826.

———, *Sermon Occasioned by the Death of . . . DeWitt Clinton, Governor of New York*. New York, 1828.

Potter, Alonzo, "Our Country Admonished" (1848), *The Discourses of Bishop Potter* (Philadelphia, 1858), pp. 211-228.

Stone, John S., *The Bearings of Modern Commerce on the Progress of Modern Missions*. New York, 1839.

GERMAN REFORMED

Muehlenberg, Henry Augustus, *Busztagspredigt*. Reading, Pa., 1812.

Nevin, John W., "Catholic Unity" (1840), *The Life and Work of John Williamson Nevin* by T. Appel (Philadelphia, 1889), pp. 217-225.

———, *The Year 1848; or, The American Epoch*. N.p., 1848.

BIBLIOGRAPHY

LUTHERAN

Schmucker, Samuel S., *Appeal to the American Churches, with a Plan for Catholic Union.* New York, 1838.

———, *The Christian Pulpit, the Rightful Guardian of Morals.* . . . Gettysburg, Pa., 1846.

———, *The Happy Adaptation of the Sabbath School System to the Peculiar Wants of our Age and Country.* Philadelphia, 1839.

METHODIST

Hamline, Leonidas Lent, "Christian Patriotism" (1841), *Works* (Cincinnati, 1871, 2 volumes), I, 396-413.

Peck, John Mason, *Fifty Year's Retrospect.* St. Louis, 1825.

Stevens, A., *An Alarm to American Patriots.* Boston, 1835.

REFORMED PRESBYTERIAN

McLeod, Alexander, *Negro Slavery Unjustifiable.* New York, 1802.

———, *A Scriptural View of the Character, Causes and Ends of the Present War.* New York, 1815. (A volume of sermons).

McLeod, John N., *Protestantism, the Parent and Guardian of Civil and Religious Liberty.* New York, 1843.

UNITARIAN

Channing, William Ellery, *Works.* Boston, 1877, 931 pp.

If John Leland epitomizes the frontier's opposition to the theocratic pattern, Channing represents the opposition of theological liberalism, though restrained by social and political conservatism.

Clarke, James Freeman, *A Discourse on the Annexation of Texas.* Boston, 1844.

Parker, Theodore, "A Discourse on the Transient and the Permanent in Christianity" (1841), *Works*, ed. by Frances P. Cobbe (London, 1864, 10 volumes), VIII, 1-30.

———, "A Letter . . . Touching the Matter of Slavery" (1847), *Works*, V, 17-84.

———, "The Political Destination of America" (1848), *ibid.,* IV, 77-110.

———, "A Sermon of War" (1846), *Works,* IV, 1-31.

Peabody, Andrew P., *The Nature and Influence of War.* Boston, 1843.

BIBLIOGRAPHY

Whitman, Bernard, *National Defence*. Cambridge, Mass., 1829.
Worcester, Noah, *The Friend of Peace; with, A Solemn Review of the Custom of War*. Schenectady, 1817.

REPORTS OF SOCIETIES

American Board of Commissioners for Foreign Missions, *Annual Reports*. Boston, 1810-1849.
A.B.C.F.M., *First Ten Reports* (Boston, 1834).
"Foreign Missions School," *Report for 1817*, pp. 18-19.
"Foreign Missions School," *Report for 1826*, pp. 103-111.
American Society for Colonizing the Free Peoples of Colour of the United States, *Address to the American Public* (Washington, 1818). Includes report by Ebenezer Burgess of his trip to Africa. *First Annual Report* (Washington, 1818).
American Education Society, *Constitution and Address*. Boston, 1818. Includes address by Eliphalet Pearson.
American Education Society, *Annual Reports*. Andover and Boston, 1822-1849.
[American] Congregational Home Missionary Society, *Annual Reports*. New York, 1827-1849.
American Protestant Association, *Address and Constitution*. Philadelphia, 1843.
American Society for Ameliorating the Condition of the Jews, *Constitution and Address* by the Hon. Elias Boudinot. New York, 1820.
American Society for Promoting the Civilization and General Improvement of the Indian Tribes in the United States, *First Annual Report* by Jedidiah Morse. New Haven, 1824. (Morse founded this "society" in 1822 but it never really materialized.)
American Sunday School Union, *Annual Reports*. Philadelphia, 1825-1849.
American Tract Society, *Proceedings of the First Ten Years*. Boston, 1824. This organization changed its name to "New England Tract Society."
American Tract Society, *Annual Reports*. New York, 1825-1849.
Board . . . for the Emigration, Preservation, and Improvement of the Aborigines of America, *Documents and Proceedings*. New York, 1829. The "Indian Board"; mostly Dutch Reformed clergymen.

BIBLIOGRAPHY

The Christian Alliance, *Report of the First Annual Meeting*, by Leonard Bacon and Edward Norris Kirk. New York, 1845.

Society for the Promoting of Collegiate and Theological Education at the West, *Annual Reports*. New York, 1844-1849.

United Foreign Missionary Society, *Address to the American Public*. New York, 1817.

CONTEMPORARY PERIODICALS

African Repository. Washington, D.C., 1825-1849.
Monthly journal of the American Colonization Society. The chief source for the progress of the colonization effort.

The American National Preacher. New York, 1824-1849.
Charles Hoover, "Criminality, Cowardice, and Cure of Duelling," XII, 67-69. (1838)
Thomas H. Skinner, "Progress the Law of Missionary Work," XVII (1843), 217-240.
David B. Coe, "War as a Means of Settling National Disputes," XX (1846), 62-72.
Robert Baird, "National Prosperity—A Thanksgiving Sermon," XXI (1847), 273-286.
William A. Scott, "The Hope of Republics," XXIII (1849), 60-76.

American Quarterly Register. Boston, 1827-1830.
Monthly report of the American Education Society.

American Baptist Magazine. Boston, 1820-1849.
Volumes X, XVII, and XVIII (1830, 1837, 1838) consulted for correspondence concerning Indian removal.

Biblical Repertory (And Theological Review). Philadelphia, 1829-1849.
"Review of 'The Difficulties of Romanism' by George Stanley Faber," I (1829), 500-520.
"Review of 'A Narrative of a Visit to the American Churches . . .' by Andrew Reed and James Matheson," VII (1835), 598-626.
"Review of 'Slavery,' by William E. Channing," VIII (1836), 268-305. (By Charles Hodge.)
"Indian Affairs," X (1838), 513-535.
"Annual Report of the Board of Missions of the General Assembly," XXI (1849), 309-331.

The Christian Advocate. Philadelphia, 1822-1849. Ed. by Ashbel Green. "The Cherokee," VIII (1830), 194.
Christian Union. New York, 1848-1850. Ed. by Robert Baird.
"Constitution and Address of the Evangelical Alliance," I (1848), 4-11.
"California," II (1849), 280-288.
The Gospel Proclamation. St. Clairsville, Ohio, 1847-1849. Ed. by Alexander Hall.
"Essay on Christianity and War," I, 211ff. (A series of Letters to the Editor.)
The Home Missionary. New York, 1829-1853.
Monthly Journal of the American Home Missionary Society. A major source of information on the evangelistic and educational efforts of the theocrats on the frontier.
Methodist Magazine [And Quarterly Review]. New York, 1818-1849.
"Constitution and Address of the Missionary and Bible Society of the Methodist Episcopal Church," II (1819), 277-279.
"Progress of Religion among the Wyandott Indians in Upper Sandusky," V (1822), 29-34.
"Report for 1823," VI (1823), 275-279.
"An Address . . . before the South Carolina Conference Missionary Society," by Stephen Olin, VII (1824), 301-310.
Wilbur Fisk, "The Science of Education," XIII (1831), 419-431.
Rev. John Johnston, "Wisdom and Benevolence of the Deity, Exhibited in the Constitution of the Atmosphere," XXII (1840), 110-120.
"Review of 'Rights of Conscience Defended in A Speech of Thomas Hertell, Esq.,'" XXV (1843), 5-23.
"Mormonism and the Mormons," XXV (1843), 111-127.
"Fourierism," XXVII (1845), 545-594.
"British Tourists in the United States," XXVIII (1846), 508-534.
"Review of the 'Twenty-Seventh Annual Report of the Missionary Society of the M.E. Church,'" XXIX (1847), 269-308.
"The Revolutions of 1848," XXX (1848), 535-552.
[The Panoplist] Missionary Herald. Boston, 1804-1849.
The official organ of the American Board of Commissioners for Foreign Missions. Published monthly. Authori-

tative source for the entire missionary program of the theocrats.
The Peace Advocate. Boston, 1840-1849.
"Resolutions on Peace," VII (1847), 133-137.
"When and How Certain People would have Ministers Preach Peace," VII (1849), 43.
Western Baptist Review. Frankfort, Kentucky, 1844-1849.
Howard Malcom, "Address to the Graduating Class in Georgetown College, Kentucky," IV (1848), 34-38.
John L. Waller, "A Central Theological School," IV (1849), 303-307.

BIOGRAPHIES AND MEMOIRS

Smith, George G., *The Life and Letters of James Osgood Andrew.* Nashville, Tenn., 1883.
Beecher, Lyman, *Autobiography*, edited by Charles Beecher. New York, 1865, 2 volumes.
Bingham, Hiram, *A Residence of Twenty-One Years in the Sandwich Islands.* Hartford and New York, 1848.
Gabriel, Ralph H., *Elias Boudinot, Cherokee, and his America.* Norman, Okla., 1941.
Cartwright, Peter, *Autobiography.* New York, 1856.
Chase, Philander, *The Reminiscences of Bishop Chase.* New York, 1844, 2 volumes.
Cone, E. W. and S. W., *The Life of Spencer H. Cone.* New York, 1857.
Tracy, E. C., *Memoir of Jeremiah Evarts, Esq.* Boston, 1845.
Brown, I. V., *Memoir of the Rev. Robert Finley.* New Brunswick, 1819.
Chambers, Talbot W., *Memoir of the Hon. Theodore Frelinghuysen, LL.D.* New York, 1863.
Garrison, W. P. G. and F. J., *William Lloyd Garrison.* New York, 1885, 4 volumes.
Garrison, together with Channing and Leland, represents consistent opposition to the theocrats. In his case, an extremely liberal, humanitarian theology combines with social radicalism and with fierce contempt for the churches of Protestant Orthodoxy.
Park, Edwards A., *Memoir of the Life and Character of Samuel Hopkins.* Boston, 1854.

BIBLIOGRAPHY

Brosnan, C. J., *Jason Lee, Prophet of the New Oregon.* New York, 1932.
Paine, Robert, *Life and Times of William McKendree.* Nashville, Tenn., 1874, 2 volumes.
Wylie, S. B., *Memoir of Alexander McLeod.* New York, 1855.
Mallory, C. D., *Memoirs of Elder Jesse Mercer.* New York, 1844.
Spring, Gardiner, *Memoirs of the Rev. Samuel J. Mills.* New York, 1820.
Henshaw, J. P. K., *Memoir of the Life of the Rt. Rev. Richard Channing Moore.* Philadelphia, 1843.
Appel, Theodore, *Life and Work of John W. Nevin.* Philadelphia, 1889.
Maxwell, William, *A Memoir of the Rev. John Holt Rice.* Richmond, Va., 1835.
Drury, Clifford M., *Marcus Whitman, M.D., Pioneer and Martyr.* Caldwell, Idaho, 1937.

MISCELLANEOUS PRIMARY SOURCES

An Address to the Public on the Subject of the African School. New York, 1816.
Alexander, Archibald, *A History of Colonization on the Western Coast of Africa.* Philadelphia, 1846.
Alexander, James Waddell, *The American Mechanic and Workingman.* New York and Philadelphia, 1847, 2 volumes.
American Peace Society, *The Book of Peace.* Boston, 1845.
An anthology of addresses and special articles.
Beecher, Lyman, *A Plea for the West.* Cincinnati, 1835.
Birney, James G., *The American Churches, the Bulwark of Slavery.* London, 1840.
Boudinot, Elias, *A Star in the West; or, a Humble Attempt to Discover the Long Lost Ten Tribes of Israel.* Trenton, 1816.
Breckinridge, Robert J., *Popism in the Nineteenth Century in the United States.* Baltimore, 1841.
Bromwell, William J., *History of Immigration to the United States, from September 30, 1819, to December 31, 1855.* New York, 1856.
Cheever, George B., *The Right of the Bible in our Public Schools.* New York, 1854.
Colton, Calvin, *Protestant Jesuitism.* New York, 1836.

BIBLIOGRAPHY

Davis, Emerson, *The Half Century.* (Introduction by Mark Hopkins.) Boston. 1851.
Dew, Thomas Roderick, *An Essay on Slavery.* Richmond, Va. (1832) 1849.
Dwight, Timothy, *Travels in New England and New York.* New Haven, 1821-1822, 4 volumes.
Finney, Charles Gradison, *Sermons on Various Subjects.* New York, 1836.
Religious Society of Friends, *Some account of the Conduct of the Religious Society of Friends toward the Indian Tribes.* London, 1844.
Hitchcock, Edward, *Reminiscences of Amherst College.* Northampton, Mass., 1863.
Hopkins, John Henry, *The Primitive Church.* Burlington, N.J., 1835.
The Indian's Advocate. Geneva, N.Y., 1817.
Jones, Charles Colcok, *The Religious Instruction of Negroes in the United States.* Savannah, Ga., 1842.
Kalley, Robert R., *Persecutions in Madeira in the Nineteenth Century.* New York, 1845.
McCoy, Isaac, *History of Baptist Indian Missions.* Washington and New York, 1840.
Mills, Samuel J. and Smith, Daniel, *Report of a Missionary Tour through that Part of the United States which Lies West of the Allegany [sic] Mountains.* Andover, 1815.
Morse, Jedidiah, *Universal American Geography.* Sixth Edition, Boston, 1812, 2 volumes.
———, *A Report to the Secretary of War of the United States on Indian Affairs.* New Haven, 1822.
Morse, Samuel Finley Breese, *Foreign Conspiracy Against the Liberties of the United States.* New York, 1835.
Murray, Nicholas (pseud. "Kirwan"), *Letters to the Right Reverend John Hughes.* First and Second Series. New York, 1847.
Nelson, David, *The Cause and Cure of Infidelity.* New York, 1841.
Nevins, William, *Thoughts on Popery.* New York, 1836.
Opinion of the Supreme Court ... in the case of S. A. Worcester, plaintiff in error, vs. the State of Georgia. Washington, 1832.
Paley, William, *Moral and Political Philosophy.* London, 1788, 2 volumes.

BIBLIOGRAPHY

Park, Edwards A., *The Associate Creed of Andover Theological Seminary.* Boston, 1883.

Parker, Samuel, *Journal of an Exploring Tour beyond the Rocky Mountains.* Ithaca, N.Y., 1838.

Polk, Josiah F., *The Claim of the Church of Rome to the Exercise of Religious Toleration during the Proprietary Government of Maryland, Examined.* Washington, D.C., 1846.

Read, Hollis, *The Hand of God in American History.* Hartford, 1850.

This book presents, though without proper organization, the complete *Weltanschauung* of the theocrats.

Rice, Nathan L., *Romanism not Christianity.* Cincinnati, 1847.

Schermerhorn, John F. and Mills, Samuel J., *A Correct View of that Part of the United States which Lies West of the Allegany [sic] Mountains.* Hartford, 1814.

Sprague, William Buell, *Lectures on Revivals.* Albany, 1832.

Sunderland, LeRoy, *The Testimony of God Against Slavery.* Second Edition, Boston, 1836.

Wayland, Francis, *The Elements of Moral Science.* Boston, 1835.

The classical textbook on ethics, representative of the theocratic viewpoint. An unusual "best seller" for its time.

———, *Elements of Political Economy.* Boston, 1837.

This was a companion volume to the former, which also passed through several editions.

———, *The Limitations of Human Responsibility.* New York, 1838.

Webster, Daniel, *Speech in Defence of the Christian Ministry and in Favor of the Religious Instruction of the Young ... in the case of Stephen Girard's Will.* Washington, 1844.

Weld, Theodore Dwight, *The Bible Against Slavery.* New York, 1837.

DENOMINATIONAL HISTORIES

Baird, Robert, *Religion in America.* London and New York, 1835, 1844, 1856.

The outstanding contemporary work on American Christianity, written originally for European readers, by a prominent Presbyterian theocrat.

Bowman, Rufus D., *The Church of the Brethren and War.* Elgin, Ill., 1944.

BIBLIOGRAPHY

Burrows, E. Lansing, *American Baptist Register for 1852*. Philadelphia, 1853.
Cox, F. A. and Hoby, J., *The Baptists in America*. New York, 1836.
Dorchester, Daniel, *Christianity in the United States*. New York and Cincinnati, 1890. (Old but still useful.)
Garrison, Winfred E. and DeGroot, Alfred T., *The Disciples of Christ—A History*. St. Louis, 1948.
Hirst, Margaret, *The Quakers in Peace and War*. New York, 1923.
Holcombe, Hosea, *A History of the Rise and Progress of the Baptists in Alabama*. Philadelphia, 1840.
MacCaffrey, James, *History of the Catholic Church in the Nineteenth Century*. Dublin and St. Louis, 1910, 2 volumes.
Manross, William W., *The Episcopal Church in the United States, 1800-1840*. New York, 1938.
Schaff, Philip, et al., *The American Church History Series*. New York, 1893-1894, 12 volumes.
  Includes standard histories of all the major denominations.
Sprague, William Buell, *Annals of the American Pulpit*. New York, 1866-1869, 9 volumes.
Smith, C. Henry, *The Story of the Mennonites*. Berne, Ind., 1941.
Sweet, William Warren, *Religion on the American Frontier*.
  Vol. I. The Baptists. New York, 1931.
  Vol. II. The Presbyterians. New York, 1936.
  Vol. III. The Congregationalists. New York, 1940.
———, *The Story of Religion in America*. New York, 1930, 1939, 1951. (The standard one-volume history.)
Torbet, Robert G., *A Social History of the Philadelphia Baptist Association, 1707-1944*. Philadelphia, 1944.

OTHER SECONDARY WRITINGS

Abbott, Edith, *Historical Aspects of the Immigration Problem —Select Documents*. Chicago, 1926.
Abrams, Ray H., "The Churches and the Clergy in World War II," *Annual of the American Academy of Political and Social Science (1948)*. Philadelphia, 1948.
———, *Preachers Present Arms!* New York, 1933.
Adams, Alice D., *The Neglected Period of Anti-Slavery in America*. Boston, 1908.

BIBLIOGRAPHY

Adams, James Truslow, *The Epic of America*. Boston, 1933.
Aptheker, Herbert, *American Negro Slave Revolts*. New York, 1943.
Bainton, Roland H., *The Churches and War*. New York, 1945. A reprint from *Social Action*, June 15, 1945.
Baldwin, Alice N., *The New England Clergy and the American Revolution*. Durham, N.C., 1928.
Barnes, Gilbert H., *The Anti-Slavery Impulse, 1830-1844*. New York, 1933.
Barton, James L., "Some Missionary Activities in Relation to Government," *International Review of Missions*, XIII (1924), 340-359.
Beard, Charles and Mary, *The Rise of American Civilization*. New York, Macmillan, 1942. Volume IV, *The American Spirit*.
Bemis, Samuel F., *A Diplomatic History of the United States*. New York, 1942.
Bennett, John C., *Christian Ethics and Social Policy*. New York, 1946.
———, *Social Salvation*. New York, 1935.
Billington, Ray A., *The Protestant Crusade*. New York, 1938.
Blied, B. J., *Austrian Aid to American Catholics, 1830-1860*. Milwaukee, 1944.
Bonn, M. J., *The American Experiment*. London, 1930.
Brawley, Benjamin J., *A Social History of the American Negro*. New York, 1921.
The Cambridge History of American Literature, edited by W. P. Trent and others. New York, 1917-1921, 2 volumes.
Channing, Edward, *A History of the United States*. New York, 1905, volumes IV and V only.
Cobb, Sanford H., *The Rise of Religious Liberty in America*. New York, 1902.
Curti, Merle E., *The American Peace Crusade, 1815-1860*. Durham, N.C., 1929.
———, *The Growth of American Thought*. New York, 1943.
———, *The Roots of American Loyalty*. New York, 1946.
This book is the most suggestive single treatment of the motives underlying the historical development of American patriotism, from the founding of the nation to this day.
Dorfman, Joseph, *The Economic Mind in American Civilization*. New York, 1946-1949, 3 volumes, II: "1789-1861."

BIBLIOGRAPHY

Eels, Myron, *A History of Indian Missions on the Pacific Coast.* Philadelphia, 1882.

Ekrich, A. A., *The Idea of Progress, 1815-1860.* New York, 1938.

Elsbree, O. W., *The Rise of the Missionary Spirit in America, 1790-1815.* Williamsport, Pa., 1928.

Fish, Carl Russell, *The Rise of the Common Man, 1830-1850.* (A History of American Life, volume v).

Foreman, Grant, *Advancing the Frontier, 1830-1860.* Norman, Okla., 1933.

———, *Indian Removal.* Norman, Okla., 1932.

Foster, Frank H., *A Genetic History of the New England Theology.* Chicago, 1907.

Foster, Herbert D., "International Calvinism through Locke and the Revolution of 1688," *Collected Papers,* Private Printing, 1929, pp. 147-178.

Fox, Dixon Ryan, "The Protestant Counter-Reformation," *New York History,* xxxiii (1935), 19-35.

Fox, Early Lee, *The American Colonization Society, 1817-1840.* (Johns Hopkins University Studies, xxxvii, #3). Baltimore, 1919.

Franklin, John Hope, *From Slavery to Freedom.* New York, 1947.

Gabriel, Ralph H., *The Course of American Democratic Thought.* New York, 1940.

Goodykoontz, Colin B., *Home Missions on the American Frontier.* Caldwell, Idaho, 1939.

Greene, Evarts B., "A Puritan Counter-Reformation," *Proceedings of the American Antiquarian Society* (New York, 1928), xvii, part 1, pp. 17-46.

———, *Religion and the State.* New York, 1941.

Greene, M. L., *The Development of Religious Liberty in Connecticut.* Boston, 1905.

Guilday, Peter (ed.), *The National Pastorals of the American Hierarchy, 1792-1919.* Washington, D.C., 1923.

Hall, Thomas C., *The Religious Background of American Culture.* Boston, 1930.

Hansen, Marcus Lee, *The Atlantic Migration, 1607-1860.* Cambridge, Mass., 1940.

Hart, Albert Bushnell, *Slavery and Abolition* (The American Nation: A History, vol. xvi). New York and London, 1906.

BIBLIOGRAPHY

Hayes, Carlton J. H., "The American Frontier—Frontier of What?", *American Historical Review*, LI (1946), 199-216.

Hillquit, Morris, *History of Socialism in the United States*. New York, 1903.

Hinman, George W., *The American Indian and Christian Missions*. New York, 1933.

Hockett, Homer Carey, *Political and Social Growth of the American People, 1492-1865*. New York, 1941.

Humphrey, Edward Frank, *Nationalism and Religion in America, 1776-1789*. Boston, 1924.

Hutchinson, Paul, "Christian Missions and Imperialism," *Christian World Missions*, ed. by W. K. Anderson (Nashville, Tenn., 1946), pp. 223-242.

Jenkins, William S., *Pro-Slavery Thought in the Old South*. Chapel Hill, N.C., 1935.

Johnson, Alvin W., and Yost, Frank H., *Separation of Church and State in the United States*. Minneapolis, Minn., 1948.

Kohn, Hans, *The Idea of Nationalism*. New York, 1944.

Krout, John Allen, *The Origins of Prohibition*. New York, 1925.

Krout, John Allen and Fox, Dixon Ryan, *The Completion of Independence, 1790-1830*. New York, 1944. (A History of American Life, vol. v).

Lauer, Paul E., *Church and State in New England*. (Johns Hopkins University Studies, Series x, #2-3). Baltimore, 1892.

Lindquist, G. E. E., *The Indian in American Life*. New York, 1944.

Lloyd, Arthur Young, *The Slavery Controversy, 1831-1860*. Chapel Hill, N.C., 1939.

Locke, Mary S., *Anti-Slavery in America, 1619-1808*. Boston, 1901.

McGiffert, Arthur Cushman, Jr., "Christianity and War," *American Journal of Theology* (now *Journal of Religion*) XIX (Chicago, 1915), 323-345.

May, Henry F., *The Protestant Churches and Industrial America*. New York, 1949.

Mecklin, John M., *The Story of American Dissent*. New York, 1934.

Meyer, J. C., *Church and State in Massachusetts, from 1740 to 1833*. Cleveland, 1930.

Moehlman, Conrad, *The American Constitutions and Religion*. Berne, Ind., 1938.

BIBLIOGRAPHY

———, *School and Church—The American Way*. New York, 1944.
Morrison, Charles Clayton, "The End of the Peace Movement," *Christendom* (1936), pp. 687-701.
Niebuhr, Reinhold, *The Irony of American History*. New York, 1952.
Niebuhr, H. Richard, *The Kingdom of God in America*. New York, 1937.
———, *The Social Sources of Denominationalism*. New York, 1929.
Parrington, Vernon L., *Main Currents in American Thought*. New York, 1927, 3 volumes.
Perkins, Dexter, *Hands Off, a History of the Monroe Doctrine*. Boston, 1941.
Post, Albert, *Popular Freethought in America, 1825-1850*. New York, 1943.
Pratt, Julius W., *The Expansionist of 1812*. New York, 1925.
Ray, Mary A., *American Opinion of Roman Catholicism in the Eighteenth Century*. New York, 1936.
Riegler, Gordon A., *The Socialization of the New England Clergy, 1800-1860*. Greenfield, Ohio, 1945.
Riley, I. Woodbridge, *American Thought from Puritanism to Pragmatism and Beyond*. New York, 1941.
Savelle, Max, *Seeds of Liberty*. New York, 1948.
Schlesinger, Arthur M., "Biography of a Nation of Joiners," *American Historical Review*, L (1944), 1-25.
Schlesinger, Arthur M., *Paths to the Present*. New York, 1949.
Schlesinger, Arthur M., Jr., *The Age of Jackson*. Boston, 1946.
Schmeckebier, Laurence F., *The Office of Indian Affairs*. Baltimore, 1927.
Shanks, Caroline L., "The Biblical Anti-Slavery Argument, 1830-1840," *Journal of Negro History*, XVII (1931), 132-157.
Shaughnessy, Gerald, *Has the Immigrant Kept the Faith?* New York, 1925.
Smith, Justin H., *The Annexation of Texas*. New York, 1941.
———, *The War with Mexico*. New York, 1919, 2 volumes.
Speer, Robert E., "Christianity and International Relations," *Christianity and Modern Thought*, ed. by Ralph H. Gabriel (New Haven, 1924), pp. 179-196.
Stephenson, George M., *The Puritan Heritage*. New York, 1952.

BIBLIOGRAPHY

Stokes, Anson Phelps, *Church and State in the United States*. New York, 1950, 3 volumes. (Especially vol. II.)

Strong, Josiah, *Our Country: Its Possible Future and its Present Crisis*. New York, 1888.

Strong, William E., *The Story of the American Board*. Boston, 1910.

Sweet, William Warren, "The Churches as Moral Courts of the Frontier," *Church History*, II (1933), 3-21.

Sydnor, Charles S., *The Development of Southern Sectionalism, 1819-1848*. Baton Rouge, 1948.

Tewksbury, Donald G., *The Founding of American Colleges and Universities before the Civil War*. New York, 1932.

Thompson, A. E., *A Century of Jewish Missions*. New York, 1902.

Troeltsch, Ernst, *The Social Teaching of the Christian Churches*. (Translated by Olive Wyon.) London, 1931, 2 volumes.

Tyler, Alice Felt, *Freedom's Ferment. Phases of American Social History to 1860*. Minneapolis. 1944.

Weinberg, Albert K., *Manifest Destiny*. Baltimore, 1935.

Zollmann, Carl, *American Civil Church Law*. New York, 1917.

INDEX

Abbot, Samuel, 16
Abbott, Abiel, 6n.
Adams, John, 100
Adams, John Quincy, 60, 245
African Education Society, 145
African Repository: official organ of the American Colonization Society, 121
African School of the Presbyterian Synod of New York and New Jersey, 125, 145
Alden, Timothy, 6n.
Alexander, Archibald, 8n., 12n., 113n., 245f.
Alexander, James Waddell, 17n., 175, 178f.
Alger, William, 8n.
Allen, Ethan, 153
American and Foreign Bible Society, 160n.
American Anti-Slavery Society, 139
American Anti-Sunday-Law Convention, 43
American Bible Society, 20, 65n., 159, 167
American Board of Commissioners for Foreign Missions, 18f., 22, 89, 96, 99
American Board's Foreign Mission School, 96, 98f., 244
American Colonization Society, 18, 20, 114, 117ff., 130ff., 147ff.,
American Education Society, 14, 15n., 16, 20
American Home Missionary Society, 20, 22, 160
American Peace Society, 229f.
American Protestant Association, 77f.
American Quarterly Register: official organ of the American Education Society, 15n.
American Sabbath Union, 20
American Society for Ameliorating the Condition of the Jews, 87n.
American Society for Educating Pious Youth, 65n.

American Society for Promoting the Civilization and General Improvement of the Indian Tribes in the United States, 100n.
American Society for the Promotion of Temperance, 184
American Sunday School Union, 20, 27, 168, 242
American Temperance Society, 20, 28
American Temperance Union, 185, 187
American Tract Society, 20, 77, 160, 167
American Unitarian Association, 24
Amherst College, 15
Anderson, Rufus, 246
Anderson, W. C., 81n.
Andover Theological Seminary, 4, 16f., 23
Andrew, James Osgood, 147, 200
Andrews, Elisha, 49
Andrews, William Watson, 211f.
anti-Catholicism, 61ff., 69, 78f.
"anti-mission" movement, 25, 162
anti-theocratic elements, 25ff., 55ff.
Appleton, Jesse, 204n.
Arminianism, 10
Ashmun, Jehudi, 121
"Associate Creed": mandatory for Andover faculty, 4

Bacon, Leonard, 122ff., 169n., 252n., 259n.
Bacon, Samuel, 120f.
Bailey, R. W., 146
Baird, Robert, 33, 78f., 122, 161n., 171, 235, 240f., 259n.
Baldwin, Elihu, 140
Baldwin, Theron, 169n.
Baldwin, Thomas, 154
Ballantine, Elisha, 237
Ballou, Adin, 26, 56ff.
Bancroft, Aaron, 87n.
Bangs, Nathan, 122, 141
Barnes, Albert, 144
Bascom, Henry Bidleman, 147
Bates, Joshua, 86, 240n.

285

INDEX

Beecher, Henry Ward, 218
Beecher, Lyman, 3, 11, 21, 24, 32, 39f., 52ff., 76f., 82n., 98, 141f., 148, 153ff., 157, 162, 168f., 174f., 181, 182n., 183ff., 240, 255f.
Belknap, Jeremy, 115
Beman, Nathan S. S., 169n., 198n., 259
benevolent associations, *see* voluntary societies
Bennett, Alfred, 56n., 58n.
Benton, J. A., 224
Bestor, Daniel P., 130
Bethune, George W., 54, 141
Bingham, Hiram, 245n.
Birney, James G., 135
Blatchford, Samuel, 204n.
Boardman, Henry, 78n., 141
Boudinot, Elias, 20f., 86
Boudinot, Elias (Cherokee), 97ff.
Bouton, Nathaniel, 124n., 125
Boynton, Charles B., 62
Bradford, William: *History of Plymouth Plantation*, 5
Braman, Isaac, 197
Braman, Milton, 218f.
Breckinridge, John, 141
Breckinridge, Robert J., 78n., 82n., 129, 148
British and Foreign Bible Society, The, 200
British societies, 18f.
Broaddus, Andrew, 122
Brooks, Charles, 171
Brownson, Orestes, 56
Bureau of Indian Affairs, 101
Burgess, Ebenezer, 123
Bush, George, 161
Bushnell, Horace, 51, 82n., 140, 155, 162, 164, 169n., 181, 237, 248f.
Butler, Elizur, 107

Calhoun, John C., 93f., 97, 100f., 208
Calvinism, 10
Campbell, Alexander, 24ff., 38f., 59, 227f., 247
Carey, William, 244
Cartwright, Peter, 164, 170
Channing, William Ellery, 23ff., 79, 179n.
Chapin, Calvin, 183n.

Chapin, Stephen, 7n., 250n.
chaplaincy to Congress, 36
Chase, Philander, 141
Cheever, George B., 43n., 75, 141, 172
Christian Association of Washington, (Pa.), 24
Christian party in politics, 46ff.
Christian Phalanx, 47
church and state, separation of, 42
city problems, 173ff.
Clark, Kendrick, 57n.
Clarke, James Freeman, 214n.
Clay, Henry, 36, 212
clergy, American Protestant: composition of, vii; definition of, viii; pattern for America, viii ff.; influence curtailed, 9; depletion of, 13; number of in proportion to population, 14; in politics, 44ff.; opinions concerning the Negro problem, 149ff.; rigid attitude toward drinking, 188
Codman, John, 155, 241n.
Coe, David B., 215
Coffin, Charles, 204
Cogswell, William, 259
college movement: initiated by theocrats, 16
College of New Jersey, 15
colleges and universities: founded by various denominations, 14f.; attended by ministerial candidates, 14-16; enrollment figures, 17n.
Colton, Calvin, 28f., 189, 255
Cone, Spencer H., 36, 82n.
Congregational Association of Connecticut, 39
Connecticut Missionary Society, 18n.
Connecticut Moral Society, 183
Cornelius, Elias, 11, 15n., 21n.
Cotton, John, 34
Counter-Reformation (Roman Catholic), 28, 255f.
"Cumberland Presbyterians," 11
Cummings, Asa, 5, 129

Daggett, Herman, 96
Davis, Emerson, 43n., 169n.
Davis, Henry, 12n.

286

INDEX

Day, Jeremiah, 12n., 141, 259
Dedham Case, 32
Dew, Thomas Roderick, 134ff.
"disinterested benevolence," doctrine of, 11
Doane, George Washington, 247
Dod, Albert B., 141
Dorfman, Joseph, 179
Douglass, James W., 146
Dudleian lectures, 63, 65
Dudley, Paul, 63
Duer, William, 141
Dwight, Sereno Edwards, 114, 236n.
Dwight, Timothy, 7, 11, 16, 32, 49, 182n., 183n., 198, 251, 256

Eaton, John H., 102
Edwards, Bela Bates, 15n., 35n., 247
Edwards, Jonathan (the Younger), 10, 115
Edwards, Justin, 11, 114n., 184f., 259
Ely, Ezra Stiles, 46ff.
Emmons, Nathanael, 8, 31f., 49, 61f., 203, 206, 221, 236
Episcopal African Mission School Society, 145
establishment, religious: forbidden by the Constitution, ix; reaction of clergy, ix; slow collapse of, 31ff.; retained in Massachusetts, 32
Evarts, Jeremiah, 11, 19n., 20, 103ff., 108, 132n., 184, 244

Fay, Warren, 184
Finlay, James B., 90, 164
Finley, Robert, 11, 118, 121, 125
Finney, Charles G., 12, 13, 139n.
First Provincial Council of Baltimore, 67
Fisher, Samuel, 35, 45, 50
Fisk, Pliny, 87n.
Fisk, Wilbur, 34, 141
Flint, Abel, 205n.
Foster, Stephen, 130
Fourierism, 177
Free Enquirer, 173
Frelinghuysen, Theodore, 21, 104
Frey, Samuel F. C., 87n.

Fuller, Richard, 144
Furman, Richard, 143f.

Gambold, John and Anna, 96
Gardner, Newport, 114
Garrison, William Lloyd, 26, 43, 56, 132, 135ff., 229
General Union for Promoting the Observance of the Christian Sabbath, 40f., 43
Gillette, A. D., 78n.
Going, Jonathan, 141
gold, discovery of, 223f.
Gold, Harriet, 98f.
Goodell, William, 88
Greeley, Horace, 188
Green, Ashbel, 12n., 127
Green, Beriah, 148n.
Greene, David, 108
Griffin, Edward Dorr, 11, 12n., 91, 125, 250
Gurley, Ralph, 120ff., 127, 130ff., 140

Hadduck, Charles B., 53
Hall, Gordon, 88n.
Hamilton and Burr duel, 182
Hamline, Leonidas Lent, 129, 242n.
Harris, Samuel, 217
Hart, Burdett, 217, 218n.
Hart, Levi, 115
Haven, Joseph, 179n.
Hawes, Joel, 12n., 259n.
Henry, T. Charlton, 91
Henshaw, J. P. K., 51
Hertell, Thomas, 187
Hewit, Nathaniel, 184
Hickok, Laurens P., 179n.
Hillyer, Asa, 141
Hinton, Isaac T., 163n.
Hitchcock, Edward, 15n.
Hodge, Charles, 4, 139, 141, 164, 241, 256
Holcombe, Hosea, 252
holidays, national: advocated by theocrats, 37ff.
Hopedale Community, 57
Hopkins, John Henry, 189
Hopkins, Mark, 252
Hopkins, Samuel, 10, 114f., 117, 121, 123
Humphrey, Heman, 4, 12n., 15,

287

INDEX

55n., 106, 154n., 155, 159n., 162, 178, 183n.

immigrants, 68, 73ff., 80ff.
"Indian College," 96
Indians: early missionaries to, 85f.; Boudinot compares them with ancient Hebrews, 86f.; missions to, 87ff., 108f.; ignorance of, 90f.; "wards" of federal government, 92; exploitation, 92; "Civilization Fund" for education of, 95; intermarriages, 97; treaties with U.S., 104, 107; removal to the West, 92f., 101ff.; and Negro slavery, 109f.
Industrial Revolution, 152
Ives, L. S., 148

Jackson, Andrew, 102, 107, 176, 186, 208
Jarvis, Samuel, 204n.
Jefferson, Thomas, 100
Jenks, William, 184
Jennings, Obadiah, 90n., 91
Jennings, Robert L., 173
Jesuitism, 28f., 66, 74
Jewish missions, 87n.
Johnson, Edward, 5
Johnson, Richard M., 26
Johnson Report to the Senate, 42f.
Jones, Charles Colcock, 146
Jones, David, 200
Jones, Evan, 107f.

Kemper, Bishop, 148
Kennaday, John, 78n.
Kingsbury, Cyrus, 88
Kirk, Edward Norris, 164
Knowles, James D., 210
Krebs, John M., 177

labor unions, 175
Lathrop, John, 199, 203
Latta, John Ewing, 202
Lee, Jason, 109, 214f.
Leland, John, 27, 33, 37, 40ff., 47, 55ff., 79, 162, 188f., 201, 228
Leo XII, 72
Leopold Foundation, 69, 72, 74, 238
Lindsley, Philip, 147, 237, 241ff.
Little, Robert, 45

London Missionary Society, 243f.
Lord, Nathan, 12n., 60
Lord's Day Alliance, 43
Louisiana Purchase, 191ff.
Ludwig Mission, 69

McCoy, Isaac, 86n., 89, 101ff., 108
McIlvaine, Charles P., 12n.
McKendree, William, 141
McKenney, Thomas L., 101f.
McLean, John, Jr., 141
McLeod, Alexander, 116n., 199f.
McMaster, Gilbert, 242
Madison, James: denounced by Samuel Fisher, 35, 50; against chaplaincies, 36; on society for welfare of Indians, 100; and War of 1812, 194ff., 198
Malcolm, Howard, 180n., 230, 238
Mann, Horace, 171
Marshall, John, 104, 106
Mason, John Mitchell, 182n.
Massachusetts Peace Society, 228n., 229
Massachusetts Temperance Society, 184
Mather, Cotton: *Magnalia Christi Americana*, 5f.
Mather, Increase, 182
Matheson, J., 38n.
Mathews, James M., 179n.
Mathews, Philip, 202n.
May, Samuel J., 229
Meade, William, 13, 121, 129
Mercer, Jesse, 44n.
Mexican War, 216-223
Milledoler, Philip, 12n., 89, 141, 179f.
Miller, Samuel, 12n., 18n., 82n., 123n., 126, 128, 181, 246
Miller, William, 251
Mills, Samuel J., 10f., 64, 88, 117f., 121, 123, 128, 158f., 166, 244
Milnor, James P., 22
Missionary and Bible Society of the ME Church in America, 90n.
missionary enterprise, 10, 232, 243ff.
Missionary Society of the Synod of South Carolina and Georgia, 91n.
missions: "foreign" and "home"

INDEX

compared, 18n.; to Indians, 87ff.; education or mission families, 94f.
Missouri Fur Company, 94
Monk, Maria, 70, 78, 83
Monroe, James, 102
Monroe Doctrine, 239f., 257
Moore, Richard Channing, 12
Morris, Thomas, 147
Morse, Jedidiah, 3, 16, 19n., 32, 49, 93ff., 103, 111f., 117, 166, 184, 198, 205, 244n.
Morse, Samuel F. B., 69ff., 77
Muehlenberg, Henry Augustus, 201
Murray, Nicholas, 222, 238

Native American party, 74
Nativist movement, 69, 76f., 80ff.
natural events as media of divine guidance, 7f.
Negroes: slavery and amalgamation condemned by theocrats, 112f.; colonization of, 114f., 117ff.; and the missionary motive, 123f., abolition of, 128ff.; education of, 145f.
Nelson, David, 161n.
Nevin, John Williamson, 51, 238
Nevins, William, 77
New England Tract Society, 160
New Harmony Gazette, 167, 173
"New Haven Theology," 12
"New Measures," 12
New York Colonization Society, 141
Newman, John Henry, 189
Nisbet, Charles, 179n.
Nott, Eliphalet, 116n., 126, 128, 182n., 259
Nubia, Salmar, 114

Olin, Stephen, 91
Onderdonk, Bishop, 148
Owen, Robert Dale, 167, 173, 176

Paine, Tom, 153
Paley, William, 116f., 139, 156, 226ff.
Palmer, Elihu, 153, 167
Panoplist: pioneer journal of theocrats, 20, 184

Park, Edwards A., 16
Parker, Daniel, 25f., 162n.
Parker, Samuel, 108n.
Parker, Theodore, 23ff., 179n.
parochial schools, state aid for, 172
Parrish, Elijah, 197, 205
Parson, Levi, 87n.
party politics, 48ff.
patriotism: definition of, vii; synonymous with Christian piety, 9
Payson, Edward, 12n.
Payson, Seth, 196f.
Pearson, Eliphalet, 13, 16
Peck, George D., 51, 82n., 177
Peck, John Mason, 22, 149, 250
Penn, William (pseudonym of Jeremiah Evarts), 104
Peters, Absalom, 169n.
Phillips, Wendell, 229
Pierce, John, 65n.
Pius VII, 65
Plan of Union, 14n., 158, 201n., 223
Plummer, William S., 148
Polk, James K., 56, 213, 223
Polk, Josiah F., 63n.
population, growth of, 13f., 62
Porter, Ebenezer, 11, 16
Porter, Eliphalet, 184
Post Office Establishment, An Act Regulating the, 39
Potter, Alonzo, 185, 238
Potts, George, 38, 45, 127
Powell, J. Hare, 27n.
presidential messages criticized by theocrats, 35
Princeton Seminary, 16f.
"Protestant Crusade," 82ff.
Proudfit, Alexander, 141
Prudential Committee, 19, 244
public school system, 170ff.
Puritan belief concerning America, 6

Rankin, John, 145n.
Rantoul, Robert, Jr., 174
Read, Hollis, 7n., 207, 230f., 236, 249
Remeyn, John B., 250n.
revivals: in first half of 19th century, 11; devices used in, 12; at Amherst College, 15
Rhees, Morgan J., 220

289

INDEX

Rice, John Holt, 17n., 42, 44, 47f., 142, 209f., 234f.
Richards, James, 11
Robinson, H. D., 174
Roman Catholics: growth of, 62, 67ff., 76; subjected to civil disabilities, 63; supported by Protestants, 66f.; schools, 67, 172; "trusteeism controversy," 67; political doctrines, 70ff.
Ross, John, 107
Ruggles, Samuel and Nancy, 245n.
Rush, Benjamin, 184

Schermerhorn, John F., 64, 107
Schmucker, Samuel S., 5, 37f., 45, 53n., 78n., 82n., 220, 252, 258f.
Scott, Walter, 227
Scott, William A., 238f.
Scott, Winfield, 107
"Second Awakening," 11f., 153, 158f.
Sessions, Horace, 121
Sharp, Daniel, 33f., 215
Skinner, Thomas H., 169n., 259
Smith, Gerrit, 135
Smith, Joseph, 180
Smyth, Thomas, 230
Society for Propagating the Faith, 66, 69
Society for Propagating the Gospel among the Indians and Others in North America, 18n., 86
Society for the Promotion of Collegiate and Theological Education at the West, 168
Society for the Propagation of the Gospel in Foreign Parts, 63
Soule, Joshua, 90n., 147n.
Speece, Conrad, 202
Spees, Samuel G., 220, 222
Sprague, William B., 12, 55n., 155n.
Spring, Gardiner, 8n., 21, 53, 144, 178, 181, 259n.
Spring, Samuel, 16
Stanhope, Samuel, 179n.
Stevens, A., 76n.
Stiles, Ezra, 114f.
Stone, John S., 248n.
Storrs, Richard S., 242
Stuart, Moses, 16, 144, 259

Sunday mails issue, 39ff.
Sunderland, LaRoy, 145n.
Superintendent of Indian Trade, 94
Swift, Elisha P., 141, 148

Tappan, Arthur, 40, 139n.
Taylor, James B., 79n.
Taylor, John, 25, 162n.
Taylor, Nathaniel W., 12, 82n.
temperance movement, 183-189
theocratic pattern: viii; cornerstone of, 3; three basic points, 6; structure, 9, 21, 29f.; roots, 52ff.; unsuccessful as applied to Indians, 110; for America, 189, 233ff.
theocrats: patriotism of, 3, 253; belief in God's direct rule of nations, 4f., 8; avoidance of doctrinal controversy, 10; theological orientation adopted by, 11f.; on "true" and "false" revivals, 12; against abolitionism, 139ff.; advocated paternalism, 176ff.; and expansion, 205-216; and war, 226-231
theological education, 16
theological seminaries a result of college movement, 16
Thomas, Thomas E., 219n.
Thornwell, James Henley, 144
Treat, Selah B., 109
Tyler, Bennet, 11
Tyng, Stephen H., 78n., 82n., 141, 259

Union Theological Seminary, 210
Unitarianism, 23f.
United Foreign Missionary Society, 89
United States Temperance Union, 184
United States as heir of ancient Israel, 5ff., 24, 232f., 240, 257

Van Rensselaer, Stephen, 40, 89, 184
Vanpelt, P. I., 201n.
"voluntary principle," 33
voluntary societies: character of, ix; inaugurated by theocrats, 13,

INDEX

17; church-sponsored, 18; national in scope, 19f.; influence on national unity, 22; target of "anti-theocrats," 26ff.; strengthened Christianity, 32; political mission, 54f.; effectiveness varied, 185f.; created to assist churches, 189

Wainwright, Jonathan, 131
Walker, Amasa, 229
Walker, David, 134n.
War Hawks, 193, 195f., 208
War of 1812: causes, 194ff.; opposed by theocrats, 196-199; attitude of clergy, 199-202; similarities between it and Mexican War, 216f.
Ware, Henry, 32, 57n.
Wayland, Francis, 12n., 116, 144, 156, 178, 184, 214, 221, 229, 240, 251
Webster-Hayne debate, 208
Weld, Theodore Dwight, 139n., 142, 145n., 148n.

the West: evangelization of, 158-165; educating, 165-170
Western Missionary Society, 90
Whipple, Charles, 229
White, William, 141
Whitman, Bernard, 41n., 47n.
Whitman, Marcus, 215
Willey, Samuel H., 224
Williams, William R., 220, 241
Winans, William, 147
Winchester, Samuel G., 4f., 54
Wisner, Benjamin, 114, 184
Witherspoon, John, 9
Witherspoon, Thomas, 144, 148
Woods, Leonard, 16, 184, 244
Worcester, Noah, 229
Worcester, Samuel Austin, 19n., 106ff., 244n.
Worcester, Samuel M., 80n., 207n.
Wright, Frances, 167, 173, 176

Young, John Clark, 17n., 113, 148, 187
Young Men's Colonization Society of Pennsylvania, 141